THE COURAGE TO BE CHRISTIAN

THE COURAGE TO BE CHRISTIAN

Entering a Life of Spiritual Passion

MIKE NAPPA

HOWARD
PUBLISHING CO.

Our purpose at Howard Publishing is to:

- *Increase faith* in the hearts of growing Christians
- *Inspire holiness* in the lives of believers
- *Instill hope* in the hearts of struggling people everywhere

Because He's coming again!

The Courage to Be Christian: Entering a Life of Spiritual Passion
© 2001 by Nappaland Communications, Inc.
All rights reserved. Printed in the United States of America

Published by Howard Publishing Co., Inc.
3117 North 7th Street, West Monroe, Louisiana 71291-2227
01 02 03 04 05 06 07 08 09 10   10 9 8 7 6 5 4 3 2 1

The Courage to Be Christian: Entering a Life of Spiritual Passion is another creative resource from the authors at Nappaland Communications, Inc. To contact the author, visit his Web site (www.Nappaland.com).

Edited by Michele Buckingham
Interior design by Stephanie Denney

Library of Congress Cataloging-in-Publication Data
Nappa, Mike, 1963–
    The courage to be Christian : creating a life of spiritual passion / Mike Nappa.
        p. cm.
    Includes bibliographical references.
    ISBN 1-58229-160-8
        1. Christian life. I. Title.
    BV4501.3 .N36 2001
    248.4—dc21   2001016586

        Scripture quotations marked (NIV) are taken from the Holy Bible, New International Version®. Copyright © 1973, 1978, 1984 by the International Bible Society. Used by permission of Zondervan Publishing House. All rights reserved. Scripture quotations marked (NLT) are taken from the Holy Bible, New Living Translation. Copyright © 1996. Used by permission of Tyndale House Publishers, Inc., Wheaton, Illinois 60189. All rights reserved. Scripture quotations marked (NKJV) are taken from the Holy Bible, New King James Version. Copyright © 1979, 1980, 1982 by Thomas Nelson, Inc. Used by permission. All rights reserved. Scripture quotations marked (NCV) are quoted from The Holy Bible, New Century Version. Copyright © 1987, 1988, 1991 by Word Publishing, Nashville, Tennessee 37214. Used by permission. Scripture quotations marked (NASB) are taken from the New American Standard Bible®. Copyright © 1960, 1962, 1963, 1968, 1971, 1972, 1973, 1975, 1977, 1995 by The Lockman Foundation. Used by permission.

for Rex Stepp, Eric Jaqua, and Kevin Heard—
three men who have often held me
up when I thought I would fall—
I love you all like the brothers you are

When the light of courage illuminates our way, we always find true richness at the end of the path.

—*Suze Orman*

When we die and it comes time for God to judge us, he will not ask, "How many good things have you done in your life?" Rather he will ask, "How much love did you put into what you did?"

—*Mother Teresa*

CONTENTS

Introduction: Christianity Isn't for Wimps 1

Part One: The Passionate Pursuit of God

Chapter 1: Courage to Pray 7
Seeking Intimacy with God through the Practice of Prayer

Chapter 2: Courage to Think 19
Seeking Intimacy with God through Understanding the Scriptures

Chapter 3: Courage to Worship 31
Seeking Intimacy with God through Acts of Worship

Part Two: The Cost of Pursuing God

Chapter 4: Courage to Give Your All. 45
Living a Life Completely Dedicated to Jesus

Chapter 5: Courage to Serve 57
Serving God by Serving Others

Chapter 6: Courage to Lead—and Follow 69
Following Jesus and Leading Others to Do the Same

Chapter 7: Courage to Say No—to Yourself and Others 79
Setting Priorities in Order to Say Yes to God's Will

Part Three: Putting Your Passion into Action

Chapter 8: Courage to Be Christian at Home 91
Being Christian in the Presence of Your Family Members

Chapter 9: Courage to Be Christian at Work. 101
Being Christian on the Job

Chapter 10: Courage to Be Christian in Your Community 113
Being Christian in Your Neighborhood and Community

Chapter 11: Courage to Be Christian at Leisure 125
Being Christian at Rest and at Play

Chapter 12: Courage to Be Christian When You're Alone 135
Being Christian in the Presence of No One but God

Part Four: Weakness and Strength

Chapter 13: Courage to Rely on God. 149
Trusting God in Everything

Chapter 14: Courage to Multiply Your Gifts and Talents 161
Assessing and Using Your Spiritual Gifts and Physical Talents

Chapter 15: Courage to Go In over Your Head—and Risk It All . 175
Stretching Your Potential for Christ to Its Fullest Limit

Part Five: Failure Is an Event, Not a Person

Chapter 16: Courage to Risk It All...Again 187
Picking Up the Pieces and Trying Again When You Fail

Chapter 17: Courage to Forgive—Yourself and Others 197
Exercising the Power of Forgiveness in Your Daily Life

Chapter 18: Courage to Choose Your Response to Life
        Circumstances 209
Choosing Love and Life in the Face of Difficult Circumstances

Part Six: When All Is Said and Done

Chapter 19: Courage to Hope 221
Focusing on Jesus and Expecting a Miracle

Chapter 20: Courage to Persevere 233
Hanging in There until Your Miracle Comes

Chapter 21: Courage to Love—No Matter What 243
Always Practicing Love—from Here to Eternity

Epilogue: Is This the End? 253
Discussion and Study Guide 255
Notes 265

Anyone who loves his father or mother more than me is not worthy of me; anyone who loves his son or daughter more than me is not worthy of me; and anyone who does not take his cross and follow me is not worthy of me. Whoever finds his life will lose it, and whoever loses his life for my sake will find it.

—*Matthew 10:37–39* NIV

Introduction

CHRISTIANITY ISN'T FOR WIMPS

Let me tell you a story about Keefy. When Keefy was a boy, his greatest passion was football, and his favorite player was a running back for the Minnesota Vikings named Chuck Foreman.

Keefy used to spend hours each day playing football in the streets of Stowe Village, a ghetto located in Hartford, Connecticut. Two on two, four on four, morning or evening—it didn't matter to Keefy. All that mattered to him was having the opportunity to emulate his hero while playing ball.

On Sundays, Keefy watched the Vikings on TV and studied the running form of Chuck Foreman. He watched as Foreman used his strength to bowl over one tackler, his speed to blow past another—whatever it took to get the job done. On Mondays (and practically every day for the rest of the week), Keefy practiced Foreman's moves: Spin away from a tackler here, lower your head and power through the opposition there, start and stop on a dime, keep the opponents guessing (and missing). If Chuck Foreman did it on Sunday, Keefy wanted to do it too.

One day Keefy and his brother were playing their usual game of street football with some of the neighborhood kids. On one play, Keefy's brother dropped back to pass while Keefy ran deep for a bomb. As the ball floated up in the air, Keefy could tell it was going too long.

1

But his passion kicked in, and he refused to give up. Summoning his courage, he put on a burst of speed and dove to catch the ball at the last possible second, stretching his fingertips as far as they would go and never taking his eyes off the pigskin. To the amazement of all, he caught the ball, landing hard on the pavement and scraping the side of his face on the gravel surface.

After making that spectacular catch, only one thought went through Keefy's head. "Did you see that catch?" he yelled to his friends as he jumped up in excitement. "That looked just like Chuck Foreman!"

His friends stared at him in wide-eyed amazement. A few said, "Ooooh! Keefy, Keefy!"

The boy could barely contain himself. He'd done it! He'd laid it all on the line—just like Chuck Foreman—and come up the hero. "Yeah, that's right!" he said. "You saw that catch! Just like Chuck Foreman." Raising the ball over his head in triumph, he shouted for the world to hear, "I'm Chuck Foreman!"

Still the other players didn't move. Finally one said, "Man, look at your ear!"

That was when Keefy felt something warm and wet on the side of his face. He touched it and discovered it was blood. A friend explained, "Man, your ear's hanging off!"

Scraping the side of his face on the gravel had actually ripped off a chunk of the boy's ear, leaving it dangling precariously on the side of his head. But Keefy hadn't even noticed. He was so courageously passionate about being a football player just like Chuck Foreman that nothing else really mattered.

Well, little Keefy got medical attention for his ear, and it healed over time. The day after his accident, he was back in the streets playing football again. And as he grew into a man, his passion for football continued to grow, eventually carrying him to the National Football League. His inspired play not only sent him to the prestigious Pro Bowl several times, it helped the Green Bay Packers win a Super Bowl championship.

Keefy—better known today as Eugene Keefe Robinson—has made his share of mistakes, to be sure. Some have been very big and very public. But his example of passionate commitment to the game of football is second to none.[1]

Imagine for a moment what would happen if Christians displayed that same kind of courageous passion in the way we approach life. If, after studying the life and actions of Jesus on Sundays, we went out and practiced his "moves" and imitated his lifestyle the rest of the week. If we made it our overriding goal, our never-ending passion, to be just like Jesus Christ.

Woohoo! Can you envision the transformation that would occur in our communities, our nation, and our world if those of us who claim to believe in Jesus had the courage to be passionate about being Christian? It'd be like a fire, an unstoppable blaze of spiritual passion sparked by thousands—no, millions—of little flames joined together as one.

And it can start with you and me.

I've got news for you. True Christianity, courageous Christianity—the kind the apostles Paul and Peter and thousands of other early Christians practiced—isn't for wimps. It's not for the fainthearted, the lukewarm, the moderately committed, or the occasional churchgoer. It's for the passionate, the ones with the courage to say, "I believe God, and I will dedicate my every waking hour to his purpose, no matter what it costs."

Not that kind of person yet? Me neither. But I want to be. And I trust you've picked up this book because you want to be too.

I'm convinced we can see this world transformed—flame by flame by flame. But we don't have to do it alone. We *can't* do it alone, in fact. Instead, we must turn to God daily and ask him to empower us to be passionate followers of Christ. We must ask him to grant us the courage to be truly Christian.

Are you ready to take that step? Are you ready to be molded by God's Holy Spirit into a man or woman of spiritual

> Courageous passion is... Desire, fueled by determination and rewarded by the *pursuit of*—not necessarily the *acquisition of*—the object of desire.

passion? Are you ready, by God's grace, to elevate your Christian life to a higher level—to be made into more than you are?

Me too, friend, me too! That's why I invite you to explore with me, through the pages of this book, what it really means to be a passionate and courageous Christian. Obviously, I (like you) fall short in many ways, and I don't claim to have all the answers as we begin this journey, but I want to at least ask the questions. And maybe if we ask them together, we'll discover a few of the answers—and kindle the flame of passion that will make us jump up and shout:

"Did you see that? That was just like Jesus!"

Forgive us that with the cross as a starting point we have made of Christian faith a bland and easy-going way of life.

Forgive us that our preference runs to Bethlehem and Joseph's garden, to poinsettias and lilies, and away from Golgotha, with its rusty nails and twisted thorns.

Forgive us that we are more willing to be instructed or reformed than we are to be redeemed.

Open us, each one, to ever new and deeper meanings in our Savior's Passion.

—a prayer of Ernest T. Campbell[2]

Part One

THE PASSIONATE PURSUIT OF GOD

As the deer pants for streams of water,
so my soul pants for you, O God.
—Psalm 42:1 NIV

And they came to an olive grove called Gethsemane, and Jesus said, "Sit here while I go and pray." He took Peter, James, and John with him, and he began to be filled with horror and deep distress. He told them, "My soul is crushed with grief to the point of death. Stay here and watch with me."

He went on a little farther and fell face down on the ground. He prayed that, if it were possible, the awful hour awaiting him might pass him by. "Abba, Father," he said, "everything is possible for you. Please take this cup of suffering away from me. Yet I want your will, not mine."

Then he returned and found the disciples asleep. "Simon!" he said to Peter. "Are you asleep? Couldn't you stay awake and watch with me even one hour? Keep alert and pray. Otherwise temptation will overpower you. For though the spirit is willing enough, the body is weak."

Then Jesus left them again and prayed, repeating his pleadings. Again he returned to them and found them sleeping, for they just couldn't keep their eyes open. And they didn't know what to say.

When he returned to them the third time, he said, "Still sleeping? Still resting? Enough! The time has come. I, the Son of Man, am betrayed into the hands of sinners."

—Mark 14:32–41 NLT

COURAGE TO PRAY

Seeking Intimacy with God through the Practice of Prayer

It's no mistake that a relationship with God most often begins with a prayer—a humiliating prayer at that. The words of the "sinner's prayer" vary from person to person, but the content is the same. In short, we come to God acknowledging that we have failed to fulfill his desires for our lives, and we beg his forgiveness (which he freely gives). And in that prayer a new life begins, a relationship starts, and our every moment from that point on is spent either growing closer to or away from our dearest friend in the world.

The trouble is that we often forget the simplistic intimacy of that first prayer. We change prayer until it becomes a laundry list of our wants and needs, a lexicon of theological language put on display, something meant for people's ears rather than God's. Oh that we could return to the passion, to the intimacy of that first prayer which introduced us to our heavenly Father!

We can.

You see, no matter how we try to change prayer—no matter what we try to make it—prayer doesn't change; we do. Prayer always remains the same from God's perspective.

So what is prayer, you ask? Let me offer this definition: *Prayer is practicing intimacy with God.*

Here's another way of looking at it: In the wardrobe of spirituality, prayer is intimate apparel. When we pray, we lay ourselves bare before God—no blemish is disguised by makeup, no "spare tire" is hidden under cotton and polyester. In prayer, nothing and no one can come between us and our Creator.

If you have trouble with the idea of intimate prayer, listen to how psychologist Lloyd Thomas describes intimacy:

> Intimacy is not sexual. We often confuse the meaning of the word "intimacy" to mean sexual contact. Intimacy is much more. Intimacy is the free and comfortable revealing to another who you really are. It means sharing what you genuinely feel, what you really want, your hopes and aspirations, dreams and fantasies, fears and resentments, successes and failures. It means being open and vulnerable, receptive and self-expressive within your own knowledge and integrity.
>
> Intimacy is the lifeblood of healthy and loving relationships...[1]

Does that describe your prayer life? It should.

You see, your prayers (and mine) are more than mere communication with God. They're greater than language, deeper than words. Like little children who've scraped their knees on the sidewalk of life, we launch ourselves in prayer through time and space right into the loving lap of our heavenly Father, all in the space of an instant, before we can even blink an eye.

Yet it takes courage to pray with that kind of intimacy and child-like abandon—courage we often feel too weak to summon. We feel too unsure of our audience to speak plainly, too uncomfortable with our words to put them together with confidence, too self-reliant to admit we're desperately lost and in need of help.

> An answered prayer is a secondary miracle. The first miracle is prayer itself.
>
> —Anthony Vespugio[2]

It takes courage to get beneath the surface with God and pray with intimate passion. God has already done his part. He sent his Son to make the way for us to have an intimate relationship with him. The next step is ours.

COURAGE TO COME AS YOU ARE

I have a confession to make. There was a time in my life when I was a champion pray-er, at least by human standards. During this period, it seemed as if everyone wanted me to pray aloud at group gatherings. So I would pray, in properly respectful yet down-to-earth tones, choosing my words carefully to meet the needs of the moment.

After these little prayer performances, well-meaning people would invariably come up to me and say things like, "That was a really good prayer, Mike." "Your prayer touched me, Mike. Thanks." "I love to hear you pray." "You pray so eloquently." Blah, blah, blah!

At first I felt a bit proud to be such a hit as a pray-er. But soon the pressure got to me. *I can't pray here,* I'd think. *I'm not ready. What if I say something stupid? What if my prayer is just average?* I was literally paralyzed by the expectation that I pray impressively! I soon quit praying in public altogether for fear of what my peers would (or wouldn't) say to me afterward.

I also found myself mimicking my public performances of prayer in my private times with God. It was during one of these times, late at night, that I heard God yawn. (OK, so I didn't *literally* hear him yawn, but that was the impression in my spirit.) I stopped my yammering for a moment and felt God speaking to my heart, impressing this phrase into my mind: *Mike, exactly who are you praying for?*

I was crushed. For months I had been so bent on shaping my prayers for human audiences that I'd forgotten I was whispering directly into the ear of God! I'd been so concerned about presenting a good image that I'd ignored the fact that God saw through my spiritual window dressing and directly into my heart—which was encased in the armor of pride.

I'm ashamed to say that moment of revelation came to me only a few years ago, even though I've been a praying Christian for two decades now. But I learned something that night—something we all need to learn. When we come to God in prayer, we must come as we are. No amount of flowery words will impress God. No religious postur-ing, no "attitude of prayer," no kneeling or bowing or crying or suffer-ing will make us more worthy in God's eyes. God knows our every impulse, our sinful thoughts, our secret desires, our inner being—and he knows them better than we do. We can't fool him with impressive praying.

No, if we want to be people who passionately pursue intimacy with God in prayer, we must first and foremost have the courage to approach him honestly, completely revealing who we are, what we've done, and how we feel each time we call his name. To do less than that is an insult to God and to the miracle of prayer he's given us.

> In prayer, it is better to have a heart without words, than words with-out a heart.
>
> —John Bunyan[3]

Imagine a wife who is unwilling to let her husband see her as she really is. As the alarm goes off in the morning, she quickly shouts, "No! Don't look at me! Stay in bed and cover your head with the pillow!" She jumps up, rushes to the bathroom, brushes her teeth, showers, blow-dries her hair, and applies her makeup. Then she runs downstairs and irons her best dinner dress, slides it over her head, pulls on her nylons, and steps into her fancy, high-heeled shoes. Finally, after draping pearls around her neck and primping one last time in the mirror, she returns to the bed-room and—fully clothed, decked out, and made up—climbs back under the covers and proclaims, "Good morning, darling. Now you can look it me."

It's a ludicrous image, isn't it?

Yet that's the way many of us approach God. We feel as though we must dress up our thoughts and words and "put on" our Sunday best in order to pray. But all God really wants is for us to turn to him—bad breath, rumpled hair, and all—and pour ourselves into his loving arms.

It takes courage to be that honest with God, but that kind of unpretentious vulnerability is part of what it means to be truly

Christian. The good news is that while God welcomes us into his presence just as we are, he never leaves us that way. Our every encounter with God changes us—sometimes obviously, sometimes subtly—in ways that mold us more into the image of Jesus.

Courage to Seek God's Will, Not Your Own

Each time I read Jesus' prayer in the Garden of Gethsemane, I'm struck by the passion and intimacy evident in his words and actions—and disappointed by the shallowness of my own prayers in comparison. Let's revisit that scene for a moment.

It's the night that will change the history of man, mere hours before Jesus Christ will be arrested, beaten, falsely charged and convicted, and finally executed by the cruel Roman custom of crucifixion. Nailed to a cross with spikes in his hands and feet, he will be left to suffer and die, mocked by the crowd that once cheered him.

His suffering is imminent, and Jesus knows it. So he does what to him is second nature: He prays.

Taking his closest disciples into a garden called Gethsemane, Jesus reveals the struggle going on inside him. "My soul is crushed with grief to the point of death," he says. "Stay here and watch with me."

Then moving a short distance away, he kneels among the flowers and shrubs in the soft silence of the night and cries out to God. "Father," he says, "everything is possible for you. Please take this cup of suffering away from me."

In this quiet hour of prayer, Jesus reveals the intimacy of a passionate relationship with God. He first calls to the *Father*—not El Shaddai, not mighty God, not the Creator of the Universe. In his most desperate moment, he seeks a family member, the one who loves him beyond comprehension.

Next he lays himself bare before God. "Please take this cup of suffering away from me," he says. Jesus has not forgotten his purpose on this earth. He knows that the reason God became man was to take the penalty for humanity's sins by dying on the cross. He knows that on the third day following his death, he will return to life once more, the gift of eternal life firmly in his grasp. And yet, facing the brutality that awaits him, he feels nearly overwhelmed—so much so, the Gospel of Luke says, that blood drips like sweat from his pores.

"Please take this cup away," he pleads. Had I been Jesus, my prayer would have ended there. "Take this suffering away!" I would have yelled. "I don't deserve it! You can't make me!" But Jesus (thankfully) is not me, and without hesitation he adds the words: "Yet I want your will, not mine."

Amazing, isn't it? In his prayer, one passion is apparent above all: Jesus wants the will of the Father, no matter the cost.

Can you and I say the same?

As I write this book, I know I will probably never have to suffer like Jesus did. But I have known my share of suffering. For the past two and a half years, I've struggled with a rare chronic stomach disease that causes me to feel some degree of nausea every day. Many times I've prayed with passion for God to heal me, begging him to release me from the chains of illness that have manifested themselves inside my body. For months after the diagnosis, I was angry, then I became depressed. I was certain that God had forsaken me.

But he hadn't—and he hasn't. He is simply teaching me to say like Jesus, "I want your will, not mine...even if it means a lifetime of disability. Even if it means poverty or embarrassment or sorrow or sacrifice. I want your will, not mine."

It takes courage to pray this way. And it takes courage to trust God with the consequences, no matter what. To be honest, I'm not yet to that point in my prayers. But each day (I hope) I'm growing a little bit closer, a tiny bit more passionate, a sliver more courageous about asking God to work his will in my life.

COURAGE TO APPROACH GOD OFTEN

If we are to be praying Christians, we must be willing to approach God at all times in all ways. The intimacy of prayer doesn't become comfortable in once-a-week intervals or powerful in occasional bursts.

It must be practiced time and time again—when we wake in the morning, when we work through the day, when we play or rest or eat or laugh or cry or watch TV or sit in a traffic jam.

There's a reason that the apostle Paul commanded, "Pray without ceasing" (1 Thess. 5:17 NKJV). It's because our very life depends on it. If we desire to truly live (and not simply to exist), we must commune with the Creator of Life—and the more often we do it, the better!

Where is God right now as you read this book? Is he in your thoughts, your mind, your very being? Can you hear his whisper? Are you asking him whether all these words Mike Nappa has written are to be believed—or just a load of bunk? You should be!

We must be courageous enough to let God invade and occupy every area of our lives, and that invasion begins with prayer. Like a sprinter who trains his muscles to explode onto the track at the sound of the starter pistol, we must also exercise the "muscles" of prayer until it becomes such a habit we do it without

> I have a theory. Unbelievers don't pray because they are afraid that God might be there. Believers don't pray because they are afraid he might not be.
>
> —*Steve Brown*[4]

thinking. That doesn't mean we must always speak formal words and sentences to God. We can often communicate better in feelings and images, and it's good to know that God speaks with nonverbal language just as well as he speaks with words.

With that in mind, we must train ourselves to acknowledge God's presence in the mundane moments of life. We must redirect our minds toward prayer at odd moments of the day—when we're cut off in traffic, when the secretary puts us on hold, when we're changing diapers, when we're playing taxi driver to get our kids to all their after-school obligations, when we're lying in bed almost ready to drop off to sleep. You see, God is our constant companion. It's time we had the nerve to stop ignoring him.

One last story and then we'll close this chapter. It seems there were three people who stood at the gates of heaven ready to account for their lives. One was a banker, and when she marched boldly to the door, Saint Peter asked, "What have you bought with your time on earth?"

The banker smiled and answered, "Why, I've bought homes and buildings and businesses. I've used money to make money, to fulfill dreams, to invest in every kind of business venture known to man."

Saint Peter responded, "That's not enough." Then he turned to the second person, a wealthy owner of a sports team. "What have you bought with your time on earth?"

The sports owner smiled broadly and spoke, "Why, I purchased a championship team, brought thrills and entertainment to millions, built a stadium that will stand decades after my death, and made a place for myself in the annals of sports history—I even have a plaque in the Sports Hall of Fame!"

Again Peter shook his head and said, "That's not enough." Turning to the last woman he asked again, "What have you bought with your time on earth?"

This woman had been primarily a homemaker, occasionally working as a secretary and supermarket clerk. Still, she had many things to brag about. She could tell how she'd been faithful in attending church, how she'd made herself available to her children and invested in their lives, how she'd managed to avoid divorce, and more.

But she passed on all those things, saying only, "I spent my days and nights, every minute I could muster, trying to seek out and enjoy the presence of God."

At those words, Saint Peter opened wide the gates of heaven, saying, "Ah, so you have been inside before. We welcome you back again to spend eternity in the presence of the one you've known on earth."

Friend, how are you spending the riches of life's moments? The greatest investment you can make on earth is to spend your time getting to know God. Do you have the courage to do that in prayer?

A Personal Invitation

I would be remiss to assume that everyone reading this book has already met God once, personally, intimately. If you have not yet become a Christian, let me tell you here how you can meet God and begin this courageous adventure of faith.

First, you must understand that you and I, friend, have failed. From day one to this moment, we have fallen short of God's expectations for our lives. The Bible calls that "sin" and is very clear in saying, "For all have sinned; all fall short of God's glorious standard" (Rom. 3:23 NLT).

That poses a problem, because sin, like a deadly virus, brings spiritual death to us. For the answer, God sent his one and only Son, Jesus Christ, to live on earth as a man. Here he bore the penalty of our sin (yes, yours and mine!) through his execution on the cross. But he didn't stop there.

On the third day after his execution, he proved his power over life and death and sin by returning to life once more. He is still alive even today and now offers spiritual life to all who would believe in him and trust their lives to his care.

Listen to what the Bible says about it:

"The wages of sin is death, but the free gift of God is eternal life through Christ Jesus our Lord" (Rom. 6:23 NLT).

"For if you confess with your mouth that Jesus is Lord and believe in your heart that God raised him from the dead, you will be saved. For it is by believing in your heart that you are made right with God, and it is by confessing with your mouth that you are saved. As the Scriptures tell us, 'Anyone who believes in him will not be disappointed'" (Rom. 10:9–11 NLT).

And so, dear friend, you have a choice. Will you begin this new life—this courageous adventure—with Jesus? Will you accept his offer of forgiveness for sin and of eternal life? Will you trust your every action, your very being, to his care and leading?

If your answer is yes, you can meet him right now. Lay down

this book and pray. Admit to Jesus what he already knows—that you have sinned and need his forgiveness. Tell him you want to receive his offer of eternal life. Ask him to help you live out his desires for you from this day forward and to help you grow moment by moment in intimacy with him.

When your prayer is finished, call someone—a Christian friend or family member, perhaps, or the pastor at a local Christian church—and tell them what you've just done! Ask them to help you learn more about how to grow in your new relationship with Jesus.

Go ahead, put the book down, and do it now. I'll meet you again in chapter 2.

Jesus, full of the Holy Spirit, returned from the Jordan and was led by the Spirit in the desert, where for forty days he was tempted by the devil. He ate nothing during those days, and at the end of them he was hungry.

The devil said to him, "If you are the Son of God, tell this stone to become bread."

Jesus answered, "It is written: 'Man does not live on bread alone.'"

The devil led him up to a high place and showed him in an instant all the kingdoms of the world. And he said to him, "I will give you all their authority and splendor, for it has been given to me, and I can give it to anyone I want to. So if you worship me, it will all be yours."

Jesus answered, "It is written: 'Worship the Lord your God and serve him only.'"

The devil led him to Jerusalem and had him stand on the highest point of the temple. "If you are the Son of God," he said, "throw your-self down from here. For it is written:

"'He will command his angels concerning you
    to guard you carefully;
they will lift you up in their hands,
    so that you will not strike your foot against a stone.'"

Jesus answered, "It says: 'Do not put the Lord your God to the test.'"

When the devil had finished all this tempting, he left him until an opportune time.

Jesus returned to Galilee in the power of the Spirit, and news about him spread through the whole countryside.

—Luke 4:1–14 NIV

2

COURAGE TO THINK

Seeking Intimacy with God through Understanding the Scriptures

Please forgive me for what I'm about to say, but all too often we Christians are a stupid lot. (I hope you noticed that I included myself in that statement!)

History tells us that Christians were guilty of atrocities during the great Crusades. Believers in Christ were the ones who spurred on the "witch hunts" of the nineteenth century. Even misguided fools of the twentieth century, claiming to be followers of Jesus, donned cloaks and sought to demean America's black population as an inferior group—using (I should say *mis*using) the Bible as justification for racial animosity.

Unfortunately, Christians today are living up to their reputation as dumb sheep—following any obscene fad that claims the name of Christ—and abandoners of the gospel in the process.

In many Christian circles, it seems we've given up the right to think, to reason, to carefully examine the message of Jesus as applied in our lives and in our world. We have weakened our minds—and thus our wills—in an effort to supposedly "live by faith." As if thinking, questioning, examining, studying, and applying God's Word aren't exercises of faith! There is no holiness in ignorant Christianity; there is only error and a susceptibility to Satan's deception when we neglect the obligation we have to be *thinking* Christians.

There are dozens of examples that illustrate what I'm talking about, but I'll only take time to tell you of two. At the time of this writing, there is great alarm throughout Christendom over a certain set of toys and videos for children. Several prominent Christians have dubbed these toys "the work of Satan" and have warned Christians to prohibit their kids from having any association with them. When I started receiving frightened e-mails from several of my readers asking my opinion, I decided to check out the toys myself. I did a little research, played the games, watched the shows, and looked for Satan within them. He might have been there, but frankly, I couldn't see him.

Next I read the arguments my Christian brothers and sisters have leveled against this toy brand. I soon realized that everything they said could be applied to *any* toy or game, not just this one kind! So I chose the most innocuous and respected game I could think of—chess—and wrote a satire, applying the same arguments.

I made ludicrous leaps of logic in this article. I insisted that because the queen in chess can go two ways (both diagonally and straight), then she must be promoting a homosexual lifestyle. With tongue firmly in cheek, I averred that the knight's L-shaped path in the game is homage to Lucifer—another name for the devil. I even said that I was going to illegally break into my brother-in-law's house and smash his marble chess set to rid him of that evil influence. At the end of my article, I gently suggested that either chess is evil or some of my Christian colleagues might be wrong about the toys they are so quick to demonize.

After the article was published on the Internet, I wasn't surprised by the hateful responses I received from many of my Christian brothers and sisters—I expected them (although I had to laugh when one woman told me I was desperately sinful for daring to disagree with a Christian leader on the subject.) What did surprise me, though, were the e-mails I got from well-meaning Christians who were ready to *join* me in a crusade against chess! Despite the fact that my title had clearly labeled the article a satire, they thought I was serious and—simply because I had said it was so—were willing to believe that chess was inherently evil.

Obviously, I sent those people an explanatory e-mail pointing out (again) that the article was merely a satire and an attempt to make people think before leaping to judgment. Still, it's scary to realize they would have followed me in my error without pausing to *think through* what I had said.

Which leads me to Christians like the pastor of a Baptist church in Kansas. Let's call him Pastor F. He and his followers have enacted a crusade against homosexuals that is hateful and vindictive—all in the name of Christ.

For the record, I believe that homosexual behavior is wrong and that it is sin in God's eyes. I do not, however, believe that every homosexual person deserves the hatred and contempt of Christ's people. Pastor Phelps believes differently.

John W. Kennedy, news editor for *Christianity Today* magazine, reports, "During the 1990s [Pastor F] and followers in his 210-member Westboro Baptist Church have picketed more than ten thousand events. In addition to messages such as 'God Hates Fags,' they brandish large, colorful signs containing slogans such as 'No Tears for Queers,' 'Turn or Burn,' and 'AIDS Cures Fags' at homosexual rights parades and funerals of AIDS patients."

Any preachers who disagree with Pastor F's actions are added to his list of the condemned. "These maudlin, kissy-pooh, feel-good, touchy-feely preachers of today's society are damning this nation and this world to hell," Pastor F says.[1]

> Rhetoric that generates violence is an offense against the second greatest commandment—"love thy neighbor."
>
> —Theologian J. I. Packer[2]

When I hear about a person like Pastor F leading my Christian brothers and sisters down the pathways of hate, I wonder *how in the world* he's managed to win over people who are followers of Jesus. I'm mystified when I hear of Christians applauding the murder of an abortion doctor or when I read in the news about another Christian-perpetrated bombing of an abortion clinic or when another David Koresh-like cult leader drags church folk away into deception and death.[3]

How can Christians believe that waging a hate-inspired war within our society's walls is the righteous act of God? It comes from being *unwilling to think*. We prefer to let others do our thinking for us—and we've become moral and spiritual paupers as a result. It's sad to say, but in the climate of today's Christianity, it takes courage to be a thinking Christian, one who asks the hard questions (even if there are no answers). It takes courage to be a passionate seeker of truth.

COURAGE TO THINK THE THOUGHTS OF GOD

The primary protection we have against the diseased thoughts and actions that bombard us from both mainstream society and certain sectors of the Christian world is to *think the thoughts of God*.

But how do we think God's thoughts? There is only one answer to that question. To think his thoughts we must first become students of his Word. Yet in spite of our great need, it is the Bible that we so quickly discard from our everyday lives; it is God's Word that we take for granted and allow to grow dusty on our shelves or on our coffee tables. The Bible is the healing antidote to poisoned thinking; yet all too often it lies undisturbed, misunderstood, and forgotten in the byways of our time on earth.

I sometimes wonder how a man like William Tyndale would feel about the callousness with which we Christians regard the Bible today. You see, in Tyndale's time—the early sixteenth century—it was illegal to possess a copy of a Bible in the English language. England used only the Latin translation of the Scriptures, which meant only the wealthy and educated had access to the Word of God. The great majority of the English population could not discover God's message for themselves; and, unfortunately, many of the clergy delivered only portions of (or distortions of) the Bible to those in their care.

Tyndale finally decided to do something about this inequity. First he petitioned the government, asking for permission to translate the Bible into English. He was denied. So he went to Germany in self-imposed exile and spent many years translating the Bible into the language of his homeland. In 1526 the first complete English New Testament was printed in Worms, Germany. Tyndale had finally given every literate Briton direct access to the thoughts of God as revealed in Scripture. But King Henry VIII rejected the English Bible and condemned William Tyndale for creating it.

Tyndale became a hunted man, a fugitive from a so-called Christian king and church! Nearly a decade later, while working on a translation of the Old Testament, he was betrayed by a supposed Christian friend, arrested, and tried. In 1536 he was declared a heretic, a voice of Satan in the church. Soon after, he was strangled and burned at the stake as a condemned criminal.[4]

And for what did William Tyndale sacrifice his life? To give people like you and me the opportunity to read the Scriptures for ourselves! He gave his life for the book that you and I often let rot undisturbed inside our comfortable homes.

Men like Tyndale, Martin Luther, and others gave our generation the greatest legacy we could ever obtain—God's Word in our own language. We now have access to at least some of the unsearchable riches of God's intellect, his emotion, and his heart for you and me. It's all in our dusty, old Bibles, waiting to be read, studied, thought about, digested, argued over, enacted, and applied.

> O God! Open the King of England's eyes!
>
> —*The last words of William Tyndale as he was burned at the stake in 1536 for the crime of translating the Bible into English. Less than a year later, King Henry VIII finally legalized an English Bible—one based largely on the work of William Tyndale before his death.*[5]

Think about it. If there were no Holy Scriptures, how would you know that God cares for you? Sure, you could read a few historical documents and gain a rudimentary knowledge of the life of Jesus Christ, but would you ever hear of his death and resurrection? Of his power to heal body and soul? Of his love and sacrifice for you? Of the hope he holds for you in heaven?

And equally important, would you have a measure by which to gauge all the "teachings of righteousness" in this world? How do I know it's wrong to pursue murder and hatred in the name of God—that the message of Pastor F is contrary to the message of Christ? Because I have been introduced to the God whom Pastor F claims to represent. I met him in the pages of my English Bible. And when I compare the Jesus that Pastor F preaches with the one I see in Scripture, I know they are not the same.

If we are to be courageous Christians who live lives of spiritual passion, we must be willing to challenge our thinking with the thoughts of God. We must be diligent to study God's thoughts revealed in the Bible, to understand them as best we can, and then to live our lives by them from here to the end of time.

SEEKING UNDERSTANDING OF THE THOUGHTS OF GOD

Sam Om was thrilled when he first received a Bible. He was living in a refugee camp in Thailand at the time, having finally escaped from five years as a virtual slave laborer and prisoner of war in Cambodia. It was 1979, and one of his few benefits in the refugee camp was his own copy of the book that held the words and passions of God within it. Sam inspected his new prize, flipped through several of the pages, and smiled. It was perfect.

Next he took out a rough pouch filled with tobacco. With careful precision, he ripped a page out of his new Bible and placed the rest of the book aside. He then proceeded to roll himself a brand-new cigarette, using the page of Scripture as the outer paper to hold his precious tobacco. Striking a match, he lit the Word of God and inhaled the nicotine smoke. Yes, there'd be plenty of good cigarettes made out of this thick book!

One day while he was rolling a cigarette, his eyes fell on the words imprinted on the page:

For God so loved the world,

that he gave his only begotten Son,

that whosoever believeth in him should not perish,

but have everlasting life. (KJV)

"It was John 3:16," Sam remembers. "The words about God's love really struck me because I was filled with such a deep hate."

All at once he began to understand. The words that had previously meant no more to him than his next cigarette suddenly had new meaning. It was truth he held in his hand, not simply cigarette papers. And in that truth, a few months later, he finally met Jesus, the one with power to save his soul. That one flash of understanding changed Sam's life—and his treatment of God's Word. Today Sam Om is the pastor of a Cambodian church in North Carolina, and he regularly returns to his home country in Southeast Asia to teach pastors and plant churches. On one recent trip back, he took with him something special: one thousand Bibles to give to other Cambodians who, like Sam in 1979, needed to be introduced to the thoughts of God.[6]

You and I may not burn the pages of the Bible with the same carelessness that Sam Om did; but if we are honest, we must admit that we too have treated God's Word with callous indifference. We have put off the understanding of this gift, neglected it, twisted its meaning, denigrated its message, and crowded out its life-giving power. As a result, we have weakened our ability to think rightly about our world and our faith. We have taken away the truth and replaced it with half-truths and lies—and that can be deadly.

Not long ago I was fortunate enough to interview Christian author and thinker Philip Yancey. We met over lunch at a restaurant in downtown Denver and spent almost our whole time together talking about God's Word. At one point I said to him, "One thing I noticed through all of your books is that you seem to be working strongly to challenge people to think [about the Bible and Christianity]. Why do you suppose that's necessary?"

Philip paused for a moment, choosing his words carefully, then he replied, "Well, the reason I emphasize that, I suppose, is that I was brought up in a church that told you *not* to think. They would say, 'Don't question. Just believe.' And the things I was told to 'just believe' I found out later were lies, a lot of them...Later I realized, 'Well, yeah, it is a bunch of nonsense, but somewhere in there is a core of truth that is the most important thing in the world.' "[7]

Philip Yancey found that core truth through his own personal journey into the pages of Scripture. By studying the Bible, he was able to guide his thinking and separate the lies he'd been taught from the truth of Christ. That effort has made all the difference in his life. It can make all the difference in our lives too.

Emulating the Thinker of the Thoughts of God

It was on a dusty plain that Jesus met face to face with Satan, the father of lies. This was not their first meeting. Surely, in the eons before his incarnation, Christ had faced the devil and his evil intent. And it certainly wasn't the last meeting between the Creator and his fallen creature.

But this appointment in the wilderness of Israel held special importance. It was a time of testing, a moment of truth for the God-Man who had not yet sinned.

I imagine a dry and barren scene. In the stifling heat of the day, I picture a weakened Savior, conserving his strength, enduring fatigue, hunger, thirst, sunburn, uncleanness, and who knows what else. The Gospel of Luke reports that Jesus didn't eat for forty days during this time in the wilderness. And he wasn't alone. In fact, the Bible reveals that Satan was with him the entire time, tempting and harassing him day after day after day. Finally, at the end of forty days, the devil had Jesus just where he wanted him: exhausted, weak, and *hungry*.

A smile crept onto Satan's face. "If you are the Son of God," he said, "tell this stone to become bread."

A simple suggestion, really, and one well within the realm of possibility. Jesus had participated in the creation of all things; certainly he had the power to turn a stone into bread. It was a healthy suggestion too. Poor Jesus needed to keep his body in top shape, right? And hadn't he already proven himself during the past forty days? Wasn't it finally time to take a break and think of himself?

Satan seemed to offer valuable advice that any decent mother would give: "You're hungry, you haven't eaten for weeks, and your body is wasting away before your eyes. Go ahead and use an infinitely small portion of your power to feed yourself before you die of starvation!"

But Jesus had taken time to think the thoughts of Scripture, and when a moment of decision came, he was ready with his answer. Quoting directly from the Old Testament, he rebuffed the insidious suggestion of the devil, recognizing its evil source. He quickly saw that the thoughts of Satan were not the desires of God. "It is written: 'Man does not live on bread alone,'" he said. Score one for the Son of God!

Twice more Satan wheedled and cajoled, even quoting Scripture out of context to support his views. And twice more Jesus the Great Thinker called upon his memory of the Bible to expose the liar's evil deceptions. Finally, Satan gave up. After forty days and nights, all his efforts had failed to confuse and mislead the Savior. Satan left, and the Bible reports that "Jesus returned to Galilee in the power of the Spirit."

Friend, I hope you see where I'm going with this. Can you imagine how different your life—your world—would be if Jesus had given in to impulse during that time of testing? If he hadn't spent time prior to that moment thinking and learning and understanding the Word of God? If he had simply followed the first reasonable-sounding argument he heard? If he'd gone ahead and done something as simple as making and eating a piece of bread? The Sinless One would have been guilty of sin, making his whole life, death, and resurrection a moot point. He would have failed in his mission before it really began!

And what of us? If you and I are to be men and women of God, we, too, must become imitators of Jesus, the Great Thinker. When we are tempted by the wiles of this world, we must be ready to draw upon the Word of God to check out the veracity of our impulse. When pastors and teachers and writers like me lay out a position or extend a call to action, we must be able to study God's thoughts as revealed in Scripture to determine whether or not that position or action is truly within the boundaries of God's truth and character.

> All Scripture is inspired by God and is useful to teach us what is true and to make us realize what is wrong in our lives. It straightens us out and teaches us to do what is right. It is God's way of preparing us in every way, fully equipped for every good thing God wants us to do.
>
> —2 Timothy 3:16–17 NLT

In short, we must endeavor to be men and women who are *thinking* Christians, steeping ourselves in the Bible each day so that we have an accurate frame of reference for the decisions we make and the temptations we face day after day. We must throw off the mantle of spiritual stupidity that enslaves much of the modern church and seek with renewed intensity to know, understand, and apply the thoughts of God in our everyday lives.

This is no easy task; in fact, it takes a lifetime of effort. I'd be lying if I told you otherwise. Yet we are not alone in this pursuit. Every moment, every day, the Spirit of Christ himself walks with us, empowering us to dig more deeply into his Word and pointing our lives toward the highest pinnacles of truth found therein.

And so I end this chapter with a question and a challenge: Friend, do you desire a life of renewed spiritual passion and courage? You'll find it by immersing your thoughts, your time, and your very self into the pages of the book we call the Bible. Only then can you become a *thinking* Christian, a person with the courage and wisdom and passion to follow the truth through this life—and beyond.

It's hard to read the Old Testament like you would read any book. Most books, I pick up from page one and start reading. I wouldn't necessarily recommend that to a newcomer to the Old Testament.

If you just keep plowing through, you hit this huge bulk of prophets, one right after the other, and they're kind of jumbled together. They're not in any kind of chronological order, so you have one prophet talking about Babylon, the next prophet talking about Assyria, and later you find out they're a hundred years apart in reverse order. [Also, the prophetic books] are a collection of sermons, a collection of speeches. It's hard to read thirty speeches in a row...

I think [the Old Testament] is confusing for a lot of people who are serious about the Bible. They don't know what of it still applies today, and that's a tricky deal. You can't figure it out at first reading. You've got to really study it...

I think we need to get an overview [first], a broad sweep, and then only gradually get into the detail.

—Advice from Philip Yancey on reading
(and understanding) the Old Testament[8]

"Sir," the woman said, "I can see that you are a prophet. Our fathers worshiped on this mountain, but you Jews claim that the place where we must worship is in Jerusalem."

Jesus declared, "Believe me, woman, a time is coming when you will worship the Father neither on this mountain nor in Jerusalem. You Samaritans worship what you do not know; we worship what we do know, for salvation is from the Jews. Yet a time is coming and has now come when the true worshipers will worship the Father in spirit and truth, for they are the kind of worshipers the Father seeks. God is spirit, and his worshipers must worship in spirit and in truth."

—John 4:19–24 NIV

3

COURAGE TO WORSHIP

Seeking Intimacy with God through Acts of Worship

There are moments in life when the supernatural invades the natural, when through a mysterious miracle the Spirit of God makes contact, however briefly, with the spirit of a man or woman. In those surprising moments we are treated to a fresh encounter with God—and a time of worshiping in his presence.

I experienced a moment like this just a week ago. It came without warning. I wasn't prepared for it, nor was I seeking it. Yet it came, nonetheless.

To tell you this story, I must first introduce you to a little friend of mine. Her name is Danielle Frandsen, and her very life is a miracle. She's the second child of our favorite family friends, Rick and Ellen Frandsen. Danielle came along after years of disappointment for the Frandsens, after more miscarriages than I care to mention. But finally, through the grace of God and the help of medical professionals, Danielle was born. At the time I write this, she is a beautiful five-year-old with long, curly blond hair and an active imagination.

Last week, my wife, Amy; my son, Tony; and I were visiting the Frandsen's home. While we were laughing, chatting, and getting ready to eat (one of our favorite activities whenever we get together!), I went over and put a CD on their stereo—A *Heavenly Place* by Christian pop star Jaci Velasquez. We'd listened to about half the album when I suddenly noticed that someone had switched the songs, fast-forwarding to a beautiful ballad on prayer titled "On My Knees."

I glanced from the kitchen to the living room to see who was messing with "my" music, and I saw Danielle step away from the stereo. Then, oblivious to the fact that anyone was watching, she began a little ballet of sorts, swaying, spinning, and bowing to the music. When the chorus came around, Jaci Velasquez sang the words, "I get on my knees…" and Danielle did just that, immediately dropping to the floor, kneeling, clasping her hands, and bowing her head in a posture of prayer.

It was a beautiful moment.

The adults were still active in the kitchen, chattering away among the clanking pots and pans. My son was happily (and loudly) playing with the Frandsens' son in the other room. But for me, time froze for just a moment as the image of this five-year-old dancer filled my eyes. Deep inside, I longed to worship with abandon the way this child was doing. It was then I felt the Spirit of Truth moving within my spirit, and all I could do was shake my head, fight back a tear or two, and think to myself, *What a mighty God we serve!*

Then just as quickly as it came, that worshipful moment left. The noise and bustle of the household reentered my mind. The CD went on to the next track, and Danielle found somewhere else to play. But even as my mind transitioned back to earthly time and space, my heart longed for the return of that momentary contact with God. Something inside me needed to worship—and still does.

Like it or not, we are all created to worship. Something within us wants to—no, *needs* to—lift up, admire, praise, and follow a power greater than our own. My brother-in-law, worship leader and lay pastor Ron Stinnett, brought this home for me once during an after-dinner conversation years ago.

Citing a rock concert he'd attended, he suggested that the next time I went to a concert or sporting event, I should watch the crowd instead of the show. So I did. Know what I saw? People raising their hands in exultation. Joyful shouting and singing. Dancing. Hand-clapping. Hugging, laughing, crying, trembling, praising. All the things Ron told me I'd find.

Each of these actions is an expression of worship. We do them naturally, not necessarily because we want to worship a rock star or an athlete, but because they spring from humanity's common need to reach toward something greater than itself. We *need* to worship, and unless we train ourselves to direct that worship to God, we can easily be distracted into acting out a pseudoworship of other things.

COURAGE TO ADMIT THE TRUTH

"Why does God want to be worshiped?" a friend asked me once. "I mean, is he that insecure in who he is that we have to keep reminding him of his supposed greatness? Or is he just a cosmic egomaniac who's not happy unless everybody in the world recites compliments to him?"

The questions may seem harsh, but they are valid, and the person who asked them is one of the most committed Christians I know. He wasn't trying to insult God; he was simply trying to understand him. Sadly, I had no answers for my friend that day, but the questions stayed with me through the years—through days of prayer and nights of studying Scripture and weeks and months of growing ever so slowly into a deeper relationship with God.

Then one day I read (for probably the thousandth time) the story of Jesus as he talked with a woman at a well. The story is found in John 4:1–43, but I'll just summarize it here for you.

A Samaritan woman, despised by Jews because of her race, came to a well to fetch water in the middle of the day. She was alone; her reputation around town as a promiscuous woman had caused her to be ostracized by her community. So when Jesus approached the well and struck up a conversation, she was no doubt surprised that he was totally undeterred by her ethnicity and her reputation. As they talked, Jesus revealed that he knew all about the woman's past, and he challenged her to move forward toward a greater destiny with God.

There is such depth in the record of John 4:1–43 that I could write a whole book on this passage alone. But I want us to focus on one seemingly obscure reference within this story—the words of Jesus in verse 24: "God is spirit, and his worshipers must worship in spirit and in truth."

What strikes me about this verse is Jesus' reference to the "truth" in worship. It seems obvious that to truly worship God we must do so in our spirit, but why did Jesus tack on that emphasis about truth?

Here's my theory: Because truth is the *central element* of worshiping God.

Does God need us to worship him because he is insecure? Of course not. Does God want our worship because he's simply a cosmic egomaniac? Ludicrous. Does he need a daily quota of compliments before he can feel good about himself? That's absurd.

So why does God demand our worship? Simply because when we worship God, when we discipline our minds and hearts to see and recite the wonders of his being, *we acknowledge eternal truth.* We finally remove our eyes from our sinful perceptions of reality and accept the truth of eternity that God is truly who he says he is. We state what is already known so that we can bring our spirits into alignment with the truth of the unseen world around us—and thus into alignment with God.

Are you getting the implications of

> The story goes of a farmer who used to sit in church for long periods of silence. When he was asked about this practice, he said of our Lord, "I look at him and he looks at me, and it is enough." We too have moments when we are struck speechless, as when we are stunned by the beauty of the snow-capped Mount Kilimanjaro in Tanzania, or the majestic roar of the Victoria Falls in Zimbabwe. Our instinctive worshipfulness then comes to the fore with all these created things; how much more when we encounter the Source of it all—God, who is Beauty, Truth, and Goodness? Then we want to fall down to worship and adore the one whose glory fills the heavens and the earth.
>
> —*Bishop Desmond Tutu*[1]

this? Do you see what this means? Worship isn't a crutch for God to use to feel better about himself. Worship is infinitely more for us than it is for God. Jesus doesn't need your puny compliments (or mine, for that matter). But *we* need to speak and act them, because in doing so we become united with the way things really are; we become partners with the truth, and thus we are changed more into his likeness, more into truth.

Fact is, God is awesome, powerful, loving, joyful, compassionate, all-knowing, all-encompassing, *all-everything*, whether we tell him so or not. The absence of our worship takes nothing away from God. Just as nighttime doesn't stop the sun from shining in its heavenly spot, lack of worship doesn't stop God from being God. He is God whether we admit it or not! We *need* to worship him simply because of the truth of who he is—and *we* are made the better for it, not him.

Consider the experience of George Frederick Handel. In 1741 this famed composer took on a new project. Using Scriptures compiled and organized by Charles Jennens, Handel was commissioned to compose a new musical work that he titled *The Messiah*.

While it was no big deal for the composer to take on such a task, what happened to Handel while he worked on the piece was not what he expected. He took the job for money—and ended up meeting God in the process.

It is said that while Handel was composing the musical masterpiece "The Hallelujah Chorus," his servant walked in and found the otherwise arrogant man broken, sobbing over his work. As Handel had been writing a chorus of simple praise to Christ that primarily repeated the word *Hallelujah* over and over, something happened inside him. For a few brief, yet precious moments, the chorus in Handel's

> America has a worship problem. Our surveys among regular church-going adults indicate that one-third of these people have never experienced God's presence. Half of all regular churchgoing adults admit that they have not experienced God's presence at any time during the past year.
>
> —Dr. George Barna, pollster[2]

heart echoed the song of heaven, and he was changed because of that worshipful encounter.

As tears streamed down his aristocratic face, Handel sat humbled before his servant and could only explain, "I did think I did see all heaven before me, and the great God himself."[3]

It's been more than two and a half centuries since George Frederick Handel wrote "The Hallelujah Chorus," but even today this aria of praise evokes a sense of wonder and worship in its listeners— and performers. Simply stating the truth of God's awesome power through the combination of orchestra and voices is still enough to facilitate a peek at our "great God himself."

To worship, then, is to glimpse the truth about God and the universe around us, to acknowledge it, to order our very being around that truth. And in doing that, we reap the benefit.

COURAGE TO WORSHIP GOD WITH WORDS AND ACTIONS

Yet we are often found lacking in this area of our lives. We assume that "worship" means simply to attend a weekly worship service at church. We figure if we sing along with the hymns and praise songs during the service, then we've done our "worship duty" for the week and can get on with the rest of our lives.

Listen to what Christian pollster George Barna has to say on that subject: "You can never give God too much worship; he revels in it. Worship is not meant to be simply a Sunday morning activity—it is not something you turn on at 11:00 A.M. on Sunday and switch off at noon, not to be worried about for the next 167 hours. Worship is meant to be a regular part of our daily existence."[4]

The story is told of a young man who wanted to reach a deeper level of spirituality, so he determined to spend a day following a monk around and recording his habits. The monk rose early and sat by a window, waiting for the sunrise. When the first rays of dawn broke over the horizon and into the monk's eyes, he smiled and said quietly, "Praise the Lord." The young man wrote the words on his notepad.

At breakfast, the monk placed a spoonful of food in his mouth and smiled. "Praise the Lord," he whispered between bites, and the young man wrote this down too. Next the monk spent the morning working in the garden, weeding, sweating, pruning, and churning the earth to bring forth healthy vegetables. While he worked he hummed a little tune. Every once in a while, words would spill out: "Praise the Lord." The young man took note.

Finally the monk stretched and cracked his back, trying to uncramp his shoulders and feel the blood flow through his limbs again. As he did, he looked toward heaven and said the words, "Praise the Lord!" The young man scribbled on the notepad.

The rest of the day went the same. The monk would do some mundane activity, stop for a moment, and utter the phrase, "Praise the Lord." At the end of the day, the young student looked through his notes. Page after page said the same thing: "Praise the Lord." The frustrated young man threw his notepad down and spoke to the monk.

"All day long, no matter what you were doing, all you did was say 'Praise the Lord.' What's the matter with you? Don't you know anything else to say? What in the world are you doing anyway?"

The monk simply smiled, put a calming hand on the young man's shoulder, and said, "Isn't it obvious? I'm practicing for eternity."

That, my friend, is the way we need to approach the thought of worship in our lives. If what we hope for in God truly comes to pass (and it will), then our days in eternity will be spent in the joyous rapture of praising our Lord. If we can't take the time or make the effort to do that now, how can we say we'll enjoy doing it in heaven?

We can't let the routines and busyness of this life keep us from the truth of God's beauty and love and peace and presence. We must summon our courage and say to ourselves, "I will worship God

A Prayer of Worship

Great is He!
One yet Three.
Let God reign.
Praise His name.
Daily He gives us
water and bread.
By His Holy Spirit our
souls will be fed.
He gives to us life even
though we be dead.
Oh, praise His name!

—Author unknown[5]

today—no matter what my circumstance, no matter what my feelings, no matter if the sun shines or the rain comes. *Today* I will worship God."

How do we do that, you ask? The ways of worship will vary from person to person, but here are a few ideas for you:

Sing.

Sing in the shower.

Sing yourself to sleep.

Whistle while you work.

Marvel at God's creation.

Take in the wonder of your spouse.

Hike through a place of beauty in nature.

Thank God.

Meditate on God's character and actions.

Serve another.

Help a stranger.

Compliment God.

Remember God's love and goodness toward you.

Laugh.

Dance.

Go on a "date" with God (take him wherever you go).

Tell someone about Jesus.

Recite scriptures.

Tap your fingers on the table.

Breathe his name.

Love, love, and love some more.

Of course there are myriad ways to focus your thoughts and heart and soul on the awesome God we serve, but I think you get the idea. Worship must be more than an hour spent at church. We must be courageous enough to seek God's presence in both the majestic and the mundane moments of life. We must be as willing to worship God while standing in the shower as we are while sitting in a pew! God hasn't changed in either circumstance—and he's certainly not embarrassed at the sight of us at any point of the day.

In short, we must live a life of total abandonment to the truth of God's greatness. And in those moments of seeking to recognize God's glory, he miraculously draws us closer to himself.

Would you like to live a life of spiritual passion? Then learn to worship Jesus, the one who has no equal. In that worship, you'll find the passion that comes from seeing—and knowing—the truth.

IN THE END, ALL THAT MATTERS IS GOD

I have many heroes. My mother, for one, who as a teenager had the courage to walk away from her family's religion (Islam) and into the arms of Jesus. My friend Ray Hummel, father of the senior pastor at my church—a decorated war veteran, a successful businessman, and a wonderful family man. When I grow up, I want to be just like him. Mark Brunell, a pro football quarterback I've never met but who inspires me by his athletic performance on the football field and his Christian example off it.

My son, Tony, who has the talent, intelligence and potential to accomplish so much more than I ever will. John Duckworth, who is already the writer I only hope to become. Charles Colson and Mother Teresa, who have changed the world simply by caring enough to act on behalf of the weak, the lonely, and the forgotten.

In the end, though, none of the accomplishments of these unforgettable people are worth a hill of beans. Don't get me wrong. I'm not saying it's sinful to admire and even desire to emulate men and women of great courage and accomplishment. But I am saying that nothing any human ever does (myself included) can match the overwhelming, mind-numbing goodness of God.

So that leaves me with a choice. Do I dedicate my life to the pursuit of—and thus, the worship of—the temporary things of my world? Or do I allow those temporary things to hone me, direct me, shape my will toward the worship of the eternal truth, the everlasting God?

If life were a test, that would be the question I'd have to answer every day of my existence. Some days (I hope) I answer it correctly by focusing my heart and actions and desire on the awesome God I serve.

Most days, though, I choose the wrong answer and spend my heart on the temporary. I am weakened when I do that, and the power of Satan's lying will is strengthened in my life. But thankfully, God continually wipes my slate clean and offers me opportunity after opportunity to take this simple test of loyalty and worship.

My very being has been designed to worship. Yours has too. And no matter where the moments of our lives find us, we are constantly presented with new opportunities to let our words, our attitudes, and our lives transform the mundane minutes of life into golden intervals of eternal praise. Because when all is said and done, when this universe unravels and all we know and comprehend has been abolished into nothingness, God and God alone will remain. Just as it was in the beginning, so too in the end: God is all that matters.

Today might be a good day to start getting used to that fact. So let's purpose, as best we can, to spend our moments worshiping God. When we do that, we will supersede the natural world and glimpse the truth and majesty of our supernatural God—the perfect one who gave his all for insignificant creatures like you and like me.

GET ME TO THE CHURCH ON TIME

One of the most basic worship actions we can do is to involve ourselves deeply and regularly in a local Christian church. Christ ordained that we should go through this life in tandem with our brothers and sisters of faith—not without them. If you need more incentive to get involved, listen to these ten reasons President Theodore Roosevelt gave for going to church:

1. In this actual world a churchless community, a community where men have abandoned and scoffed at or ignored their religious needs, is a community on the rapid downgrade. It is perfectly true that occasional individuals or families may have nothing to do with church or religious practices and observances and yet maintain the highest standard of spirituality and of ethical obligations. But this does not affect the case in the world as it now is…

2. *Church work and church attendance mean the cultivation of the habit of feeling some responsibility for others and the sense of braced moral strength which prevents a relaxation of one's own moral fiber.*

3. *There are enough holidays for most of us which can quite properly be devoted to pure holiday making…. Sundays differ from other holidays—among other ways—in the fact that there are fifty-two of them every year…. On Sunday, go to church.*

4. *Yes, I know all the excuses. I know that one can worship the Creator and dedicate oneself to good living in a grove of trees, or by a running brook, or in one's own house, just as well as in church. But I also know as a matter of cold fact the average man does not thus worship or thus dedicate himself. If he stays away from church he does not spend his time in good works or in lofty meditation. He looks over the colored supplement of the newspaper.*

5. *He may not hear a good sermon at church. But unless he is very unfortunate, he will hear a sermon by a good man who, with his good wife, is engaged all the week long in a series of wearing and humdrum and important tasks for making hard lives a little easier.*

6. *He will listen to and take part in reading some beautiful passages from the Bible. And if he is not familiar with the Bible, he has suffered a loss….*

7. *He will probably take part in singing some good hymns.*

8. *He will meet and nod to, or speak to, good, quiet neighbors…. He will come away feeling a little more charitably toward all the world, even those excessively foolish young men who regard church-going as rather a soft performance.*

9. *I advocate a man's joining in church works for the sake of showing his faith by his works.*

10. *The man who does not, in some way, active or not, connect himself with some active, working church misses many opportunities for helping his neighbors, and therefore, incidentally, for helping himself.*[6]

Part Two

THE
COST OF
PURSUING
GOD

After this, Jesus went out and saw a tax
collector by the name of Levi sitting at his tax booth.
"Follow me," Jesus said to him, and Levi got up,
left everything and followed him.

—Luke 5:27–28 NIV

Now as He was going out on the road, one came running, knelt before Him, and asked Him, "Good Teacher, what shall I do that I may inherit eternal life?"

So Jesus said to him, "Why do you call Me good? No one is good but One, that is, God. You know the commandments: 'Do not commit adultery,' 'Do not murder,' 'Do not steal,' 'Do not bear false witness,' 'Do not defraud,' 'Honor your father and your mother.'"

And he answered and said to Him, "Teacher, all these things I have kept from my youth."

Then Jesus, looking at him, loved him, and said to him, "One thing you lack: Go your way, sell whatever you have and give to the poor, and you will have treasure in heaven; and come, take up the cross, and follow Me."

But he was sad at this word, and went away sorrowful, for he had great possessions.

—Mark 10:17–22 NKJV

4

COURAGE TO GIVE YOUR ALL

Living a Life Completely Dedicated to Jesus

Li Dexian was ready when they came for him in January of 2000. True, his heart beat a little faster and worry stole into his mind, but this was the eighth time he'd been "detained" in just the last three months—not to mention the numerous other arrests he'd suffered during the 1980s and 1990s. Li knew what to expect. At least, he hoped he did.

He went quietly, without a fuss. He said good-bye to his wife then walked calmly out the door with the police officers of the Chinese Republic. God willing, he'd be allowed to come home before too long. God willing.

Li's mind flitted back to memories of previous arrests by China's communist officials. One "visit" in prison stood out—the time police beat him until he vomited blood, the result of broken ribs at the hands of his guards. There had been other beatings and threats and arrests— even the arrests of his wife and visiting friends from other countries. You see, China believes Li Dexian is a notorious criminal, a desperate lawbreaker with a penchant for illegal behavior.

Li's crime? He is a Christian and the pastor of a medium-sized Protestant church in Yongming Village in Gwangzhou (Canton), China. Every Tuesday—if he's not in jail—he leads two Bible studies attended by about six hundred people. That makes him a wanted man by the Chinese government—and a man exempt from the protection normally provided to Chinese citizens by the police.

> I trust in my Lord God, who put His mind, will, and affection in my heart, and choose to lose all my worldly substance, and my life, too, rather than deny His known truth.
>
> —Bishop Nicholas Ridley, Christian martyr who was burned at the stake in 1555[1]

"Li Dexian is Gwangzhou's illegal religion organization's leader," one government report states. During an arrest in 1998, police told Li that he was "creating a public disorder by illegal preaching."

In spite of this kind of opposition to his faith, Li Dexian refuses to give up on Christ. "I will preach until I die," he says, knowing full well that his Christianity could bring that about sooner rather than later.[2]

CHRISTIANITY IS NOT A SAFE RELIGION

Why do I tell you this story? Because there's something very important that you should know: Christianity is not a safe religion.[3]

One look at Christian history should be proof of that. The hallways of Christianity's past are better described as graveyards because so many of our forebears sacrificed their lives for the cause of our Christian faith. In fact, the roll call of martyrs for Christ is so long I would venture to bet that it would make the list at the Vietnam War Memorial seem short by comparison.

"Ah, but Mike," you say. "This is America. Surely we are safe as Christians in this country, at least."

Possibly. And possibly not. True, we do have more freedom to practice faith in Christ in the United States than in places like China or the Middle East. Still, we are blind if we don't recognize that the social climate of our country at the start of the second millennium indicates a greater and greater intolerance toward the Christian faith.

We've all experienced the thinly veiled contempt of peers who call Christians "Jesus freaks" or "right-wing nuts" or "doctor killers" or "intolerant bigots" or...well, you get the idea. In a country where freedom of expression is one of the highest ideals, Christian expression is often looked down upon and even derided by otherwise centrist-thinking citizens. Why, even in the presidential primary elections of early 2000, one front-running candidate courted "mainstream America" by publicly denouncing several prominent Christian leaders of our day. Political strategists applauded his move, saying that his critical attack on religious leaders made him a more appealing candidate.

> Save in order to give your life away, not to retire comfortably.... The gift of our life is something to be used up in the ministry of God.
>
> —Lynn Miller[4]

But that's not all. Consider this sampling of recent news reports telling of anti-Christian sentiment readily accepted by our society:

- University of Nebraska football player Aaron Wills was reprimanded by his coach and athletic director for taping a small white cross to the front of his face mask. A former drug abuser, he had been rescued from that habit by a conversion to Christianity. He put the cross on his face mask, he says, "to remind me that Jesus has to come before me on every play." Some fine, upstanding Nebraska fans saw the cross and called into the athletic director's radio show to complain about Wills's personal Christian "display." Soon after, Wills was ordered to remove the cross.[5]

- When the American Civil Liberties Union spotted players and a coach praying together after a University of Colorado basketball game, they protested the practice to university leadership. The protest effectively put an end to the voluntary practice of prayer after games.[6]

- Recently, a federal circuit court banned voluntary, student-led prayer in high schools in three states. As of the writing of this book, the case was pending appeal on the docket of the United States Supreme Court.[7]

- After the horrendous Columbine High School shooting tragedy in 1999, carpenter Greg Zanis erected thirteen crosses (one for each person killed) at Clement Park in the Denver metropolitan area as memorials for those slain in the attack. The crosses became places of mourning for relatives, neighbors, and friends of the victims. Hundreds streamed to the display, leaving letters, flowers, balloons, and other mementos at the base of the crosses. But the Freedom from Religion Foundation complained, calling the place of emotional healing a "monstrous, Christian-oriented memorial." The local government agreed with that sentiment and ordered that the crosses be torn down.[8]

- In March 1998, a Christian couple in east Denver, David and Diane Reiter, began hosting a women's Bible study in their home. Around eight to twelve women usually attended—until October of that year. That was when the Reiters' neighbors complained to the city government about the Christian gathering. In response, Denver city officials declared that the Bible study was in violation of zoning law and declared the meeting illegal. In a compromise effort, the government said it would allow one—and only one—Bible study each month. It took more than a year for that anti–Bible-study order to be overturned (which it was in December of 1999), and only then after the American Center for Law and Justice, a Christian-based legal organization, protested the order in court.[9]

- Sometimes the most vocal opponents to our Christian faith are other Christians themselves. Witness the hoopla surrounding a proposed community service and evangelism initiative in Chicago. In early 2000, Baptists planned an outreach strategy in that area that included block parties, food and clothing drives for the city's underprivileged population, and church planting. Critics of the plan spoke out immediately, likening the effort to an "invading army" of Baptists. The Council of

Religious Leaders of Chicago also threw in their two cents, saying the outreach would foment "faith-based prejudice" and lead to "hate crimes"—and thus should be canceled.[10]

- In a separate incident, Baptists printed a prayer guide and encouraged Christians to pray for Jews and Hindus to come to Christ. The Anti-Defamation League angrily branded this as "an attack on [Jewish] integrity and commitment." Hindu leaders were equally outraged that Christians would dare to pray for them and lashed out with threats of a "holy war"—all because Christians dared to pray.[11]

Add to these the numerous reports of church burnings, church shootings, and the like, and it's obvious that Christianity is not on any "most-favored-religion" list. I'm not telling you these stories to plant fear or suggest that Christians need to "strike back" at our godless society. I *am* telling you because you need to know that within your lifetime, it's possible that Christians could be seriously oppressed by our society and our government.

When (or if) that happens, how will you respond? Will you have the courage to pursue your relationship with Christ when it means you must give up everything? When it costs you a job or a reputation or assets or wealth or position or status or a home or property or relationships? That, my friend, is something you and I need to decide today, before we ever face such an oppressive, costly situation. Otherwise, we are doomed to enter the coming persecution weak, unprepared, and defeated before we begin.

COURAGE TO DO MORE THAN DIE

But there is more to a passionate Christian life than being willing to welcome death rather than compromising a relationship with Jesus. Which is more difficult, to *die* for Christ or to *live* for Christ?

That's a question that sometimes haunts me. I can't guarantee how I would respond if I were faced with the choice of death or denying Christ. I like to believe that (by God's grace) I would choose to join the

One reporter, while acknowledging that Prison Fellowship did good work, challenged my "exclusivist" message. "All roads lead to heaven," he insisted.

I asked if he approved of Mother Teresa. "Of course," he replied, others nodding approvingly.

"Do you know why she helps the dying?"

"She's a great humanitarian," the reporter shrugged.

"No," I answered. "She does it because she loves Jesus—the one who says he is the only road to heaven. And that's why I do the work you like in the prisons. I wouldn't do it for a moral teacher."

There were no more questions.

—Charles Colson[12]

ranks of the martyrs rather than compromise this great relationship God has given me.

But the truth is I'm faced with a more important decision each time I roll out of bed in the morning: Am I willing to *live* this day for Christ? Or will I blithely deny him through my attitudes, words, and actions as the minutes turn to hours and the sun slowly sets on another piece of my life?

If any cause is worth dying for, it is the cause of Christ. But even more, a relationship with God is worth *living* for! Still, a life lived in passionate devotion to Jesus is easier said than done. It costs more than we care to admit—everything we are and everything we have, minute after minute, hour after hour, day after day. Choosing that kind of life is difficult, and all the more so if you are blessed with an abundance of life's finer things.

Don't believe me? Just ask the one we know as the rich young ruler. His story is told in Mark 10:17–22, but let me retell it for you here.

The story takes place on a dusty road somewhere in first-century Judea. Jesus, as usual, has been teaching and healing and helping people in the area. Now he is ready to move on, and he begins to walk away and head out on another trip around the Judean countryside.

A young man whose name isn't mentioned has been standing nearby, witnessing the power and work of Christ and hearing the truth that has been spilling from the Messiah's lips. Longing stirs up deep within him. Whatever it is that this Savior has, he wants it—and he wants it now.

Seeing Jesus turn and walk away triggers something in the man. The adrenaline rushes into his bloodstream, and before he knows it, he is racing down the road to catch Jesus.

The running straggler catches the Lord's eye, and Jesus stops and waits. Breathlessly the man asks the question burning in his heart. "Good Teacher," he says, "what shall I do that I may inherit eternal life?"

In my mind's eye, I picture Jesus pausing a moment, looking this young man over from head to foot, from heart to soul. Is this young man serious? Perhaps.

Jesus responds with the standard answer: Keep the commandments; don't commit adultery; don't murder; et cetera, et cetera, et cetera. Then he waits.

The young man knows there is more; he can feel it in his spirit. "Teacher," he says, "all these things I have kept from my youth."

And now Jesus is ready to give this young man the chance of a lifetime—the chance to walk with God. I picture a smile coming across Christ's face, a hand reaching out to touch the man's shoulder, a level gaze going uninterrupted from the eyes of God to the eyes of this man. Then Jesus drops the bomb.

"Go... sell whatever you have...take up the cross, and follow me."

Pow! Suddenly, unexpectedly, the man realizes what the Lord is asking. The ticket to eternal life is more than just a life lived by proper guidelines and rules. It will cost him everything—everything he owns, everything he is.

Silence reigns in that moment. Jesus waits. The young man adds things up, but the tally finally gets too high. Sadly, he chooses the temporary instead of the eternal. He turns his back on God and walks away—a rich man unwilling to part with his wealth, even for the prize of eternal life.

Jesus presents that same demand to you and me today. He asks not only that we have the courage to die for him; even more, he demands that we have the courage to *live* for him.

That means we give up all right and title to anything we are and anything we own and place it in his hands. We courageously attempt to live out our daily experience in ways that are pleasing to him, ways of integrity, honor, and truth. We freely walk away from sin and into his arms of grace every moment, every hour, every day. We give up our dreams and ask God to give us his dreams instead. We pray daily for God's desire for our lives to become our own desire for our lives—whatever that means and whatever the cost.

If only it were as easy to do these things as it is to talk about them! Fact is, we *can't* do them. We, in our own strength, face an impossible task if we want to pursue God with that kind of passion and abandonment. Only the strength of the Holy Spirit can empower us to live this kind of life for Christ, which means our primary responsibility is this: We must constantly plead for God's Holy Spirit to make this lifestyle possible—and then follow his leading when that power comes.

And that leads me to one last thought I'd like to share in this chapter.

SIXPENCE NONE THE RICHER

God demands our all in a relationship with him; that much is obvious. What isn't always so obvious, though, is that everything God demands of us he gives to us first! That's so true it bears repeating:

We can give nothing to God that he hasn't already given to us.

Forgive me, now, for appealing to late-night television to underscore this point, but a segment of the *Late Show with David Letterman* explains exactly what I'm trying to communicate here. In July 1999 Letterman was interviewing guest Leigh Nash, lead singer for the pop music group Sixpence None the Richer. He asked Nash to explain how her band got that unusual name.

She replied, "It comes from the book *Mere Christianity* by C. S. Lewis. A little boy asks his father [for] a sixpence [coin]…to get a gift for his father. The father's happy with the gift but also realizes he's not any richer for the transaction because he gave his son the money in the first place."

David Letterman summed it up then, saying, "He bought his own gift."

"That's right," Nash continued. "C. S. Lewis was comparing that to his belief that God has given him and us the gifts that we possess, and to serve [God] the way we should, we should do it humbly, realizing how we got those gifts in the first place."

Letterman, though certainly not a theologian or even a professed Christian, took in that concept and had only one thing to say: "Well, that's beautiful."[13]

And good ol' Dave is right. It is beautiful that God would not ask anything of us that he is not willing first to give.

Our world, our talents, our intelligence, our beauty, our efforts, our work, our interests, our abilities, our very lives—all are gifts we received from the Maker. Like a father who owns all the toys and furniture and appliances the children use in his house, God simply asks to be allowed to use with us the "home furnishings" we call our lives. He asks that we share them for his purposes, not hoard them for ourselves like selfish and spoiled sons and daughters.

At some point in our lives we need to take a hard look at everything we call our own, both the tangible (possessions, money, time, talents) and the intangible (personality, relationships, hopes, dreams). Then we must ask ourselves: Are we willing to give these to God, regardless of the cost? Will we trust God's plans for these gifts—even if it leads us into dangerous territory?

Yes, it's true that passionate Christianity is not a safe religion. It could very well cause your death. But even if it doesn't, it still costs you your life.

Are you courageous enough to give your all to God? To ask for the Holy Spirit's help as you recommit every minute, every thought, every hope, every asset, every action to Jesus and his plans for you? Maybe now is a good time for you to close this book and ask God to help you consider how you've answered these questions in the past—and how you will answer them from this day forward.

Remember, it will cost you everything to say yes.
And it will be worth every bit of it.

WHAT ARE YOU HOLDING BACK FROM GOD?

*What in your life are you unwilling to give completely to God?
Look prayerfully over this list as a starting point for answering that
question. Then if you find areas of concern, begin by telling God
that although you are unwilling to completely give those areas to
him, you are at least willing to be made willing to give him your all.*

Ambitions	Cars	Children
Church involvement	Comforts	Conveniences
Desires	Dreams	Education
Entertainment	Family	Friendships
Goals	Habits	Health
Hobbies	Homes	Intellect
Interests	Jobs	Marriage
Ministry	Money	Parents
Prejudices	Prestige	Pride
Self-image	Sex	Strengths
Stubbornness	Talents	Thoughts
Time	Weaknesses	

Jesus knew that the Father had given him power over everything and that he had come from God and was going back to God. So during the meal Jesus stood up and took off his outer clothing. Taking a towel, he wrapped it around his waist. Then he poured water into a bowl and began to wash the followers' feet, drying them with the towel that was wrapped around him.

Jesus came to Simon Peter, who said to him, "Lord, are you going to wash my feet?"

Jesus answered, "You don't understand now what I am doing, but you will understand later."

Peter said, "No, you will never wash my feet."

Jesus answered, "If I don't wash your feet, you are not one of my people."

Simon Peter answered, "Lord, then wash not only my feet, but wash my hands and my head, too!"

Jesus said, "After a person has had a bath, his whole body is clean. He needs only to wash his feet. And you men are clean, but not all of you." Jesus knew who would turn against him, and that is why he said, "Not all of you are clean."

When he had finished washing their feet, he put on his clothes and sat down again. He asked, "Do you understand what I have just done for you? You call me 'Teacher' and 'Lord,' and you are right, because that is what I am. If I, your Lord and Teacher, have washed your feet, you also should wash each other's feet. I did this as an example so that you should do as I have done for you. I tell you the truth, a servant is not greater than his master. A messenger is not greater than the one who sent him. If you know these things, you will be happy if you do them.

—John 13:3–17 NCV

5

COURAGE TO SERVE

Serving God by Serving Others

I was thirty-two years old when I had my ear pierced. Some claimed I was trying to "recapture my lost youth," but the truth is I did it for two reasons. One, I liked the way it looked; but the greater motivation came from a story I heard about ancient Israel.

As you are probably aware, slavery was a common thing to ancient people, and Israel was no exception. There were several ways one could become a slave, one of them being a means to pay off a debt. And that happened often. A man would find himself unable to pay what he owed and thus would promise to serve as a slave to the owner of the debt. According to the Jewish law, that slave was bound by the terms of this servitude for seven years. At the end of seven years, the master was obligated to set the slave free and consider his debt paid in full.

Now here's the interesting part: Upon being set free, any slave could willingly *choose* to remain with the master. When presented with freedom, that slave could *refuse* it, choosing to remain a slave.

Why would a slave do that? Biblical historians tell us that (contrary to much of America's slave history) slaves in ancient Hebrew homes were often well treated—even considered valued members of the family. In such cases, a slave might have reasoned that life as a servant in a prosperous and healthy family atmosphere was a fate better than that of a poor, hungry freeman who would likely find himself in debt again and eventually enslaved by another master—perhaps a cruel one this time.

If a slave chose to give up the right to freedom, that person submitted to having his or her ear pierced in a legal ceremony. The slave would announce the intent to remain in service to the master; then the master would lead the slave to a doorpost of the house and pierce the slave's ear with an awl, pinning it to the post. From that day on, the slave bore the mark of voluntary servitude, and anyone who saw that pierced ear would know this person had loved the master so much that he or she chose to remain a slave when freedom beckoned.[1]

On July 15, 1980, as a sixteen-year-old, I, too, made a choice to serve a loving master, and I gave my life completely to Jesus Christ. And so now, in a very small way like those servants of old, I bear the mark of a slave—a testimony that I'm no longer my own. Rather, I am a bond-slave to Jesus Christ.

COURAGE TO BE A SERVANT AT ALL TIMES

Now here's an interesting fact I discovered later, at thirty-three: My choice as a Christian is not whether I will or will not be a servant. If that were so, my servanthood would be defined only by what I do. The truth is I *am* a servant, whether I choose to serve faithfully or not. My servanthood is not defined by what I do; *it's defined by who I am* and then *expressed by what I do.*

That means as Christians, you and I are God's servants at all times. The only thing in question is whether we are faithful servants—or lazy, disobedient, selfish ones!

> Life is so unnerving for a servant who's not serving!
>
> —Lumiere (as portrayed by Jerry Orbach) in Disney's Beauty and the Beast[2]

Let me share with you two examples of what I mean. As a professional writer, I am often approached by well-meaning individuals who say something like this: "You're a writer, huh? I want to be a writer too. I know I've got a book in me somewhere."

Whenever someone says that to me, I always ask, "What are you writing right now?"

Ninety-eight percent of the people get flustered at this question and sputter, "Oh, well, I haven't written anything yet. But someday I'm going to. Or better yet, how about I tell you my idea and you write it for me?"

I always nod politely and excuse myself from the conversation at that point. Want to know why? Because a person isn't made a writer by publishing a book. (In fact, I know a man who has published more than ten books and never written a word in any of them!)

Writers write because they can't help but write—because something within the core of their being demands that words be put down on paper. Perhaps he's a teenager who makes up stories during free time in class. Or she's a doctor who keeps a journal of poetry. Or she's a mom who writes and directs Bible plays for her kids' Sunday school class. Or he's a dad who composes love letters to his wife—just because.

You see, writers write because that's an essential part of who they are. To ask a writer not to write—whether the words are published or not—is like asking a flower not to bloom or a bird not to sing. Likewise we are not made servants of Christ by what we do; we serve him because of who we are. Not to serve would simply be out of character for any Christian.

I see you shaking your head out there. You're still not convinced, are you? Then let me share another, more personal example.

In December of 1996 I had surgery to remove a diseased gallbladder. For most folks, the body adjusts to that change within about two weeks, and life goes back to normal. For me, however, that didn't happen. Instead, my body kept working as if my gallbladder were still there, and the result has been chronic nausea.

For six months, from Christmas 1996 until June of 1997, my doctors had no idea what was wrong with me. The nausea was so severe that I could barely keep any food down. I lost weight and became weak and disabled. (Imagine having a stomach flu for about six months and you've got a good picture of what I was like during that time.)

For six long months I spent most of my life lying in bed, exhausted and nauseated, praying I wouldn't throw up. I dropped out of leadership on the youth ministry team at my church. I quit speaking at churches and other gatherings. I could barely even write, and my wife ended up taking on several writing assignments I'd previously committed to doing.

Was I no longer a servant of Christ? Of course not. My prolonged illness didn't mean I was kicked out of Jesus' service. My inability to perform my previous servant functions (speaking, teaching, leading, and so on) didn't redefine my existence and place me among the non-servants of God. Even when I could literally do nothing for him, Christ still welcomed me into his family of servants. I was his servant then, and I am still his servant now. My actions didn't define who I was; who I was defined my actions.

It's the same with you, friend. Think about it. If you are ill and take a sick day off work, does that mean you're no longer an employee of your company? Of course not. You still retain your title and responsibilities in spite of the fact that you are unable to fulfill them during your illness. And it's the same in the kingdom of Christ. As a Christian, you are a servant. Now you get to choose what kind of servant you'll be.

COURAGE TO ACCEPT A SERVANT'S TREATMENT

My wife, Amy, has a familiar saying that she's always happy to remind me of when I grumble about having to take out the trash or do a load of laundry: "Everybody wants to be known as a servant, but nobody wants to be treated like one!"

I'd laugh at that saying, except it's all too true! After reading the Scriptures, though, I have to add one element to her wisdom: "Everybody wants to be a servant, but nobody wants to be treated like one—except for Jesus."

John 13:1–17 gives us a most unusual picture. On the night before his crucifixion, Jesus gathered his disciples for a Passover meal. The men had walked to Jerusalem, hurrying to make it in time for this evening ritual. The sandals they wore were no doubt crusted over with dirt, their feet likely swollen and smudged with sweat and sand and stench. And so they all reclined at the table for the meal. Then the Lord of All, the one they called Master, God's omnipotent Messiah, did the unthinkable.

During the meal Jesus stood up and took off his outer clothing. Taking a towel, he wrapped it around his waist, making himself into an image of a lowly slave. Then he poured water into a bowl and began to wash his followers' feet, drying them with the towel that was wrapped around him.

I've seen some dirty feet in my time. I've even had stinky ones myself. But the thought of cleaning off the soles of a dozen desert travelers repulses me! What's more, the image of Jesus Christ willfully making himself a slave to his followers shocks and appalls me. I have to admit that had I been there, I would have reacted the way Peter did when Christ came to him. While the other disciples watched in stunned silence, Peter protested. "You will never wash my feet," he said.

Peter knew that to wash someone's feet was a debasement like few others. It was the task of worthless, lowly servants—not one for the King of Kings. Yet in the conversation that ensued, Jesus commanded Peter to allow the Christ to be his slave. Wow.

In this picture of Jesus the slave recorded in John 13, I find five principles that define what it means to be a faithful servant of Christ. For lack of a better term, I'll call them the Five Laws of Servant Living:

Law #1: A faithful servant sees the need—and meets it. The Bible gives no record that Jesus' disciples grumbled about the fact that no servant had come to wash their feet (as would have been customary). There's no indication that anyone even recognized this as a problem. But Jesus did. With the eyes of a slave intent upon a task, Jesus, the Lord of everyone there, saw the dirty sandals. He saw the mud caked between the toes of several of his followers, maybe even smelled the remnants of camel dung accidentally walked through by a disciple or two. When no one else saw a need, he alone recognized the opportunity to serve—and then acted upon that opportunity without being asked.

Consider the perspective of a slave. A slave sees all of life from the viewpoint of slavery. He does not see himself as possessing the same rights as free men and women. Please understand me, when this slavery is involuntary it is cruel and dehumanizing. When the slavery is freely chosen, however, everything is changed. Voluntary servitude is a great joy.

—Richard Foster[3]

Law #2: A faithful servant does the dirty work. You can imagine what it must have been like for Jesus to stick his hands and face near the disciples' smelly feet! I don't even like to get near my wife's tennis shoes, let alone get close enough to wipe them out and make them clean. Jesus, on the other hand, had no such qualms. If he were on the staff of a church today, he'd be the kind of pastor who'd pitch in to help clean the rest rooms with the janitor or join the gardener in the sweaty work of tending the church lawn. There was no task "beneath" the Creator of All, whether it was cleaning the dust and dirt off his creations' feet or sacrificing his own life to save those he'd made.

Law #3: A faithful servant is determined to serve. Seeing Jesus as a servant was a new idea for his disciples. Simon Peter even begged him not to wash his feet! But think of this: Jesus knew that as he wiped the streaking mud from the feet of Judas Iscariot, he was serving the one who would betray him in just a few short hours. Yet he let no obstacle come between him and the service at hand. He would serve these men, and nothing they could say or do would keep him from it.[4]

Law #4: A faithful servant seeks no reward. After he had finished washing the disciples' feet, Jesus didn't stand with his palm out, like a bellhop waiting for a tip. He didn't demand that somebody wash his feet in return. He provided the foot-washing service completely free of charge—no hidden fees, no special commendation expected, nothing. He didn't even ask the men to say thank you! That's because Jesus' motivation was to serve, period—not to serve in hopes of gaining a reward in response.

Law #5: A faithful servant leads by example. The time was short. It was only hours before Jesus was to be falsely accused, tried, and executed. But even in that hour, Jesus was the ultimate example of godliness—and he proved it by being the ultimate example of faithful servanthood. "If I, your Lord and Teacher, have washed your feet, you also should wash each other's feet," he said. We would be wise to follow Christ's example —and lead by demonstrating that example to others.

We have a high calling, you and I. As followers of Jesus Christ, we are called to be followers of his example of servanthood. Out of passion for our Lord, we must join him in giving ourselves in faithful service to God and to those in our world. You see, in God's kingdom, the highest calling is the lowest one of all. And just as Christ was willing to debase himself and faithfully serve, we too are expected to be faithful servants—and to *be willing to be treated* as servants.

I'll tell you right now, this kind of servanthood is terribly hard for me. It probably is for you too. But we can be secure in the knowledge that we *will* be rewarded for our service—not in this lifetime, perhaps, but in our eternal life with Christ that is to come.

COURAGE TO SERVE GOD AND TO SERVE OTHERS

So how exactly are we to faithfully express our servanthood to God? If we are indeed servants already, how can we train ourselves (with the Holy Spirit's help, of course) to be *faithful* servants? The answer is twofold. First, we must act out our servanthood to God in spiritual discipline; and second, we must serve God by serving others.

There's a reason that I started this book with chapters on prayer, Bible study, and worship—because practice of those spiritual disciplines is fundamental to a passionate Christian life! It's through prayer, reading and meditating on Scripture, and worship that we grow in intimacy with the Lord. And it's through these spiritual disciplines that we discover his purpose for us, the reasons he has made us as we are and the tasks he intends for us to fulfill.

The story is told of a man who owned a chain of shoe stores. As was his custom, every few months he visited each store in person to see how it was doing and to offer advice for improving the store's performance.

Upon arriving at one particular store, the owner noticed that everything was in disarray. The display window was half-empty, and the shoes that were there were strewn around in no particular order. Stepping inside the store, he found price tags switched, signs lying in a heap on the floor, and shoes stacked randomly around the room instead of ordered on the shelves as they were supposed to be. The few customers in the store were scratching their heads as they dug through the piles, trying to find shoes that fit their feet and their fancy.

Searching frantically, the owner finally found a salesclerk chatting happily on the telephone behind the counter, oblivious to the melee around her.

"Excuse me," said the owner, "what are you doing?"

Pausing her conversation for a moment, the girl said, "Oh, I work here. Did you want to buy something?"

"No," the owner replied, reaching behind the counter to pull out the store manual. "But if you work here, why are the prices all mixed up? Why are customers waiting on themselves? Why haven't you set up the displays like this manual describes?"

"Oh, that," said the clerk. "Hey, this is a busy store. I don't have time to read some thick old manual. I figured this way was working, so why change it?"

"But why didn't you at least call the district manager or the owner for help? Those people could have helped you understand the manual, and then you could have made this store one of the best!"

"Oh, them," the girl said. "Why would I want to bother them? Besides, my friends call the store a lot, and I wouldn't want them to get a busy signal."

With that, the owner stepped behind the counter, hung up the phone, and ushered the clerk to the door. "Young lady," he said, "I own this store that you've let go to rot. You may claim to work for me, but I can assure you that you do not—you never have! If you did, you'd be interested in learning and implementing my plans for this store. Now, get out!"

Unfortunately, we sometimes act out that clerk's lackadaisical attitude toward employment in our service to God! We assume God is pleased with our work but spend more time ignoring him than pursuing him—and the result is a life gone to wreck. We must always remember that our first obligation as a servant of Jesus is to seek him, to know him, to learn from him, and to desire him most of all.

As we grow closer to God through the spiritual disciplines, the fires of passion that we have for him are turned up, and we are motivated to faithfully serve others for his sake. Such passionate service has the ability to literally change our world for Christ.

Perhaps you've heard of a little woman who lived through most of the twentieth century. She really was nothing special. Stood only four feet, eleven inches tall and weighed less than one hundred pounds. Yet kings and presidents bowed in her presence, listened to her rebukes, and encouraged others to follow her example.

> There should be less talk; a preaching point is not a meeting point. What do you do then? Take a broom and clean someone's house. That says enough.
>
> —Mother Teresa[5]

That little woman was Mother Teresa, whose only claim to fame was this: She faithfully served Christ by serving the poorest of the poor.[6] In so doing, she earned a Nobel Prize and, more importantly, became a physical illustration of Christ for her world.

One more story and then I'll close this chapter. As I mentioned earlier, there were many months when my chronic illness left me nearly bedridden. With a battery of medicines, I'm now able to manage the daily bouts with nausea and lead an almost normal life. But during the summer of 1997, that simply wasn't the case.

It also happened that (thanks to age and a particularly vengeful hailstorm) the paint on our house had been stripped and chipped, leaving bare wood showing in many places. The house had to be painted, but I was too ill to do the work, and we couldn't afford to hire someone to do it for us. My wife, Amy, tried to begin the daunting task, working each day to scrape and sand the outside of the house in preparation for painting. She worked for weeks and had only managed to sand down a small corner on the east side.

Then suddenly one Saturday about a dozen people from our church showed up at our front door. Wearing their "grubbies," they'd come to do the sanding for us—and had even brought their own tools and ladders! For the next few hours they laughed and scraped and accomplished in one morning what Amy and I hadn't been able to do in weeks.

A few days later they showed up again, this time bringing their own paint (which matched our house's original color) and paintbrushes. They climbed on the roof and knelt on the ground and handled those brushes everywhere in between until, in a matter of hours, our house had a fresh, professional-looking coat of paint from top to bottom. Then munching doughnuts and giving hugs all around, they cleaned up every stitch, leaving the yard looking better than when they'd arrived. And just before they left, they stopped to spend time praying for me.

When I look back on that expression of love now, I realize these friends of ours had for a few short hours perfectly fulfilled the Five Laws of Servant Living. They'd noticed the need and done something about it; they'd cheerfully done my dirty work; they'd refused to quit until every last task had been done—and done well; they'd asked for nothing in return; and they'd been an example to those around us of what it means to be a faithful servant of Christ. Our neighbors were talking for days about "those happy people who painted your house!"

Probably the thing I most appreciate about that experience, though, was something I didn't even know was happening at the time. A few months later, my son's Sunday school teacher asked the children to draw a picture of a servant of Jesus. Tony brought the picture home, and Amy and I both got choked up looking at it.

He'd drawn a picture of himself, painting a house.

By reaching out to serve us with ladders and paint and smiles, our friends had given Tony an example of the foot-washing Savior in a way that Amy and I never could. None of our lives will ever be the same.

———————————

How would I react, I wonder
If You [Lord] pointed to a basin of water
And asked me to wash the callused feet
Of a bent and wrinkled old woman
Day after day
Month after month
In a room where nobody saw
And nobody knew.

—Ruth Harms Calkin[7]

As Jesus went on from there, he saw a man named Matthew sitting at the tax collector's booth. "Follow me," he told him, and Matthew got up and followed him.

While Jesus was having dinner at Matthew's house, many tax collectors and "sinners" came and ate with him and his disciples.

—*Matthew 9:9–10* NIV

6

COURAGE TO LEAD—AND FOLLOW

Following Jesus and Leading Others to Do the Same

We in the Nappa household are great movie fans. Some of our favorite moments are those spent sharing a video together—and talking about it afterward. Not long ago all three of us (father, mother, and ten-year-old son) gathered around our TV set to watch the classic movie *Spartacus*.[1] It took us two nights to finish the whole thing (it's a long one!), but we all sat in rapt attention as the story unfolded before our eyes.

If you haven't seen this award-winning film, you may want to skip the next several paragraphs because I'm about to ruin the ending for you! The plot goes something like this:

Spartacus (played to simmering perfection by Kirk Douglas) is a slave of the Roman Empire in the time before Julius Caesar ascended to the throne. Young, strong, and angry at his chains, he is trained as a gladiator—the ancient Roman version of a killing machine. After another gladiator spares his life, Spartacus successfully leads a rebellion and overruns the gladiatorial school where he is held prisoner.

Thus begins Spartacus's life as a hero and leader of warrior slaves. Before long, he forms an army of ex-slaves whose one goal is to march across Rome to the freedom that awaits on the high seas. He is joined by Antoninus (portrayed by Tony Curtis), a former house slave for a

Roman general. Through battles and more, the two men bond as if father and son.

Finally the army of gladiator-trained slaves reaches the coast—only to find out they've been betrayed and set up by the Romans! In the end, the Roman legions are too much for Spartacus and his army. Thousands are killed, and thousands more are captured by General Crassus of Rome (played with cruel elegance by Laurence Olivier). Rome wants Spartacus dead, but there's one problem: No one in the Roman army knows what he looks like.

And then comes the scene I love best in this movie. Hundreds of battle-weary, beaten slaves sit shackled and bleeding on the country-side. Beside Spartacus sits the faithful Antoninus. Crassus surveys his defeated foes then promises life to each of the captured slaves if they'll only tell him which man among their ranks is Spartacus. If they refuse, all will die a long, cruel death by crucifixion.

The camera focuses in on Spartacus, and there's no hesitation in his eyes. He obviously won't let these men die to protect him. Spartacus begins to stand to reveal his identity, unaware that Antoninus is watching his every move.

Suddenly, before the slave general can respond, Antoninus pushes Spartacus aside, leaps to his feet and shouts, "I am Spartacus!"

A split second later, another slave soldier also jumps to his feet and declares, "No, I am Spartacus!" Then another, and another, until hundreds of the beaten, ragged men are raging the chorus, "I am Spartacus! I am Spartacus!"

> The mark of a great leader is not in what he does, but in who follows him—and how far.
>
> —Anthony Vespugio[2]

Every time I see this scene I wonder to myself, *What kind of man can inspire people to follow him with such passion?* With nothing but death to gain, these so-called slaves willingly lay down their very lives for the man who managed for a fleetingly short time to set them free.

The scene of these men shouting their loyalty—and signing their death warrants—still lingers in my mind. I'll ask you the same question

I asked my family that night: "What would it be like if Christians followed Jesus with the same total abandon and then led others to do the same?" Perhaps we would all—every one of us—be a Spartacus for our own time.

EVERYBODY IS A LEADER TO SOMEBODY

True, we will probably never be called upon to lead an army of slaves against an oppressive government like ancient Rome. Yet in our own ways we are all Spartacuses, all leaders with the power to inspire—or disappoint—others within our circle of influence. Think of a mother who leads her children in learning the social graces, a brother who gives a younger sibling a first drink of alcohol, a student who challenges her peers to excel for God, an uncle who shares pornography with a nephew, a child whose gentle smile reminds Dad that family is more important than work, and...well, I think you get the idea. Each of us can lead others—for better or for worse.

What has that got to do with living a life of spiritual passion, you ask? Quite a bit really. You see, we Christians are being watched—both by fellow Christians and by non-Christians. Others are taking their cues from us, making decisions about Christ based on what they see in our lives. I'm reminded of a quote I'm told is attributed to India's great leader, Mahatma Gandhi. I'm certain I don't have the words exactly right, but the gist of it was this: "I would become a Christian, but I've met too many Christians."

You don't have to strive to be a leader—the very fact that you believe in Christ makes you one. The real question is, Where are you leading your followers? Where are you taking those who look to you for direction? Your spouse, your children, your children's friends, your peers, your coworkers, your football buddies, your church acquaintances—if they follow your lead, where will they end up? Gandhi considered following Christians, but he saw too many who claimed the name of Christ but did not live up to their claim. We must not be guilty of the same thing.

COURAGE TO LEAD BEGINS WITH A PASSION TO FOLLOW

Our goal in leadership should never be simply to rally others to our way of thinking or to assemble a core of people who will follow us to hell and back. The one, overarching aim of all our leadership endeavors should be this: to lead those around us directly to the one we are most passionate about following—Jesus Christ.

When I was a sophomore in high school, I must admit I had certain dramatic aspirations. I eagerly tried out for just about every school play and won roles in a number of them. One lesson I learned early in that sophomore year has stuck with me (probably because my drama teacher repeatedly pounded it into my thick head). "When you are onstage," she'd say, "focus your attention on the person who is talking." More than once she'd shout out, "Cut! Mike, why are you looking offstage?"

"Um, I heard a noise and wanted to see what it was."

"No, no, no!" she'd tell me again. "You must realize that even if you are not the center of the scene, as long as you are onstage, the audience will look toward whatever you are looking at. You must lead them—by your posture, by your expression, by your undivided attention— *to where the action is.* If you look offstage, they will too, and then they'll miss the story. But if you focus on the story, they will follow your lead and enjoy the story for themselves."

> Leaders must understand that little things *do* mean a lot and that everything they do is magnified in the minds of those they lead; every word, gesture, smile, or frown takes on a new significance when it comes from a leader. A follower's day can be ruined without a word of greeting from his or her leader. Conversely, a follower can be inspired and energized by the slightest positive comment from a leader.
>
> —Bob Briner and Ray Pritchard[3]

I quickly learned that this little truth worked offstage as well. Sometimes my friends and I would find ourselves in a crowded mall or other public location, and we'd do an experiment. First one of us, then another, then another would stop and stare in a certain direction.

Sometimes we'd look up, sometimes we'd focus on some part of the scenery, and sometimes we'd start staring at a particular person. It never failed. Within minutes, people around us would stop and stare in whatever direction we were staring, curious to know what had caught our attention. Then we'd quietly slip away, chuckling as we left people wondering exactly what it was they were staring at!

In a spiritual sense, that's what happens when we learn to focus our lives on Jesus. With him firmly in the center of our attention, others can't help but follow our lead and shift their gaze his way too.

In just a few brief words, Luke, author of the third Gospel, gives a beautiful example of that "focus shift" happening in real life (5:27–29). Let me set the stage. In this corner of life (we'll call it "stage right") sits a dishonest man. His name is Matthew (also known as Levi), and he is a tax collector—a man even more despised than today's IRS auditor.

You see, with Israel under Roman rule, a tax collector like Matthew has two strikes against him. For choosing his profession, Matthew, a Hebrew, is regarded as a traitor. He willingly gathers money from fellow Jews and gives it to the hated Roman rulers, thus helping to finance the Romans' oppressive policies toward his own people.

He is also known as a thief. Tax extortion is a common practice in occupied Israel—meaning Matthew probably demands more in taxes than is actually due to Rome, and he pockets the difference. That practice of legal skimming has made Matthew a rich man—and a hated one. (Interestingly, in Jewish society today, the job title *tax collector* has become synonymous with the word *sinner*!4)

So here sits Matthew at his tax-collector booth, pen and ink in hand, no doubt grinning like the thief he is as he rakes in more cash that day. Suddenly, out of the corner of his eye, he glimpses a man entering "stage left"—Jesus.

I picture Jesus smiling, looking straight into the crooked man's eyes as he says two simple words, "Follow me."

The response is instantaneous. For the first time in years, money has no meaning to Matthew. Position and power are relics of a useless past. Eyes that had previously been dazzled by the glint of gold and the flash of silver are now blinded to money's strong attraction. At that very moment, Matthew gets up and follows Jesus—leaving behind all the coins he collected that day!

That's a wonderful story about becoming a follower of Jesus, isn't it? But Matthew's story didn't end there. No, this follower of Christ was transformed into a leader of people. That very first night, a crowd gathered for dinner at Matthew's house. They had witnessed Matthew's miraculous change, and they wanted to take a closer look at the one who had captured the former tax collector's gaze.

Later, with an unblinking eye on his Savior, Matthew took up his pen and wrote a God-inspired biography of Jesus' life that we now call the Gospel of Matthew—the first book of the New Testament. As theologian Herbert Lockyear explains, "When he rose and left all to follow Christ, the only things Matthew took out of his old life were his pen and ink. It is well for us that he did."[5] Truth is, Matthew became a magnet for millions upon millions of others—leading us step by step, verse by verse to the Christ who said, "Follow me."

I sometimes imagine what it must have been like to be Matthew. I imagine myself going about my life when suddenly an amazing man— Jesus, the Son of God—interrupts my feeble existence with two simple words: "Follow me." Suddenly my life is radically changed, and I pledge to follow him for the rest of my days.

Then I realize: *That's happened to me already. It's my story too!* And I hope it's yours. Only by following Christ can we truly become people with the courage to lead.

COURAGE TO TRUST

"Mike," you say. "I've got it. I understand that to somebody—my family, my coworkers, my children, my neighbors, *somebody*—I am a leader. I understand that to be a passionate Christian leader I must first learn to point myself in God's direction and endeavor to always stay focused on him. But is there anything else I should know?"

Ah, my friend, I'm glad you asked.

The last part of this leadership equation is always the hardest. Now it's time to trust. You must turn over the results of your leadership to the capable hands of God's Holy Spirit. You must rely on him to bring fruit out of your weakened efforts, to bring focus to your life when you're distracted from Christ, to point out priorities that need to be addressed in your life, and to bring into your sphere of influence the followers he wants you to lead. You see, without the Holy Spirit's enabling power in our lives, we are helpless to become the leaders God desires. But with his grace at work in us and in those who follow us, we cannot help but lead others to him.

I'm reminded of two stories. The first is of a farmer who went out to plant seeds in his cornfield. His five-year-old daughter accompanied him and watched as the man carefully tilled the soil, spaced out the field, planted the seed, applied the fertilizer, and drenched it all with water.

"Now what happens, Daddy?" the little girl asked.

"Now we wait and tend our fields."

"But where does the corn come from, Daddy? How can that little seed become a tall stalk of corn?"

Patting the child on the head, the farmer said simply, "That, my dear, is God's business. If we are faithful to do our business—watering, planting, weeding, and the like, God will be faithful to do his business—bringing life to the seed and making it grow."

> I planted the seed, Apollos watered it, but God made it grow. So neither he who plants nor he who waters is anything, but only God, who makes things grow.
>
> —The apostle Paul in 1 Corinthians 3:6–7 (NIV)

And that, dear friend, is the attitude we must take as we lead on for Christ through this life. Our job is to focus wholeheartedly on following Jesus today—and trust God to worry about the fruit that will grow from our leadership tomorrow.

The second story is about a famous tightrope walker of old named Blondin. One fine day in 1860, this acrobat stretched a rope—one thousand feet long and 160 feet above the ground—over the tumbling waters of Niagara Falls. Blondin then proceeded to amaze the crowd by walking back and forth (without a net) over the raging waters on that tiny cord. At one point he even pushed a wheelbarrow all the way across and back again.

Upon his return to the applauding crowd, he spied a young boy staring open-mouthed at the feat. Blondin turned to the child and asked, "Do you believe I could take a person across in the wheelbarrow without falling?"

"Yes sir, I really do," answered the boy.

"Well, then," Blondin said with a smile, "get in, son!"[6]

History doesn't record that boy's response, but I think the challenge is a beautiful picture of what it means to courageously trust God as we lead—and follow—our way across the tightrope of life. If we trust solely in our own talents, we will inevitably fall straight into the raging waters! But if we take a step of faith and follow God into that spiritual wheelbarrow, he will carry us all the way across—and enable us to bring others along for the ride.

GOD LEADS BACKWARD

I'm going to tell you a secret now that took me more than two decades as a Christian to learn. It's this: God leads backward.

Let me explain. When I first became a follower of Jesus, I unconsciously assumed that I was now in a race with God. He, being God, had already gotten off to a big head start and was running way ahead of me. My job was to "follow his dust"—to keep my eyes on the trail Jesus left behind, ever in search of the elusive Christ and the track he was paving for me. Sometimes, if I ran fast enough, I could be like Moses and catch a glimpse of the back of God. That brief sighting would be enough to spur me on farther.

I have to tell you, that's a tiring way to live. It wasn't long before I realized I could never run fast enough (spiritually speaking) to catch up with Jesus. I seriously thought about quitting.

But then, suddenly, I opened my eyes and saw an amazing sight: not the back of Christ zipping away from me, but the face of Christ calling me toward him.

This Christian life, I discovered, is less like a race and more like a father teaching a toddler to walk. Kneeling down to my level, eyes locking hard on mine, hands outstretched in my direction, Jesus leads me through this life. And like a daddy carefully leading a diaper-clad boy, each forward step I take means a backward step for him. But that's OK. He knows where we're going without ever having to take his eyes off me.

So my job in this life isn't to chase after the back of Jesus; it's to be ever searching for God's face instead. Because, you see, God leads backward, turning his face toward me and his back to my future. I'll get to that future soon enough. In the meantime, he's teaching me to walk—step after tottering step—until I finally arrive and fall into his loving, caring arms.

Then Jesus began to tell them that he, the Son of Man, would suffer many terrible things and be rejected by the leaders, the leading priests, and the teachers of religious law. He would be killed, and three days later he would rise again. As he talked about this openly with his disciples, Peter took him aside and told him he shouldn't say things like that.

Jesus turned and looked at his disciples and then said to Peter very sternly, "Get away from me, Satan! You are seeing things merely from a human point of view, not from God's."

—*Mark 8:31–33* NLT

7

COURAGE TO SAY NO—
TO YOURSELF AND OTHERS

Setting Priorities in Order to Say Yes to God's Will

I'm always a little embarrassed for Simon Peter when I read about his encounter with Jesus in Mark 8:31–33. I suppose it's because what happened to him could have happened to me. I'm often closer to error than I think I am—and farther from God's will than I want to be.

The story goes like this: Jesus and his disciples are walking along the roads of Caesarea Philippi in Israel, slowly making their way toward Jerusalem. Moments earlier, Peter had won the admiration of his peers by rightly identifying—once and for all—that Jesus was the promised Messiah, the Son of God.

Now the walk continues, and Jesus grows very serious. He begins to warn his disciples of what is to come in the days ahead—that soon public sentiment will turn against him and he will be arrested and killed. As the gruesome realities become clearer in Peter's mind, I can visualize him looking concerned, then frustrated, then shaking his head in disagreement. Finally he decides something must be done.

Moments after declaring Christ the Son of God, Peter apparently feels that Jesus has made a mistake! Pulling Jesus aside—so as not to embarrass him, I assume—Peter begins to rebuke his Messiah, telling Jesus that his death (and subsequent resurrection) must not be.

Jesus pauses, turning to look at his disciples on the road. Then forcefully, Jesus makes his intentions clear. Turning to face Peter directly, he says, "Get away from me, Satan! You are seeing things merely from a human point of view, not from God's" (NLT).

I always cringe at this point in the narrative, knowing that Peter must've felt about as low as the underbelly of a snake. But I also realize that if Jesus had said yes to Peter's way of thinking, he would've been saying no to me (how else could I have been rescued from the penalty of sin?)—and worse yet, he would have been saying no to God's will.

In spite of the horrible cost, in spite of advice to the contrary from his friends, Jesus refused to back away from what he knew to be God's perfect intentions. He determined to say yes to God and no to Peter, and we—along with millions upon millions throughout history—are the benefactors of that selfless dedication.

SAYING YES ALSO MEANS SAYING NO

To say yes to God, we must be willing to say no to anything and anyone else.

That doesn't mean we'll always be *required* to say no to others in this life. But it does mean we must be *willing* to refuse anything that doesn't conform to God's desires for us. When our world conflicts with God's Word, we must say no to its temptations. When our selfish desires attempt to lead us away from God's best, we must say no to ourselves and yes to God. When those around us spell out expectations for our lives that are contrary to God's expectations, we must be strong enough to just say no.

Let me clarify something here. I'm not suggesting that we all become disagreeable, distrusting, inflexible people. But I am suggesting —no, *insisting*—that to be fulfilled Christians, we need to learn when to say yes and when to say no.

I have a friend—let's call him Reed—who is now in his thirties and still unmarried. He laughs whenever the topic of marriage comes up. That's because over the course of his life he's had several women insist that it was God's will for them to marry Reed. He tells me that each one, at different stages in his relationship with her, has "received a word from God" that he was to be her husband.

"So which woman is it?" he asks. "Or is God just fickle, changing his mind with each new girl I date?" The bottom line, Reed says, is that none of those women was pursuing God's will for his life; they just wanted to be married and found Reed to be a suitable prospect. They were trying to impose their own will upon God's will—with potentially disastrous results.

You're laughing now, aren't you? Don't be so quick to judge those starry-eyed women. From time to time, you and I are just as guilty of misappropriating God's intentions for our own lives. Personally, I've long hoped it would be God's will for me to be a millionaire—but God seems to have other plans!

We must remember that our responsibility as Christians is to do our best to match our priorities with God's priorities. That means we must always say no to wrong things—and sometimes we must even say no to *good* things. As Zig Ziglar is fond of saying, "I've got to say no to the good so I can say yes to the best."[1] All too often we confuse personal wants and desires for God's will and find ourselves living unhappy, unfulfilled Christian lives in spite of all the good things we are doing!

I'm going to let you in on a little secret that just might be life changing: *Ability doesn't always equal obligation.* Yes, there are some things that all Christians are obligated to do—love God, love one another, and so on. But when it comes to other endeavors, just because we *can* do something doesn't mean we necessarily *should.*

Perhaps this is best illustrated by an example from my past career in ministry. My first "real" job at a church was as an assistant pastor for a junior high group in Southern California. The way the job was structured, I worked about forty-five hours a week, Sunday through Friday. Saturday was my day off (unless there was a special event scheduled, like a trip to an amusement park or something). It was hard but rewarding work, and I relished it.

Then the senior pastoral staff decided to implement a Saturday night church service—a good idea for the busy area we served, but a problem when it came to staffing. So the junior high pastor and I worked out a system. I would take over all Sunday responsibilities for our group, and he would handle all Saturday responsibilities. That meant he would get Sundays off and I would get Saturdays off.

The senior pastoral staff objected. They reasoned that since it was God's will to implement a Saturday service, all staff members would have to be present for that service—or they'd be forced to leave. When the junior high pastor and I tried to explain that their plan would mean I'd be working seven days a week, they dismissed us as simply being out of God's will for the church. Our families and our lives outside the church walls had to be secondary to the church's goals. I was asked to leave the pastoral staff for being unwilling to work a seven-day week!

> Never let someone else determine God's will for your life. No one else can understand God's unique call on your life as clearly as you. So many waste years trying in vain to please others when they would be far more productive living as God designed them to live.
>
> —Bob Briner and Ray Pritchard[2]

The good news is that I was soon hired as an assistant youth pastor for another church nearby. The bad news is that my former church suffered many more losses during the next few years. The junior high pastor found another job within two years. Two members of the pastoral staff had extramarital affairs—including the senior pastor. Within five years the church was gone. The pastoral staff had gone through so much turmoil that people left by the droves until the remaining congregation was finally absorbed back into the original church that had planted it.

Was I capable of leading that Saturday service for junior highers? Yes. Was I qualified to do the job? Yes. Was it God's will for me to put my family on the back burner so I could lead a program at the church? No. My ability to do the job didn't mean I was obligated to perform it. It meant I was to seek God's will first and *then* use my abilities within the context of his priorities for my life.

Looking back now, I'm grateful I was spared the trauma that the rest of that church had to go through in the years after I left. But I often wonder what would've happened if I hadn't been willing to say no and walk away from a job I loved in order to maintain what I believed to be God's priorities for my life. Knowing my weaknesses as I do, it's possible I would have contributed in some way to the breakdown of that church, despite my good intentions.

And now we are back to you. Do you truly desire to say yes to God and to his will for you? Then determine in your heart that you will also be willing to say no to anything that threatens to steer you away from God's purposes for your life.

COURAGE TO PRIORITIZE

So how, exactly, do you know when to say yes and when to say no? The answer lies in the way you prioritize your life values and resources.

Here's a poem that pretty much sums up my view on priorities. It goes like this:

If in the course of traveling life's road
You find yourself choosing
Between another dollar and the smile of a child,
Choose the smile, for it'll bring happiness long after the dollar is gone.

If you encounter a patented program guaranteed to make millions
And a person willing to give a listening ear,
Choose the listening ear, for money is deaf to your sorrows.

If you find a diamond mine filled with gems of great value
And a person who will love you for life,
Choose the lover, and make gemstone memories of your life together.

And if you find the choice is between
God and anything else,
Choose God, for then you've chosen eternal life.

You see, in the end it's not what we accumulate in life that matters but the relationships we cultivate each day. When this life is over, relationships are the only things we can bring with us into the afterlife —a relationship with God and relationships with family members and friends. Only people are eternal. Everything else is just temporary.

Therefore, when we organize our lives, it's best to prioritize with eternity in mind. What's truly important in your life may be something you take for granted or something others think is of little or no value. It might even be right under your nose!

I'm told that when the great luxury liner *Titanic* was sinking, people's priorities came quickly into focus. One woman pushed her way onto a lifeboat about to be dropped into the roiling ocean. Suddenly she realized she was about to leave behind something very important. She begged the crewman in charge of her lifeboat for just a few extra moments to retrieve something from her stateroom. The sailor granted her request but warned her sternly to *hurry* or they'd leave without her.

She jumped back into the sinking ship and raced toward her room. On her way she passed the gambling room and discovered that ankle-deep mounds of money had been shoved into a corner. She kept running. Once in her stateroom she saw piles of her jewelry and fine clothes, but she simply pushed them aside. Finally she reached her treasure: three small oranges she'd nonchalantly stashed away some time before. That was all she took back with her to the lifeboat—a possession more valuable than any gaudy jewel or stack of cash. You see, the oranges alone had the ability to sustain her life.[3]

That, I think, must be the criteria we use when assessing our resources and prioritizing the demands of our lives. Does this priority give life in some way? If not, it must be relegated to a value lower than those that do.

For instance, does a relationship with Jesus give life? Absolutely— greater life than we can dream of or attain by ourselves. That relationship, then, must be our first priority. Does a family give life? Yes. In large and small ways, the folks we call our relatives—father, mother, brothers, sisters, spouse, children, cousins, grandparents, and more— plant within us the core of who we are. They help define our happiness and bear our sorrows. They contribute life to us from the first day to the last. In any list of priorities, the family must be near the top.

Ministries, careers, homes, investments, entertainment—*everything* can be measured by the amount of life it brings. When we are faced with a choice between any two (or more) of our priorities, the wisest response is to choose first the one that gives the most life, then work our way down from there.

After all, isn't that what Jesus did when he went to the cross? When faced with the choice of preserving his human life or saving the lives of people like me and you and the millions of others who would trust him, Jesus chose to invest in our lives—and say no to his own.

LEARNING TO SAY NO WITHOUT SAYING NO!!!

There's one last thing I want to point out before we end this chapter. Yes, it's true that in your life as a Christian, you must say no to some things in order to say yes to God's will. And it's true that carefully prioritizing your values will help you know when to say yes and when to say no. But it's also important for all of us to learn to say no without saying NO!!! That is, we need to learn how to decline an option without harming or putting down the presenter of the option.

For instance, if my neighbor invites me to join him in barhopping and carousing this Saturday night, my response is an obvious no. Does that mean I should say to him, "No way, you heathen, you ungodly, sinful man! The Bible teaches me not to get drunk and to remain faithful to my wife, and there's no way I'm going to join you for this kind of debauchery and sin! Now get out of my face, you miserable miscreant, or I'll call down fire from heaven to consume you on this very spot"?

Of course not! That kind of response, though essentially true, is totally inappropriate. The better answer? "Thanks for the invitation, but I'll pass. Still, I would like to spend some time with you. How about coming over to my house for dinner Saturday night instead?" This allows me to say no without harming my neighbor *and* keeps me in relationship with him—a relationship that perhaps can lead him into an eternal relationship with God.

> Put first things first and
> we get second things
> thrown in; put second
> things first and we lose
> *both* first and second
> things.
>
> —C. S. Lewis[4]

So how do we learn to say no without saying NO!!!? First, we must learn to be people of our word. As Jesus said in Matthew 5:37 (NIV), "Simply let your 'Yes' be 'Yes,' and your 'No,' 'No'; anything beyond this comes from the evil one."

That means you shouldn't say no when you really mean "convince me," or "maybe," or "not right now." And you shouldn't say yes when you really mean, "I'll think about it," or "When I have time, I'll get around to it," or "I don't want to do this, but I can't think of a good excuse not to, so I guess I'll give it a try until I get tired of it." If you make a promise, keep it. If you don't want to make a promise, don't make it. If you're asked a question, answer it tactfully and honestly—even if your answer is simply, "I can't answer that question right now." If you need time before you can make a confident decision, take it—with no apologies.

If you are known as a person of your word, you'll find it easier to say no when the time is appropriate because then people will believe you really mean no! And you won't have to say NO!!! because people will understand you the first time.

Second, we must remember that Jesus loves every person—even the most disagreeable, unkind degenerate on the planet (or on your street!). So while it is necessary to say no to sin, to unrighteousness, to injustice, and to many opportunities, both good and evil; it is usually not necessary to harm the person who asked.

True, sometimes it's impossible not to disappoint another person when you say no, and sometimes you must be extremely firm in drawing a line that you will not cross in your conduct or attitudes. But you don't have to add insult or pride or unkindness to the way you say no.

Some years ago I visited a Christian bookstore in Southern California and asked a clerk to show me a particular product that was behind the Bible counter. While he was getting the item, another customer came in and asked to see a certain Bible.

Now, really, all that clerk had to do was say something like, "I can't help you just yet, but I'll be happy to get it for you after I finish with this customer." Instead, he ignored the woman, acting as if she hadn't spoken. This obviously didn't sit well with the woman, and she let the clerk know about it, asking again to see the Bible.

The clerk started fuming and said a few curt words to the woman. She was astonished. She repeated again that she simply wanted to look at a Bible behind the counter. "I can't believe you would be so rude to a customer!" she added.

His response? He looked her straight in the eyes and shouted, "Get thee behind me, Satan!"

Her response? She stared right back and shouted, "No, *you* get thee behind *me*, Satan!"

My response? I figured that if there were two Satans in that store, that was two too many for me. I put down the product I was examining and left, deciding I'd rather make my purchase someplace where Satan didn't shop or work!

Sure, it was necessary for that salesclerk to temporarily say no to that other customer while he was waiting on me—but it was completely unnecessary for him to call the woman "Satan." Besides, if those two really are Christians, they'll someday have to live together in heaven!

The lesson for us is this: When the passion of our relationship with God requires us to say yes to him by saying no to someone else, we need to remember to say no without saying NO!!!

'Nuff said. I'll meet you again in chapter 8.

TEN PRINCIPLES FOR PROPER PRIORITIZING

1. *Always remember God is first—no matter what.*

2. *Invest in your family, and you'll earn "joy interest" for the rest of your life.*

3. *Remember that you reap what you sow. Let your actions and attitudes today sow seeds you'll be glad to harvest tomorrow.*

4. Before making a decision, ask, "Which of my life priorities does this conflict with? Coincide with? Which is the greater priority?"

5. Be aware of your physical, emotional, spiritual, and relational resources—and know their limits. Use your resources to the limit, but don't go beyond them until God extends the limit.

6. It's better to say "no" right now than "I'm sorry" later.

7. When it comes to opportunities, not every open door is one you should walk through. Wait until you see God on the other side before you take that step of faith.

8. When you say yes, let your actions and attitudes confirm your promise.

9. Satan is a liar. Don't believe his promises—no matter how pretty they look.

10. Every minute of your life counts. Live in such a way that each of your minutes says yes to God's will.[5]

Part Three

PUTTING
YOUR
PASSION
INTO ACTION

In the same way, faith by itself,
if it is not accompanied by action, is dead.

—James 2:17 NIV

One day some parents brought their children to Jesus so he could touch them and bless them, but the disciples told them not to bother him. But when Jesus saw what was happening, he was very displeased with his disciples. He said to them, "Let the children come to me. Don't stop them! For the Kingdom of God belongs to such as these. I assure you, anyone who doesn't have their kind of faith will never get into the Kingdom of God." Then he took the children into his arms and placed his hands on their heads and blessed them.

—*Mark 10:13–16* NLT

8

COURAGE TO BE CHRISTIAN AT HOME

Being Christian in the Presence of Your Family Members

Ever wonder what it might be like if Jesus walked through your front door around dinnertime tonight? If he announced that he'd decided to live in your home for a while? How might having Christ as a houseguest affect the way your family relates to each other? To him?

Truth is, if you or anyone else in your house is a Christian, then Christ has already taken up residence with your family. The question isn't whether or not he is there; it's how much of him your family members see in your attitudes and actions.

Sometime ago M. Scott Peck told the story of five elderly monks living in a forgotten and decaying monastery. The monks, all over the age of seventy, began to despair about the fact that no young men were interested in joining their order. They realized that the work of this little monastery would literally die out when they did.

Nearby there lived an old hermit who was widely regarded to be a prophet of God. The monks decided to visit him and ask for advice about how to attract new blood to their work and mission. Upon arriving, the hermit welcomed them kindly but admitted he had no great advice for them. Shrugging, he said sadly, "Hardly anyone cares much for the old things anymore."

Disappointed, the five monks got up to leave. "I can tell you one thing though," the hermit added. "One of you is an apostle of God."

The monks bade their hermit friend farewell and traveled back to their monastery, each one lost in his own thoughts. *What did he mean, one of us is an apostle of God?* they wondered. *Which one of us?*

Perhaps it's Brother Thomas, thought one.

Maybe it's Brother Elred, thought another. *He's a little cranky—but just as often, he is right.*

Slowly they turned the possibilities around in their heads until each monk came to this exciting thought: *Maybe the apostle of God is...me!*

The next weeks, months, and years saw a change in the old men. The knowledge that an apostle of God was in their midst affected everything they did. The kindness they offered to each other was no longer given grudgingly, but freely, with the excitement of knowing that they just might be serving God's apostle. They began to enjoy their time together, treating each other with the respect and kindness due an apostle—and acting with the grace and dignity that an apostle might express.

Before long, word got out about this remarkable monastery where old men served with joy and respect for each other. People came to picnic on the monastery's grounds and stayed to chat with the monks. Then one young man asked to join the group of monks. And another. And another. Within a few short years, the monastery was once again a thriving, active place—all because five old men had begun treating each other as valued, respected Christians. [1]

I wonder what changes might occur in our families and homes if we approached life with our spouse, children, grandparents, and other relatives in the same way those five monks did. If we determined—with the Holy Spirit's help—to exhibit the qualities of Christ in our relationships with our family members. After all, when you boil it all down, becoming a representation of Christ to those with whom we share our lives is what being Christian at home is all about.

Of course, the qualities of Christ include all that is good and holy, but with our *families*, we would be wise to concentrate on reflecting three of Jesus' most obvious traits: love, joy, and peace.

COURAGE TO LOVE DAY IN AND DAY OUT

Jesus once said, "By this all men will know that you are my disciples, if you love one another" (John 13:35 NIV). Unfortunately, many Christians seem to have forgotten that truth when it comes to loving their families. In fact, many Christians don't even love long enough to stay in their families!

A recent study of nearly four thousand Americans by the Barna Research Group revealed that Christians are actually *more likely* to divorce than non-Christians. Twenty-seven percent of "born again Christians" in America have ended their marriages, compared to only 24 percent of non-Christians. Among non-denominational Protestant church members, fully one in three (34 percent) has divorced.[2]

I understand that some situations (such as an abusive spousal relationship) require a different approach. But it seems we Christians have become guilty of a fickle brand of love that simply isn't what Christ intended—nor what he modeled for us. If we are to be lovers like Christ, we must commit ourselves to being *stay-ers* like Christ.

Imagine how different your life would be if Jesus had said, "That's it. I give up. I've tried and tried, and these stubborn people just won't listen. We've got irreconcilable differences. I'm outta here!" Friend, you and I would be the most hopeless of all in God's creation! But he didn't give up on us; Jesus stayed with us—and continues to stay to the very end.

I think that Jesus' encounter with children (recorded in Mark 10:13–16) is the greatest picture (besides the cross) of familial love that Jesus gives us. As Jesus and his disciples were out ministering to

> It used to take courage—indeed, it was the act of courage par excellence—to leave the comforts of home and family and go out into the world seeking adventure. Today there are fewer places to discover, and the real adventure is to stay at home.
>
> —Alvaro de Solva[3]

people, some parents brought their children to the disciples and asked for Jesus to bless them. The disciples figured Jesus was too busy to waste time on a few little brats, so they told the children (and their parents) not to bother the Master. I imagine at this point the parents must have felt embarrassed and a little disappointed. I imagine the children must have felt even worse! If the Son of God didn't have time to love them, who would?

That's when Jesus stepped in. The Bible tells us he was "very displeased" with the disciples' actions—so much so that he uttered those now-famous words, "Let the children come to me. Don't stop them!" You see, the Son of God is never too busy to love a child. We shouldn't be either.

We'll talk in more detail about love later in this book, but for now I want us to briefly explore how Christ modeled familial love in this passage. As I study his example in meeting with these children, I see four principles of love displayed.

Principle #1: Love desires the best for the object of love. It's important to note that Christ loved both the children *and* his disciples through his actions in this passage. For the children, he wanted the best thing of all—the opportunity to experience firsthand the love of God—so he welcomed them into his loving arms. For the disciples, he also wanted the best—the practical understanding that no one is unimportant to God—so he demonstrated his love for them by disciplining them, pointing out their error in trying to keep the children away and encouraging them to change their attitudes and actions for the better.

God's love always desires the best. He is always willing to encourage and discipline with the best interests of the loved one in mind. That's something we would do well to remember as we relate to the children God has placed in our lives.

Principle #2: Love demonstrates unconditional acceptance without compromising principle #1. The things that Jesus *didn't* say or do in this passage speak volumes to me. He didn't say, "Let the children clean themselves up before they come to me." He didn't say, "Let the holy children come to me, and tell the sinful ones to get their act together first." He didn't say, "Let the pretty ones come and the talented ones, but make sure the ugly and misfit ones stay away."

You see, Christ doesn't require holiness before he will love. He doesn't require beauty or talent or success or righteousness or good deeds or perfect church attendance or angelic behavior

> No matter what you've done for yourself or for humanity, if you can't look back on having given love and attention to your own family, what have you really accomplished?
>
> —*Elbert Hubbard*[4]

before he will love. His is a love that says, "Come to me just as you are, and together we will become more than you can ever dream." We would be wise to practice that same kind of love with our children, our spouses, and all the people who live in our homes.

Principle #3: Love is affectionate. I love it when I read that Jesus "took the children into his arms." Isn't that a beautiful picture? God himself wasn't afraid to touch, to be affectionate, to communicate his love and blessing for these children in a physical way, strangers though they were! There is power in a touch, strength and acceptance in a hug, affirmation in a gentle squeeze on the shoulder or a pat on the leg. Jesus hugged children. Maybe you and I should too!

Principle #4: Love protects and encourages. When they were turned away as irrelevant by Jesus' disciples, those children received more than disappointment. They were wounded emotionally by God's men. Christ's response was first to reach out and protect their tender hearts. At that moment their feelings were more important to Jesus than the feelings of the men he called his disciples. "Let the children come to me," he commanded. Then, one by one, he blessed those children, encouraging them and assuring them of God's promises for their lives.

When was the last time you protected and encouraged your loved ones? Your spouse? Your children? Why not take a hint from Jesus' example and do it today!

DILIGENCE TO PLANT JOY

Christian scholar and author Philip Yancey once said, "People liked being with Jesus; where he was, joy was."[5] How true! That means that if we want to represent Jesus to those who inhabit our homes with us, we must desire to plant joy in their lives.

I love the parenting advice that award-winning children's author Karyn Henley once shared during an interview with my wife. "*Enjoy your children.*" Karyn said. "A lot of parents, they get so uptight and doubt, 'Am I doing it right? Am I going to ruin my child?' And you know, they're probably not. They're probably going to do just fine. Relax!"[6]

To Karyn's advice I would add this: Enjoyment of your family isn't something that just happens—it's something that you make happen, both for your family and for yourself.

Every year on my son's birthday we go see the Ringling Brothers and Barnum and Bailey Circus. And every year we crack up at the zany antics of the circus clowns. We enjoy the silly, slapstick comedy so much that we keep going back for more.

Last year I happened to glance in the circus program and read a bit about the work that goes into a typical four-minute clown act. According to Director of Clowning Robert Shields (who is one-half of the comedy duo, Shields and Yarnell), hours of effort are spent developing clown characters and plots for each clown segment. Take, for example, the segment called "The Bakery," in which nine clowns participate in a slapstick comedy along with two buckets of baby powder and fourteen shaving cream pies.

> Who decreed that kids should cringe in fear when mom says, "Wait till your father comes home"? Let's live so they jump for joy at those words instead.

"People might think doing a gag like this is just put on your makeup and throw pies," says Ringling Brothers' Boss Clown, Max Richardson, "but there's more to it than that."

For "The Bakery," Shields wrote out detailed character descriptions for each of the nine clowns in the skit. Then Shields and all nine clowns spent three weeks plotting and choreographing the four-minute sketch. "We did about eleven seconds a day," says Richardson. "But by the time we were finished, we'd established every movement in the gag, right down to the last head twitch."

The work didn't end there. Once they had the characters, the plot, and the choreography down, the clowns dove into three-a-day rehearsals that lasted five more weeks. After each run-through of the skit, the clowns would then gather and dissect their work on videotape, taking notes and practicing ways to improve the gag.

Only after they'd spent months working on "The Bakery" were the clowns finally ready to put on their four-minute show. Why did these clowns put so much work into preparing for this 240-second perform-ance? Says Richardson, "It's so satisfying getting a positive response to something we enjoy doing." [7]

If circus clowns can put that much effort into making children happy for four minutes, surely you and I can invest a little effort into planting joy in the lives of our kids and spouses as well! How do we do that? Like Karyn Henley said, relax. And enjoy. Smile. Laugh. Play. Participate. Bend the rules. Purposefully plan to enjoy your family—and plan so that they enjoy you as well. Remember, heaven will be a place of eternal joy and happiness. Let's get ready by practicing a little joy and happiness with our families today.

Passion for Peace

In Isaiah 9:6 the Bible prophetically calls Jesus Christ the "Prince of Peace." Unfortunately we often do not allow the Prince of Peace to reign in our homes and in our relationships.

"But Mike," you say, "you don't know my situation! My kids are rebellious and unkind. My daughter has tried to run away twice. My son is experimenting with sex and drugs. My spouse yells at me and the kids all the time. Even the dog barks too much! How can you blithely tell me my Christian home should be one characterized by peace?"

Please know that I understand some of the heartache—and warfare—that goes on within a family unit. My own childhood was less than perfect, and many days I felt that coming home from school was like coming home to a battlefield. But as I grew to maturity, I discovered something important: My peace at home didn't have to depend on whether or not others in my family were fighting. My peace depended only on my relationship with the Prince of Peace. You see, Jesus is still the Prince of Peace even when the world (or our family) is at war. If I intend to spread peace within the walls of my home, I must first pursue peace within myself.

Funny thing about peace: It's quietly contagious. I know of a young man who lived in a home where tempers were often short—his included. As he grew into the teen years, he became a Christian and felt the Holy Spirit prodding him to contribute peace, not anger, to his family relationships.

One day, as he and his mother were having an argument (again), the young man saw that his cutting words and sarcastic comments were visibly enraging his mother. Listen to how he describes what happened next:

> We were going at it, as usual, and every time my mom had an insult for me, I had one ready to fire right back. Then, suddenly, through all the noise of our angry words, I felt the Holy Spirit penetrate my hurt feelings and speak to my heart, saying, "Shh. Be quiet. Listen."
>
> So I shut my smart alecky, teenage mouth and saw not my mother, but a single mom doing the best she could with limited resources, frustrated with her life in general and with me at that moment. She looked a lot like me, and I realized my fighting verbal battles with her wasn't going to bring peace to my home.
>
> While she yelled, I listened. I tried to recall times of tenderness between us, times when she helped me while I was sick. Times when she cheered while I played sports or performed in dramas. She continued fighting, but it's hard to fight when no one fights back. After a few more minutes, her anger subsided, and mine did, too. We talked then and calmly reached a solution to

our problem that we were both happy with. And we didn't have to fight to get our way.

It only happened after I declared peace, not war. And to this day, our relationship has never been the same.[8]

Peace in a household is a priceless thing. Like you, your family members want to come home to a place of safety and rest. They want to live in peace. But pursuing peace doesn't mean you'll always get along with each other! Rather, it involves a choice. How will you choose to impact the emotional climate of your household? Will you choose to be one who warms the house with the peace of Christ—or one who contributes to a cold, warlike atmosphere?

Choosing peace is a daily, hourly, minute-by-minute decision. It means choosing first to pursue peace in your own relationship with God. It means calling on Jesus to fill you with his peace each day. It means praying to God for help and power. It means fighting spiritual battles with prayer and discernment against the forces of darkness that would plant discord among your family members. It means attacking problems while refusing to attack people.

It means being a Christian at home—today, tomorrow, and beyond.

So what do you say? Want to give it a go? Trust me, you'll be glad you did—and so will your family.

A PRAYER OF ST. FRANCIS OF ASSISI

Lord, make me an instrument of your peace.
Where there is hatred, let me sow love,
Where there is injury, pardon,
Where there is doubt, faith,
Where there is despair, hope,
Where there is darkness, light,
Where there is sadness, joy.[9]

Again, it will be like a man going on a journey, who called his servants and entrusted his property to them. To one he gave five talents of money, to another two talents, and to another one talent, each according to his ability. Then he went on his journey. The man who had received the five talents went at once and put his money to work and gained five more. So also, the one with the two talents gained two more. But the man who had received the one talent went off, dug a hole in the ground and hid his master's money.

After a long time the master of those servants returned and settled accounts with them. The man who had received the five talents brought the other five. "Master, he said, "you entrusted me with five talents. See, I have gained five more."

His master replied, "Well done, good and faithful servant! You have been faithful with a few things; I will put you in charge of many things. Come and share your master's happiness!..."

Then the man who had received the one talent came....

His master replied, "You wicked, lazy servant.... Take the talent from him and give it to the one who has the ten talents. For everyone who has will be given more, and he will have an abundance. Whoever does not have, even what he has will be taken from him. And throw that worthless servant outside, into the darkness, where there will be weeping and gnashing of teeth."

—*Matthew 25:14–30* NIV

9

COURAGE TO BE CHRISTIAN AT WORK

Being Christian on the Job

Ah, work! That enterprise of life that consumes half (and sometimes more) of our waking hours!

How do you feel about your job? Perhaps you're like the preschooler who just learned to tie his shoes. One day the child's mother found him crying as he laced up his new sneakers. "What's wrong, sweetheart?" the mother asked.

"I...I have to t...tie my shoes!" the boy wailed.

"But you already learned how to do it. It isn't that hard, is it?"

"N...no," sobbed the boy, "but I'm gonna have to do it for the rest of my life!"[1]

Does the thought of working the rest of your life leave you feeling like that forlorn little boy? Or are you more like the father who hadn't quite achieved all he'd hoped to in his career? One day he saw his teenage son lazily passing a day away. "You ought to be ashamed!" he scolded the youth. "When Abraham Lincoln was your age, he was building rail fences. And you? You won't even do your homework!"

The youngster simply yawned and replied, "Dad, when Lincoln was your age he was already president of the United States!"[2]

Fortunately, with Christ's involvement in our work lives, we don't have to dread our future jobs (like the preschooler) or mourn our past

101

lack of accomplishments (like the father). No matter what the occupation, we can approach each day with the power and fulfillment found only in doing our best for God. You see, being a successful Christian doesn't necessarily mean having the best job, the most perks, the highest pay, or any other job accomplishment. What it means is that we work first for Christ; and when we do, our companies, our employers, our clients, and our customers reap the benefit.

PUT YOUR MIND ON YOUR WORK AND YOUR HEART ON THE LORD

In Matthew 25:14–30, Jesus tells a parable that has the primary purpose of encouraging us to be ready for his imminent return. However, I believe this "workplace" parable contains an added bonus: It sheds a little light on God's standards for workers.

The story goes like this: A man is preparing to leave for a long journey. He calls in three of his servants and gives each a sum of money to invest and multiply while he is gone. When he returns a "long time" later, he calls them in again to see what kind of results they've had with his investment. The first and second servants report that they've been busy doing the master's business and have yielded good gains. The third servant reports he did nothing while the boss was gone—and thus earned nothing.

The result? To the faithful workers the master says, "Well done, good and faithful servant! You have been faithful with a few things; I will put you in charge of many things. Come and share your master's happiness!" (NIV). But for the third worker the master reserves only punishment.

> Come then: let us to the task, to the battle, to the toil—each to our part, each to our station.... There is not a week, nor a day, nor an hour to lose.
>
> —Sir Winston Churchill[3]

As I said, I know the primary point of this parable is to encourage us to be faithful with what God has given us until the day of Christ's return. But it's important to note that Jesus used *standards of good business* as the basis for this story. He showed us the value of a positive work ethic—that is, the motivation and ability to get work done without having a boss breathing down your neck—that can be applied to any workplace situation. When we live out this work ethic in all our business endeavors, we find that we are faithfully using our God-given talents and opportunities to the best of our ability—thus fulfilling Christ's main intent!

The best way I can encapsulate this concept for you is like this: When it comes to job responsibilities, *we need to keep our minds on our work and our hearts on the Lord.*

Earlier in this book (chapter 3), I told you about Danielle Frandsen, the preschool daughter of my good friend Rick Frandsen. Now I'd like to take a moment to introduce you to Rick.

I first met Rick when I took a job as a customer-service representative for Federal Express. As a "newbie," I was quickly overwhelmed by the massive amount of information I had to learn just to answer phones for FedEx—and so were the other dozen or so new employees in my training group.

While we rookies were cramming facts and figures that first day on the job, the veteran employees went about doing their work—and ignoring us. They knew that some of us wouldn't last past the training, so they didn't bother to even acknowledge us.

On the second day of training, we stopped for lunch and made our way to the break room to eat. Several veterans were on one side of the room, eating and chatting away. Silently all of us trainees grabbed our lunch bags and went to an empty table to eat by ourselves. It reminded me of being back in high school, when the "nerds" sat at one table, the "jocks" sat at another, the "smokers" sat in the back, and so on. We're talking "Clique City" here. And this was among adults in their thirties and forties!

Suddenly one—and only one—of the veterans separated from the "cool" side of the break room and (gasp!) came over to the trainee table.

"Hi," he said warmly. "My name's Rick. Thought I'd come over and welcome you all to Federal Express." Then he sat and spent the rest of his lunch hour chatting with us, offering pointers, and telling stories about life on the job. Every day after that, Rick always stopped by our table to chat. He even began introducing us to some of the other veterans (thereby getting us accepted into the "cool" crowd).

After Rick's second visit, I went home and told my wife, Amy, "I think I met a Christian at work. He hasn't said he's a Christian, but he's the only guy I've seen there so far who has *acted* like a Christian."

Sure enough, it wasn't long before we all knew about Rick's faith in Christ. It came out naturally in casual conversation, prompting a good discussion about religion in general and Christianity specifically.

The thing that made Rick credible to us "newbies" wasn't so much that he stopped to chat, but that he knew his job cold and did it well. Because we respected his expertise, we also were happy to have his company. He helped us to succeed at our jobs—and presented a model of Christian love at the same time. He managed to keep his mind on his work and his heart on the Lord, and we all benefited from it.

How can you best display passionate Christianity in *your* workplace? I suggest you do exactly what Rick did: Do excellent work, exhibit a positive attitude, help your coworkers succeed, and let Christ shine through you naturally in your words, attitudes, and actions. Being faithful in these little things will make you a "good and faithful servant"—both to your boss and to God.

LET INTEGRITY BE YOUR CURRENCY

I read recently about a little ethics experiment the Port Authority of New York and New Jersey conducted in 1993. They placed a classified advertisement announcing job openings for "electricians with expertise using Sontag connectors." They failed to mention, however, that there's no such thing as a "Sontag connector." Didn't stop applicants though. The Port Authority received 170 résumés from job seekers claiming a proficiency in working with this fictional device![4]

Unfortunately, this kind of thing happens all too often in today's America. In fact, a landmark sociological study by James Patterson and Peter Kim revealed that:

- Nearly one out of three American workers say their employers engage in one or more "unethical activities."

- The average American worker spends more than 20 percent of his or her time at work "totally goofing off."

- Nearly half of all American workers admit to calling in sick when they are not sick—and doing it regularly.

- One out of every six Americans uses drugs or alcohol while on the job.

- Three-fourths of American workers say they do not "give work their best effort."

- One out of every two American workers agrees with the statement: "You get ahead not through hard work but through politics and cheating."

- One out of every four Americans "expects to compromise their personal beliefs in order to get ahead on their current job."[5]

In spite of these prevailing attitudes, honesty and integrity are actually moneymaking assets to a person's career, according to researcher Thomas J. Stanley. In 1998 Stanley surveyed more than seven hundred millionaires and asked them to rank thirty different "success factors" according to their importance in their careers. The number one success factor these millionaires chose? "Being honest with all people."[6]

If the millionaires in Stanley's study are correct, it means that Christ's way is the best way in business and in life. Not only does our moral success depend on a commitment to the truth, but economic success often depends on it too.

I have to tell you some sad news at this point. Often those of us who call ourselves Christians have difficulty following Jesus when it comes to business ethics. I've worked in Christian publishing for more than a decade now, and if my experience is any barometer, we Christians can be just as greedy and deceitful as any non-Christian out there. I personally have been lied to, cheated, stolen from, insulted, plagiarized, blackballed, bullied, and more by many otherwise "fine, upstanding Christian leaders." And more than once I've been asked by employers to do the same to others—something I hope I've always been strong enough to refuse. I find this kind of experience in any business endeavor to be disappointing, but when it happens in Christian circles, it's especially painful.

Unfortunately, I'm not the only person with this kind of experience. Not long ago I had the opportunity to interview one of the best-selling authors in Christian publishing. This woman has sold literally millions of books and has impacted even more lives through her work. I won't mention her name here, but I will tell you that when I asked her to share with me her biggest surprise after working for years in the Christian publishing industry, her response was eye-opening.

> Most people work just hard enough not to get fired and get paid just enough money not to quit.
>
> —George Carlin, comedian, 7

"My biggest surprise has been to see how hard Satan fights the spreading of God's Word," she said, "even to the point of using Christian people to steal, intimidate, manipulate, lie, and destroy out of fear, greed, and a focus on money.... There is an ungodly contentment that permeates some publishing companies—contentment with mediocrity, contentment to live with a little bit of sin, and contentment with head-knowledge of God instead of an intimate heart relationship with the Father."

Why do I tell you this about Christian publishing? Because I want you to know that we Christians aren't exempt from the temptation to do whatever it takes to get ahead in business—and that includes me and you. Therefore, if we want to be truly Christian at work, regardless of the occupation, we must purpose in our hearts to become people whose currency is integrity and whose priority is truth, even if it costs us in salary or prestige.

My good friend Bob Hunt is an example of someone who applies his Christian principles on the job. He owns a used car dealership here in my hometown. Used car sales is often ranked as one of the "sleaziest" of all occupations. In fact, in the Patterson and Kim study I told you about earlier, car salesmen ranked sixty-seventh out of seventy-three in the category of honesty and integrity. They ranked well below lawyers and just barely above politicians, prostitutes, organized crime bosses, and drug dealers![8]

But Bob is out to change that statistic. He has posted a sign in his office notifying all customers that he intends to run his business by Christian principles—and inviting them to hold him accountable to that promise. Before he sells any car on his lot, it has to pass a thorough mechanical inspection. If it doesn't, Bob insists on having the vehicle repaired until it is safe and in running order.

The idea that a used car salesman would act with integrity is a surprise to some of Bob's customers. Not long ago a gentleman bought a used car from Bob, and two days later it broke down. The customer was furious, thinking he'd been duped into buying a "lemon." He came straight to the car lot to let Bob know about it, using a few choice, unprintable words in the process!

Bob's response was immediate. He apologized for the trouble and promised to have the car repaired at his expense right away. According to the sales contract, Bob was not obligated to make the repair, but that didn't matter. What did matter was that he'd sold a car that had broken down, so now he was going to fix it.

Ben Franklin on Work

- Sloth (like Rust) consumes faster than Labour wears: the used key is always bright.

- Lazy bones! Dost thou think God would have given thee arms and legs if He had not design'd thou should'st use them?

- No gains without pains.

- Plough deep while sluggards sleep; and you shall have corn to sell and corn to keep.

- Work as if you were to live one hundred years, pray as if you were to die tomorrow.[9]

The customer kept right on yelling, cursing, and threatening to sue. Finally Bob interrupted him and said, "Excuse me, sir. I don't think you understood what I just said. *I'm going to get your car fixed right away.*"

The customer was so dumbfounded he couldn't speak. He found it hard to believe that Bob would voluntarily repair the car. He sat down in silent shock. Finally he apologized, shook Bob's hand, and the two of them worked out the details for getting the car to the mechanic.

Bob did two things that day: First, he honored God by exercising integrity at his work. And second, he won a customer for life. Let's be wise enough to do the same by letting integrity rule in the way we conduct our work in this world.

NEVER LET SUCCESS OVERSHADOW FAITHFULNESS

There's one last thing I'd like to talk about before we close this chapter, and that's success. As one anonymous author put it, "Success has made failures of many people!"

Some Christians might be surprised to know that God does not call us to be successful; he calls us to be faithful. You see, success for a Christian doesn't come at the cost of faithfulness. It doesn't come before we have the opportunity to be faithful to God's desires for our lives.

Faithfulness comes first, and then—God willing—success will follow. Remember the master's words from Matthew 25:23? "You have been faithful with a few things," he said to his servant. "Now I will put you in charge of many things."

Sometimes faithfulness to God and his plan for our lives actually means less success here on earth. As passionate Christian people, we must be willing to pursue faithfulness in our work first and success after that.

I don't know if you keep up with Christian music or not, but recently I read about an interesting decision made by Jamie Rowe, lead vocalist for the Christian hard-rock band Guardian. Early in 2000, Jamie got a call from the popular mainstream hard-rock band RATT. An established band with a loyal following, RATT has seen its songs ride high on the heavy-metal charts and routinely performs in sold-out concert halls around the world.

It seems that RATT's lead singer had just left the group, and the other members of RATT were interested in having Rowe fill that prestigious slot in the band. To do so would mean instant fame in the mainstream for Rowe, as well as greater financial rewards for his work. And of course, many of Rowe's contemporaries (Amy Grant, Sixpence None the Richer, Bob Carlisle, and others) had already made millions by successfully crossing over into the mainstream music market.

Jamie flew to California for the tryout and was thrilled when he was indeed invited to join the band. He returned home and began making preparations to join RATT on a full-time basis. But something just wasn't right, and Jamie could feel it. Finally, after spending time in prayer, he knew what he had to do.

He explains, "When I got home I realized that while I think very highly of the members of RATT and it was a good match musically, my personal, outspoken Christianity just would not fit into the band situation.... It's a good feeling to know that the mainstream music world recognizes my talents and to be considered was an honor, but I feel my place in the music world is in the Christian music environment where I have an outlet to speak freely of my personal spiritual convictions."

So Jamie Rowe said no to the fame and fortune that RATT offered and chose to remain faithful to his first calling in Christ.[10]

What about you? What do you do when that opportunity for a big promotion finally comes along? Or when a headhunter picks you out of a crowd and tempts you to jump to a bigger, better job? Or when your boss lays out a task and says, "This would look really good on your annual review"?

Of course, none of those things is bad in and of itself. But before you jump at any new opportunity in the work-a-day world, remember first what Christ has personally called you to do in life. If the success that's dangled in front of you is compatible with Christ's specific purpose for you, then great! Go for it. But if pursuing success means you must be unfaithful to your priorities as a Christian—at home, at work, in ministry, anywhere—then please be willing to walk away.

After all, when everything in your life is said and done, Jesus won't ask if you managed to become vice president of a corporation, or if you made enough money to retire comfortably, or even if you won a World Series title. All he will want to know is whether or not you were faithful at serving him.

How will you answer?

Have you ever sensed a lack of purpose in your work? Have you struggled to see the reward for all your effort? Is it all getting a little wearisome?

Why go the extra mile for this company? They'll never reward me for it.

Why put fabric softener on his shirt? He'll never notice anyway.

He never says anything about my new recipes. Why do I keep trying?

Why should I put myself out on this English assignment? It'll be graded by some graduate assistant anyway. The prof will never see it.

Maybe—just maybe—you've been doing your work for the notice and praise of men. Maybe you've been laboring for your own personal gratification. Talk about tiresome! That kind of service can get very old and stale. Fast.

It's the motive that counts. Doing your work wholeheartedly "as for the Lord" can transform virtually any task you're called on to perform...whether it's counting widgets in a widget factory, writing a term paper in economics, cleaning the kitchen for the umpteenth time, or giving loving care to someone who fails to acknowledge or appreciate you.

The Lord Jesus will neither overlook nor forget the tasks you perform in his name. Nor will he fail to reward you.

—Joni Eareckson Tada[11]

[Jesus] was met by a man from the city who was possessed with demons; and who had not put on any clothing for a long time, and was not living in a house, but in the tombs.

Seeing Jesus, he cried out and fell before Him, and said in a loud voice, "What business do we have with each other, Jesus, Son of the Most High God? I beg You, do not torment me."

For He had commanded the unclean spirit to come out of the man. For it had seized him many times; and he was bound with chains and shackles and kept under guard, and *yet* he would break his bonds and be driven by the demon into the desert.

And Jesus asked him, "What is your name?" And he said, "Legion"; for many demons had entered him.

They were imploring Him not to command them to go away into the abyss.

Now there was a herd of many swine feeding there on the mountain; and *the demons* implored Him to permit them to enter the swine. And He gave them permission.

And the demons came out of the man and entered the swine; and the herd rushed down the steep bank into the lake and was drowned.

When the herdsmen saw what had happened, they ran away and reported it in the city and *out* in the country.

The people went out to see what had happened; and they came to Jesus, and found the man from whom the demons had gone out, sitting down at the feet of Jesus, clothed and in his right mind; and they became frightened.

Those who had seen it reported to them how the man who was demon-possessed had been made well.

And all the people of the country of the Gerasenes and the surrounding district asked Him to leave them, for they were gripped with great fear; and He got into a boat and returned.

But the man from whom the demons had gone out was begging Him that he might accompany Him; but He sent him away, saying, "Return to your house and describe what great things God has done for you."

So he went away, proclaiming throughout the whole city what great things Jesus had done for him.

—*Luke 8:26–39* NASB

10

COURAGE TO BE CHRISTIAN
IN YOUR COMMUNITY

Being Christian in Your Neighborhood and Community

Something strange was happening at Wal-Mart. It was Christmastime, and the outer lobby of the store seemed unusually packed, even for this time of year. The heat was inside—so why were all these people standing in the chill?

Grumbling to myself, I edged my way through the door, hoping to get in and out as quickly as possible. That's when I noticed a table set up on one side of the lobby. Behind it were four or five people wrapping gifts for Wal-Mart shoppers.

Ah, another fund-raiser, I thought. *Bet they're raking in the money today!*

A few steps closer I saw the sign: "Free Gift Wrapping. Compliments of Church of the Good Shepherd." Behind the table the workers chatted and laughed as they rolled out sheets of wrapping paper and spools of ribbon and carefully taped up their customers' holiday packages.

I finally made it into the store, bought the gift I was looking for, then made my way toward the door again. The outer lobby was still packed. Now I was really curious! Standing off to one corner, I took a moment just to watch.

A woman came out of the store with a basket full of packages. She did a double take when she saw the sign. She leaned over the table and asked in surprise, "Is this really free?"

The volunteer responded brightly, "You bet! Would you like us to wrap anything for you?"

The stunned shopper pointed to her overflowing cart. "What's the limit on the number of packages you'll wrap for free?"

The volunteer laughed. "No limit! C'mon, let's get started on some of these." Calling another volunteer over to help, she got right to work while the lady watched in open-mouthed delight.

An older gentleman walked in carrying a large bag. "I, um, bought this at another store. Will you still wrap it for free, or is there a charge since it's not from Wal-Mart?"

"No charge!" said another volunteer, smiling as she reached for the bag. She pointed behind her where several rolls of wrapping paper were stored. "Which color paper would you like?"

Another gentleman walked out of Wal-Mart, waited in line, then placed a box on the table that was easily three feet tall. Shaking his head he said, "This one's too big for you, isn't it?"

"Of course not," chided a volunteer. "We've got enough paper for this box, and then some!"

While she was wrapping the giant box, the gentleman just shook his head in disbelief. Finally he asked, "Why are you doing this?"

Without missing a beat on her wrapping job, the volunteer smiled and responded, "Well, we believe that God has given us the greatest Christmas gift by sending his Son, Jesus, to earth. This is just our way of saying thanks and giving a little something back to our community."

I kept waiting for the hard sell to come—one of the volunteers slipping a

> Jesus left few traces of himself on earth. He wrote no books or even pamphlets. A wanderer, he left no home or even belongings that could be enshrined in a museum. He did not marry, settle down, and begin a dynasty. We would, in fact, know nothing about him except for the traces he left in human beings. That was his design.
>
> —Philip Yancey[1]

tract inside a gift's wrapping paper, or someone reciting the Four Spiritual Laws to the customers while they were "trapped" waiting for their present. Didn't happen! Whenever somebody asked, the people behind the table were happy to talk about Jesus or about their church. But there was no forceful evangelistic outreach—just a bunch of happy Christians wrapping presents for anyone and everyone who wanted the service.

Watching those Christians making a positive contribution to our community made a big impression on me. And judging by the number of visitors the Church of the Good Shepherd gets over the holiday period, it has made an impression on others in this city as well!

Their example also challenges me. It makes me wonder what kind of impact I'm having as a Christian in my community. What am I doing to be a positive force for Christ here in my neighborhood, in my school district, in my city at large? If you're asking yourself the same question, then read on, friend. We'll try to come up with the answer together.

LET YOUR ATTITUDE COMMUNICATE YOUR AUTHOR

It's been said that each person's life is a story God is telling; each new day is a page to be filled by the Author of Life. If that's true, then the lives of passionate Christians ought to reveal their Author (God!) to those they encounter on any given day.

How do we do that? The easiest—and best—way to communicate the presence of our loving, caring God in our lives is with our attitude. Good works done with a bad attitude don't show Jesus' love to those around us—they only show that Jesus makes us grumpy! But a loving, giving, cheerful attitude speaks more loudly than a thousand trumpets and communicates Christ better than ten thousand Sunday sermons.

Listen to how Selwyn Hughes, the British theologian and founder of Crusade for World Revival, explains this concept:

> One of the terms used by communicators is the phrase, "the medium is the message." This means that it is impossible to separate

a message from the manner in which it is given. The message is wrapped up in the messenger.... The Greeks recognized that oratorical skill without a caring heart added up to nothing. "Eloquence without love," said the apostle, "is a sounding brass and tinkling cymbal." An American evangelist, Floyd McClung, put it succinctly when he said, "People don't care how much we know until they know how much we care."[2]

"The medium is the message." In other words, the attitude we express when we deliver a message is as important as the message itself!

Let me illustrate. Suppose I were to introduce you to my wife, Amy. "Friend," I say, "This is my [cough] lovely wife. She is the...hang on, I've got to see this football play on TV...[pause]...the most important thing in my life besides God." I yawn and roll my eyes as I continue, "She's a great conversationalist." Then I grimace in your direction and say, "Isn't she a beauty?"

Now the truth is that Amy *is* lovely, and she *is* the most important person in my life besides God, and she *is* a great conversationalist, and she most definitely *is* beautiful! But if I were to introduce her to you in the way I just described, would you believe my words were true? Of course not! My attitude would have negated every word I said, miscommunicating my true feelings for my wife.

> What we've got here is failure to *communicate.*
>
> —Captain (as portrayed by Strother Martin) in Cool Hand Luke[3]

What if I complained to you every week about going to church—what would my attitude tell you about my relationship with Christ? If I then told you that I loved Jesus, that my devotion to him was at the center of my life, would you believe me? You would be right not to!

Or what if I volunteered to do a favor for you then grumbled about it all day and did just barely enough to complete the task before excusing myself? What would you think about the job I'd done? You see, more often than not, it's the attitude we remember more than the service. And we are attracted to those people who have positive, enjoyable attitudes. The ones who are grumpy or disrespectful or discontented or arrogant or easily annoyed are the people we most often try to avoid.

What kind of attitude do you exhibit most of the time? Please know that people in your community—your neighbors, your church acquaintances, your kids' schoolteachers, the cashier at Wal-Mart, the golf-course attendant, and anybody else who hears of your faith—will associate Christ with you. God has given you a great honor; he has placed you as his ambassador in the area where you live. Don't let your negative attitude be a reason for anybody in your community to turn away from Jesus' love.

TOUCH THE WORLD FROM WHERE YOU ARE

As a young man, I often heard missionaries make impassioned pleas for people to go to the foreign mission field. In college, respected leaders told me that if I didn't go outside the United States to reach my world for Christ, then I was a disappointment to God—and I had better "get right with God" and get moving!

Now I know that foreign missionaries are invaluable. They work hard and do irreplaceable work for the kingdom of God. I would never want to discourage someone from entering a career in missions, but I also think there's another truth that my well-meaning leaders skipped over in their call for more missionaries: Your first mission field is the place right where you are.

Listen to this story from Luke 8:26–39: It seems there was a crazy man living in the area of Gerasenes, a primarily non-Jewish region within sailing distance of Galilee. Inhabited by demons and certifiably insane, the man lived naked and wild among the tombs of that area. He possessed a supernatural strength, and when the demons took control, few shackles could hold him.

Into his miserable life sailed Jesus (literally!). One encounter with the Son of God and *pow!* Jesus cast out the thousands of demons that were terrorizing him. Not long after, the people of that community came out to see what was going on. They found the crazy man dressed, peaceful, in his right mind, and sitting at the feet of Jesus. The sight of this madman no longer insane was too much for those people. Terrified of Jesus and his power to heal this poor man, they asked Christ to go away.

Just before Jesus left, though, the former crazy man *begged* to be allowed to come along with him. Like Peter, James, and John, he wanted to spend his life following Christ, traveling as one of Jesus' disciples.

Here's the surprising part: Jesus said no!

Turning the man away, he said, "Return to your house and describe what great things God has done for you." And that's exactly what the man did. The Bible reports that he "went away, proclaiming throughout the whole city what great things Jesus had done for him." He had just become the first Christian missionary—and he did it by staying right at home.

Do you want to reach the world with your passion for Christ? Then like that rescued demoniac, begin by touching the world right where you are. Begin by letting your daily life dictate your opportunities to be Christian in your community. Begin by being "salt" that God can shake into the lives of those people who surround you each day.

YOU ARE SALT—GET READY TO BE SHAKEN

You've probably heard the old joke, "Wherever you go, there you are." What you might not have heard is, "Wherever you go, there God is, empowering you to touch your world for Christ." Once you became a Christian, you also became God's ambassador. In a spiritual sense, you were transformed into a candle that brings the light of God's fire to those around you; you were changed to salt and sent out to season the lives of the people in your life.

So what does it mean to be spiritual "salt" that's shaken out into your community? How do you season the world around you with your passion for Christ? Let me answer by telling you a few stories.

The first one is about a young man named Justin Bundschuh. Justin is the bass player for the Christian band Spooky Tuesday. His father (and the band's manager), Rick, describes Justin's grueling touring schedule this way: "Six nights a week, nine months a year, forty-eight states, and lots of long highways!"

> Jesus, today place me fully aware in this world I live in…this world you loved so much you gave your life for it. Your world. Love it through me, Jesus!
>
> —*Susan Lenzkes*[4]

It was during one such tour in the winter of 1999 that Justin and the band found themselves driving through the night on a desolate stretch of desert highway. The band pulled off the road simply to change drivers and suddenly found that God had thrown them right into the middle of a tragedy.

In a ditch in the median where the band just "happened" to stop were the remains of a terrible traffic accident that had occurred only moments earlier. I'll let Rick tell you what happened next:

> The swirl of light from arriving truckers showed one adult female (the driver) in bad shape. Another truck driver with a flashlight spotted the passenger, a young high school girl, lying fifty feet away in the snow-flecked high desert sand.
>
> While some band members assisted with the driver, Justin grabbed his sleeping bag and sprinted back to the critically injured—but conscious—girl. Wrapping her in his sleeping bag, he began to talk to her.
>
> She told him her name: Sarah. He talked to her about school, friends, and anything else to keep her mind focused. He discovered she was a Christian.
>
> Suddenly, as the truck driver holding the flashlight helped Justin adjust the sleeping bag on the shivering girl, they discovered she'd lost her right arm in the accident. The truck driver laid his flashlight on the ground and walked away. Justin was alone.
>
> Mustering everything he could remember from high school first aid class, Justin warned Sarah that he was going to hold her tight, and it might hurt a bit. He squeezed shut the flow of blood with pressure from the knotted sleeping bag. Moments later

paramedics arrived on the scene and found the pair praying together. Sarah and her mother—the driver—survived the crash.

On the way home from the tour, Spooky Tuesday returned to Sarah's home church in Elko, Nevada, for a benefit concert. The whole town showed up. Sarah, now fitted with a prosthetic arm, is their biggest fan.[5]

The next story I want to tell you is about a man named Ed Gerecke. Ed was a military chaplain at the end of World War II and found himself assigned to duty in Nuremberg, Germany, in 1945. Specifically, Ed was assigned to be the chaplain for fifteen Nazi war criminals on trial in the now famous Nuremberg War Trials. Among the men in his charge were such infamous propagators of Hitler's "Final Solution" as Rudolph Hess, Hermann Goering, and Albert Speer. These men had been in Adolf Hitler's inner circle and had been substantially responsible for the political and military machinery that exterminated the lives of more than six million Jews and foreigners.

Ed Gerecke quickly felt that God had made a mistake, that he'd "shaken" Ed into a world that was too overwhelming, too evil. *How can a humble preacher, a one-time farm boy, make any impression on disciples of Adolf Hitler?* he asked himself time and time again.

Still, Ed mustered up his courage and began meeting with the fifteen men and their families. Several of the men—including Goering—rejected Ed outright. Others—like Goering's wife and daughter—saw a glimpse of Christ in the outmatched chaplain. Once Ed asked Goering's daughter if she said her prayers, and the little girl responded, "I kneel by my bed and ask God to open my daddy's heart and let Jesus in." The father didn't, but that little child did.

Fritz Sauckel, chief of German slave labor, also responded to Ed's Christianity. Ed documented one conversation with the hated war criminal that went like this:

"Do you believe that you are a sinner?" Ed asked.

"Yes, I am a sinner," said Sauckel.

"Are you sorry for your sin?"

"Yes, I am sorry I have sinned against God."

"Do you hope to be saved?"

"Yes, such is my hope."

"In whom then do you trust?"

"In my dear Lord Jesus Christ."

When the trial ended in August of 1946, Ed found himself accompanying five of his charges, one by one, to the gallows where they would be hung. He prayed with the men who now faced a death they had so easily imposed upon others. And through his work, we will now spend eternity with some of history's most hated war criminals—but they are criminals no more! Through the ministry of one overwhelmed Christian, Ed Gerecke, Christ met them where they were and changed them forever.[6]

Finally, I want to share a story about my wife, Amy. Last year one of our teenage neighbors made a stupid mistake. He and a buddy, out to have a good time, thought it would be fun to break into a local school. So they did. Then they vandalized school property, causing thousands of dollars in damage and outraging just about everyone in our community. Of course, they were caught, and now that young man is serving prison time.

Most people—including people from our church—took pleasure in knowing the young vandal had been severely punished for his crime. But Amy could only think about the boy's mother. She felt that mother's heartache and sensed the shame that mother felt over the deeds of her son. Several times she made a point to call the mother and just listen. She visited the boy's mother, and the women prayed together. She even went along with the mother to court dates for the son. Afterward Amy mentioned how surprised she was that no one else—no friends or family—came along to support that mother during those difficult days in court.

In the end, the boy was sentenced and the mother had to deal with her pain. But at least with Amy there, she didn't have to deal with it all alone.

So what am I saying by telling you these three stories? Just this:

Sometimes God will "shake" you into unexpected circumstances in your community (or outside it). When that happens, be available to be used. Be compassionate. Be involved in the lives of the people who cross your path in your little corner of the world.

Don't hide your Christ away behind the doors of your home and church. Open those doors and step boldly, cheerfully, into community projects, civic clubs, professional organizations, city celebrations, local volunteer organizations, and the like. The world lies just beyond your driveway. Taking Jesus at your side, step out to meet it with Christ's love. When you do that, you will not only have shown the courage to be Christian in your community; you will literally change your world.

COMMUNITY QUIZ

Use this quiz to help you see where you might be able to inject a little of Christ's love into your community:

1. *What are the five greatest needs of the community in which you live?*
2. *What are specific, tangible ways you can contribute to meeting any one of the needs you listed in question #1?*
3. *What's stopping you from doing anything you listed in question #2?*
4. *What are you going to do about it?*

On the third day a wedding took place at Cana in Galilee. Jesus' mother was there, and Jesus and his disciples had also been invited to the wedding. When the wine was gone, Jesus' mother said to him, "They have no more wine."

"Dear woman, why do you involve me?" Jesus replied. "My time has not yet come."

His mother said to the servants, "Do whatever he tells you."

Nearby stood six stone water jars, the kind used by the Jews for ceremonial washing, each holding from twenty to thirty gallons.

Jesus said to the servants, "Fill the jars with water"; so they filled them to the brim.

Then he told them, "Now draw some out and take it to the master of the banquet."

They did so, and the master of the banquet tasted the water that had been turned into wine. He did not realize where it had come from, though the servants who had drawn the water knew. Then he called the bridegroom aside and said, "Everyone brings out the choice wine first and then the cheaper wine after the guests have had too much to drink; but you have saved the best till now."

This, the first of his miraculous signs, Jesus performed at Cana in Galilee. He thus revealed his glory, and his disciples put their faith in him.

—John 2:1–11 NIV

11

COURAGE TO BE CHRISTIAN AT LEISURE

Being Christian at Rest and at Play

- "I'll never watch an R-rated movie."
- "I don't follow sports. Why should I spend my time 'worshiping' some athlete when I should be worshiping God?"
- "Mainstream music is of the devil! I don't listen to it—and neither should you!"
- "Television is Satan's missionary in the home. I refuse to own a TV, let alone watch one."
- "Dancing? Leads to extramarital sex. That makes dancing a sin, and I won't do it."
- "We don't play cards here. It teaches kids to gamble."
- "I'll never let my kids read a Harry Potter book—it's got magic in it!"

Do any of these sentiments sound familiar? If not, you probably haven't been around Christians lately! I've heard variations of all these statements repeatedly in my Christian life—and I'm betting you have too. Are they right? Are they wrong? The answer doesn't matter at this point. What does matter is the larger issue they raise: How does faith in Christ impact a Christian's leisure-time activities? A Christian's hobbies? A Christian's interests and entertainment choices?

Unfortunately, many Christians spend more time debating

whether or not dancing is wrong than they do debating methods for reaching people for Christ. We've got crusaders against television, crusaders against books, crusaders against movies, and crusaders against athletics. If there is an activity Americans do in their leisure time, there's probably a group of Christians crusading against it.

It reminds me of the story of a group of protesters marching on Capitol Hill. As they marched in a circle on the sidewalk, they waved placards in the faces of the passersby and shouted, "No! No! It must go!"

Finally, one curious bystander noticed that, despite their vigorous opposition to whatever they were protesting, the marchers' signs were blank. During a brief break, the bystander approached the leader of the picketing group.

> From silly devotions and from sour-faced saints, good Lord deliver us!
>
> — *St. Teresa of Ávila*[1]

"Excuse me," he said. "I've been watching your demonstration here, and I just had to ask: What are you protesting against?"

Without hesitating, the leader replied, "What've you got?"

You may chuckle at that illustration, but it's often all too true—especially among Christians. No wonder we're viewed as negative and inflexible people! Just as the Pharisees and Sadducees of Jesus' time were guilty of adding hundreds of unnecessary "laws" to God's Word, today we Christians are often guilty of making up all kinds of unhealthy rules for Christian living. Then, despite our holy motives, we gradually replace a vibrant relationship with Christ with adherence to rules that we ourselves made up.

Should a Christian watch an R-rated movie? Read a fantasy book? Play cards, dance, watch football, and so on? Rather than give you an easy, yes-or-no answer, I want to share with you a principle I've found to be helpful in my life.

LET YOUR RELATIONSHIP GOVERN YOUR RULES

I don't want to waste your time and mine debating whether or not a rating by the Motion Picture Association of America speaks for God and his standard, or whether or not playing bridge with friends will lead you to become addicted to gambling. But I will say that when it comes to leisure-time entertainment, we Christians spend too much time making rules and not enough time in relationship.

My advice? When it comes to entertainment, *Let the relationship govern the rules—and not vice versa.*

Here's what I mean. Next time you are deciding whether or not to participate in some form of leisure pursuit, ask yourself, "If Jesus were physically with me right now, would I be comfortable having him join me in this activity?"

By doing this, you bring into focus your relationship with Jesus and allow that relationship to govern the rules you abide by in your life. Considering a movie? Jesus has already seen it (he *is* God, remember?). Would you feel comfortable viewing it with him and then discussing it with him afterward? If the answer is yes, go, and afterward take time to talk it over with God. If the answer is no, don't go, and find something else for you and Jesus to do together.

Like to follow a particular sports team? Ask yourself if you'd feel comfortable sharing that interest and your commitment to it with Jesus. If the answer is yes, then you and God get together and enjoy a good game. If the answer is no, reevaluate your commitment until you reach a point where you feel comfortable sharing it with Christ.

One warning though: Don't assume—or insist—that your entertainment rules will always apply to the lives of other Christians. Outside of obvious biblical commands (such as worship God only, don't commit adultery, and so on), God has actually given us remarkable freedom to choose our everyday activities. That's why the apostle Paul could write with confidence, " 'Everything is permissible for me'— but not everything is beneficial. 'Everything is permissible for me'—but I will not be mastered by anything" (1 Cor. 6:12 NIV). And that's why he could say that for some Christians, eating meat that had been sacrificed to idols was OK—and for others it was not (see 1 Cor. 10:23–33).

What about parties, hobbies, and the like? I thought you'd never ask!

REMEMBER GOD CREATED PARTIES
—AND ATTENDED THEM TOO

I think it's very interesting that Jesus chose to perform his first public miracle at a party—a wedding party in Cana, to be exact. Here's what the Bible tells us happened: Jesus, along with his mother and his disciples, had been invited to attend a wedding ceremony in nearby Cana. Apparently Mary and Jesus were family friends of one of the families involved in the wedding. As was customary, the wedding festivities lasted seven days and were filled with feasting and drinking. On the third day, however, a crisis occurred. The wedding party ran out of wine for the guests—which was especially troublesome since the festivities were expected to last several more days.

> Moral passion without entertainment is propaganda, and entertainment without moral passion is television.
>
> —Rita Mae Brown[2]

Enter Jesus' mother. She of all people knew about her son's true identity, and she knew that he could do something about the problem. So out of concern for her friends in the wedding, she called Jesus over, told him what was going on, and commanded the servants to do whatever Jesus said to do.

At first Jesus hesitated. Then, motioning to six large stone jars, he gave this command: "Fill the jars with water."

The servants rushed to obey, and before long they had them ready. Then, without any fanfare or ceremony, Jesus commanded that some of the water be taken to the master of the banquet. Only then was it discovered that Jesus had changed more than one hundred gallons of water into more than one hundred gallons of the finest wine!

In his extremely helpful book, *The IVP Bible Background Commentary: New Testament*, theologian Craig Keener reveals several interesting cultural dynamics that were at play during this episode. Listen to what Keener says:

To run out of wine at a wedding was a social faux pas that would become the subject of jests for years; the host was responsible to provide his guests with adequate wine for seven days.

The women's quarters were near the place where the wine was stored; thus Mary learns of the shortage of wine before word reaches Jesus and the other men. Her words probably suggest that he should do something; guests were to help defray the expense of the wedding with their gifts, and it seems that their friend needs some extra gifts now....

The description of the stone jars indicates that they contained enough water to fill a Jewish immersion pool used for ceremonial purification. Although Pharisees forbade storing such water in jars, some Jews were less strict; thus these large jars were being reserved for ritual purposes. Stone jars were common because they were less likely to contract ritual uncleanness than those made of other substances.

Using the jars for another purpose would temporarily defile them; Jesus shows more concern for his friend's wedding than for contemporary ritual....

God had often manifested his glory by doing signs (Exod. 16:7).... Moses' first sign was turning water into blood (Exod. 7:20; cf. Rev. 8:8); Jesus' first sign is turning water into wine.[3]

I think it's also interesting to note that after the miracle, Jesus and his disciples simply returned to enjoying the banquet. We have no record that Jesus condemned the partygoers for getting drunk or dancing. No indication that he called down fire from heaven to consume those who went to excess in the celebration. In fact, Jesus spent an entire week partying with the wedding families!

Now what would you say if, after that party, one of Jesus' disciples—say, Peter—told you, "Hey, I went to a wild party last week. In fact, it lasted seven days! And there were tons of food and lots and lots of wine and dancing and gobs of pretty girls and—well, to be honest, I can't really remember everything that went on, it lasted so long!"

Chances are you'd think he had spent the week deep in sin—but you'd be wrong! In fact, he had spent the entire week in the presence of God—and probably enjoyed every minute of it.

Funny thing about Jesus, he was known as quite the partygoer in his time on earth. The Pharisees even complained that he must be unholy because he spent so much time at parties—and with sinners! (Read Luke 7:34, Matthew 9:9–14, and Luke 19:1–10 to see what I mean.)

> Those who decide to use leisure as a means of mental development, who love good music, good books, good pictures, good plays, good company, good conversation—what are they? They are the happiest people in the world.
>
> —*William Lyon Phelps*[4]

I am in no way suggesting that we Christians should go out and get drunk every Saturday night and wobble into church with a hangover on Sunday morning. But I am suggesting that, done within God's standards, celebrating the joys of life with friends is a holy thing to do. In fact, God himself is the creator of many parties! You can't go far in the first five books of the Old Testament without coming upon another God-ordained celebration or festival. Add to that other celebratory Christian events like communion, baptism, and so on, and it seems that God must be quite the joyful God!

So why are we Christians known as such sour people? Food for thought, my friend—and something to remember the next time you're invited to a party.

REMEMBER GOD CREATED REST

There's one more thing we need to discuss before we leave the topic of being a Christian at leisure: rest.

For some reason, modern American Christianity seems to associate busyness with godliness—but that's just not right. The concept of resting came straight from God's creative hand at the beginning of the world. "By the seventh day God had finished the work he had been doing; so on the seventh day he rested from all his work. And God blessed the seventh day and made it holy, because on it he rested from all the work of creating that he had done" (Gen. 2:2–3 NIV).

When was the last time you slept in on a Saturday morning and were called "holy" for doing it? The reason Christians frown on taking time off isn't Christian at all—it's cultural. The United States was born out of hard work and industry. We admire people who achieve great success due to a near-constant focus on work and getting ahead. The only trouble is, God does not.

Even Jesus took time away from the crowds to rest and refresh. Mark 6:31–32 (NIV) reveals a time when Jesus made rest a priority for both himself and his disciples. It says, "Then, because so many people were coming and going that they did not even have a chance to eat, he said to them, 'Come with me by yourselves to a quiet place and get some rest.' So they went away by themselves in a boat to a solitary place." Once Jesus was even caught sleeping during a raging storm while his disciples were hard at work trying to keep their boat afloat for him! (See Mark 4:34–41.)

My point?

If you're not making time for rest and relaxation, you are not acting out Christian values in your private life. Period.

Let's also remember that our hobbies can be a form of rest. Do you enjoy a good volleyball game? Find a moment's peace bass fishing? Relax by playing games with friends? Unwind through the pages of a good novel? Find yourself renewed by sewing? Reduce stress simply by hanging out with your family?

At the risk of sounding unorthodox, friend, I would say to you that those kinds of positive, restful activities are not only allowed by God but *encouraged* by God. I would even go so far as to say that your taking time to rest through a hobby or vacation or even to loaf around the house and read the paper is not just relaxing—it's holy!

I love the story Chuck Swindoll tells about the first time he went parasailing. ("Four and a half minutes of indescribable ecstasy sandwiched between a few seconds of sheer panic. Talk about fun!" he laughs.) Hovering somewhere between a bright blue sky and a turquoise sea in the vacation mecca of Puerto Vallarta, Chuck found freedom and rest.

Listen to how Chuck describes his moments of flight:

> I must confess, for those few minutes I lost all concern for things that otherwise occupy my attention. Self-consciousness vanished. Worries fled away. Demands and deadlines were forgotten, strangely erased by the swishing sound of the wind. *It was glorious!* I don't believe that as an adult I've ever felt quite so free, so unencumbered, so completely removed from others' expectations and my own responsibilities.
>
> Such are the benefits of leisure. True, authentic, carefree relaxation. The kind Jesus had in mind when he encouraged his twelve to come apart and rest awhile. How easy to forget the necessity of recreation; how quick we are to discount its value![5]

Friend, one of the great gifts God has given us in this life is the gift of rest. Let's determine to be courageous Christian men and women and disregard the work-a-day world that calls for complete submission to its will. Instead, let's be people completely dedicated to God's will—which includes the divine desire for us to rest, to celebrate, and to manage our leisure time with Jesus in mind.

I can think of no better way to close this chapter than with the words of Tim Hansel from his book *When I Relax I Feel Guilty.* I only wish I'd been wise enough to write them first! Listen:

> If I had my life to live over again I'd try to make more mistakes next time.
>
> I would relax, I would limber up, I would be sillier than I have been this trip.
>
> I know of very few things I would take seriously. I would take more trips.
>
> I would be crazier. I would climb more mountains, swim more rivers, and watch more sunsets.

I would do more walking and looking. I would eat more ice cream and less beans....

If I had to do it over again I would go places, do things and travel lighter than I have.

If I had my life to live over I would start barefooted earlier in the spring and stay that way later in the fall.

I would play hooky more. I wouldn't make such good grades, except by accident.

I would ride more merry-go-rounds. I'd pick more daisies.[6]

Amen, Brother Tim, amen!

Serenity, another form of rest, comes largely through leisure and play. In this case, rest means "repose," "refreshment," and "restoring equilibrium to one's body." It is not merely taking a "pause that refreshes" (in order to get back to work as soon as possible), as Robert Johnson once characterized the Protestant view of play. Rest is good simply for its own sake.

—Theologian R. Paul Stevens[7]

After the people saw the miraculous sign that Jesus did, they began to say, "Surely this is the Prophet who is to come into the world." Jesus, knowing that they intended to come and make him king by force, withdrew again to a mountain by himself.

When evening came, his disciples went down to the lake, where they got into a boat and set off across the lake for Capernaum. By now it was dark, and Jesus had not yet joined them.

—John 6:14–17 NIV

12

COURAGE TO BE CHRISTIAN
WHEN YOU'RE ALONE

Being Christian in the Presence of No One but God

I find it interesting that one of the most severe punishments of any penal code is solitary confinement—when a prisoner is locked away and deprived of human contact for an extended period of time. Simply the act of being alone is regarded as retribution for lawlessness; some people even consider it "cruel and unusual punishment."

While studying prisoners in solitary confinement, psychiatrist Henry Weinstein discovered that many suffer serious symptoms ranging from "memory loss to severe anxiety to hallucinations to delusions.... Under the severest cases of sensory deprivation, people go crazy."[1] And the toll is more than mental. Dr. Ron Pies, clinical professor of psychiatry at Tufts University, reports, "In a Norwegian study by Gammen (1995), solitary confinement was found to be associated with more health problems than less restrictive settings. The most common complaints were various aches and pains.... The complaints tended to last for the whole period of solitary confinement and were difficult to treat while the prisoners remained secluded; most patients recovered when the seclusion was terminated."[2]

One of the core fears of humanity, it seems, is simply the idea of being alone! Yes, too much aloneness has its downside (especially when it doesn't come by choice). But it's also true that the opposite—

that is, no time alone—can be equally harmful. As Christians we must come to terms with this truth: *Just as we must learn to be at peace when we're among people, we also must learn to be at peace when we're alone.*

I'm reminded of a parable about three men who volunteered for a scientific experiment. Each person agreed to spend one week isolated inside a one-room containment chamber. In the chamber was a week's worth of food and water, a bathroom, a dim light—and nothing else.

The first man went into the chamber on a Monday. Twenty-four hours later he was banging on the door of the chamber, screaming to be let out. The scientists released him, and he came flying through the door with bloodshot eyes and terror on his face. "I'll never, ever, be trapped like that again!" he said. "It was terrifying—so silent and alone!" Then he broke down into sobs and finally was taken home.

The second man was ushered into the chamber on Thursday. Much to the scientists' relief, he lasted all seven days. But when he came out, he had a strange look in his eye.

"Wait!" he said, as they were about to close the door. "You forgot to let Fluffy out!" The mystified scientists watched as the man got on one knee and called, "Here, Fluffy, Fluffy, Fluffy! Here, Fluffy!" When, of course, nothing emerged, the man got very angry with the scientists. "What have you done with Fluffy? That little dog hasn't left me all week! Well, except when I spanked her for trying to bite my finger...and when I accidentally stepped on her tail...and...." The poor subject just rattled on as they led him away.

Finally, the third man entered the chamber the following Saturday. A week later he exited, looking well rested and calm. Subsequent tests revealed no unusual aftereffects.

"Why is it that this chamber drove one man crazy and another to irrational fear," the scientists asked, "but it had no effect on you?"

The third man shrugged and responded, "Well, I was nervous at first. But then I realized that the same God I knew outside the chamber was also with me inside it. Once I remembered that, there was nothing else to do but enjoy the time alone with God."

That, friend, is the perspective we need as we consider the concept of being Christian while alone. Solitude is not only a good thing; it can be a wonderful thing.

COURAGE TO SEEK GOD IN SOLITUDE

Theologian Paul Tillich once said, "Our language has wisely sensed the two sides of being alone. It has created the word *loneliness* to express the pain of being alone. And it has created the word *solitude* to express the glory of being alone."[3]

My good friend (and semitheologian himself!) Michael Warden has taught me much about what "the glory of being alone" means—about how we are not only to seek God when we're alone, but also to *seek to be alone with God*. Michael is one of the few people I know who actually plans for such time—and guards it well. Periodically he schedules what he calls "spiritual retreats" with God, going off by himself for a few days simply to dig deeper into his spiritual being and draw closer to Jesus.

Not long ago, I asked Michael to share with me exactly what he does on these retreats and why. Listen to what he had to say in his e-mail response:

> Mike—Talk about questions out of the blue! But I've come to expect such wackiness from you, so...
>
> My spiritual retreats have been, for the most part, similar to any other retreats that couples or singles go on—except that I go alone. Often I have planned out the retreat just like I would if I were planning a retreat for a group of teenagers or adults, with planned Bible study times, activities, and free time, all built around a certain theme or question. The question or theme generally has come out of my life—things like, "How should a Christian deal with pressure?" or bigger issues like, "What really matters in life? What's essential, and what's fluff?"
>
> Generally, the retreats have involved journaling in some way, or tape recording, so that I've had a permanent record of my

discoveries or insights. I have always found these times away with God to be essential for keeping me humble and focused on the right things in the right way. It's sort of a spiritual realignment. We tune up our cars, and they're just machines. If I'm willing to do that for my car, then why not for my soul, which is eternal and of far more value than a machine?[4]

It takes a rare kind of courage to seek this kind of solitude with God—and it was exactly that kind of courage that Jesus modeled for us when he walked this earth. John 6:1–13 records the now-famous miracle that Jesus performed when he fed five thousand men (plus women and children) with five loaves of bread and two fish. What's not so famous is what happened afterward.

In John 6:14–16, the Bible reports that the people were so astounded by Christ's miraculous multiplication of dinner portions that they wanted to revolt against Rome on the spot and make Jesus king of Israel by force! And what was Jesus' response to such a heady scene?

He left.

Specifically the scripture says he "withdrew again to a mountain by himself" (NIV). Here Jesus was, at the height of his popularity on earth, and he walked away from it all! I think it's important to note two things in this verse. First, Jesus walked away not only from the crowds, but also from his disciples, his closest friends. He deliberately removed himself from *everyone* but the Spirit of God, seeking solitude that only a mountainside could offer.

The second thing to notice is the word "again." The Bible tells us that Jesus

> If one sets aside time for a business appointment, a trip to the hairdresser, a social engagement, or a shopping expedition, that time is accepted as inviolable. But if one says, "I cannot come because that is my hour to be alone," one is considered rude, egotistical, or strange. What a commentary on our civilization, when one has to apologize for it, make excuses, hide the fact that one practices it—like a secret vice!
>
> —Anne Morrow Lindbergh[5]

not only sought solitude; he did it *again*. Do you see what that implies? The practice of solitude wasn't simply an occasional thing for Christ—it was a way of life for him. And if solitude is something that Jesus pursued, we would be wise to follow his example in our own lives.

Yet few people do. In fact, some people would do *anything* to avoid being alone! They live with their television set constantly turned on simply to have the artificial company of a TV talking head. Or they fill their days with all kinds of busyness and activity—work, school, physical fitness, sports, dates, bars, and more—just so they can wear themselves out by bedtime and not have to deal with the silence.

Take a look at the classified advertisements in your home newspaper if you want more proof. Chances are that literally hundreds of people have put an ad in the "personals" section in the hope that they'll meet someone who can relieve them of the prospect of being alone.

It certainly isn't wrong to seek companionship, or even to fill our lives with activity. But if we do that to the exclusion of solitary time with God, then we are missing a beautiful, meaningful experience of meeting God one on one.

Many others have written about the importance of solitude—with much more eloquence than I ever could. Let me share some of their wisdom with you now:

> Solitude is such a potential thing. We hear voices in solitude we never hear in the hurry and turmoil of life; we receive counsels and comforts we get under no other condition.
>
> —Amelia Barr, nineteenth-century author

> Be able to be alone. Lose not the advantage of solitude, and the society of thyself.
>
> —Sir Thomas Browne, English physician and author

> This [is] great misfortune—to be incapable of solitude.
>
> —Jean de La Bruyère, French author and moralist

> Solitude, though it may be silent as light, is like light, the mightiest

of agencies; for solitude is essential to man. All men come into this world alone; all leave it alone.

—Thomas De Quincey, English essayist

Solitude is the beginning of all freedom.

—Supreme Court Justice William Orville Douglas

The great omission in American life is solitude...that zone of time and space, free from the outside pressures, which is the incinerator of the spirit.

—Marya Mannes, author and former columnist
for the *New York Times*

Solitude, in the sense of being often alone, is essential to any depth of meditation or of character; and solitude, in the presence of natural beauty and grandeur, is the cradle of thought and aspirations which are not only good for the individual, but which society could ill do without.

—John Stuart Mill, British philosopher and economist[6]

To all these words let me add just this: Even in solitude, we are never alone. God is always nearby, closer than our next thought, nearer than our very soul. Let us take courage in that truth and become Christians who dare to seek God in solitude.

FREEDOM TO REVEL IN THE SILENCE

Probably the most powerful aspect of solitude is silence. It's in the silence that we come face to face with who we are, who we want to be, and (hopefully) with God and who God wants us to be.

I love Mother Teresa's comments on this subject. "We need to find God," she once said, "and he cannot be found in noise and restlessness. God is the friend of silence. See how nature—trees, flowers, grass—grows in silence; see the stars, the moon and the sun, how they move in silence...we need silence to be able to touch souls."[7]

I also believe David Tyson Gentry beautifully summed up the nature of silence in a relationship with God when he said, "True friendship comes when silence between two people is comfortable."[8]

Are you comfortable being silent with God? Or do you feel the need to fill that silence with requests or "busy talk"?

> Who you are when you are alone—that's who you really are.
>
> —*Anthony Vespugio*[9]

Try an experiment for me. Right now, if you're willing. Place your thumb on this page to mark your place, then simply close your eyes and listen for a moment or two. Go ahead, I'll wait for you.

Back now? What did you hear when you were listening? Were there noises from your neighborhood—cars whizzing by, dogs barking, children laughing in the yard? Household noises—the whir of an air conditioner, the ticking of a clock, the sound of a family member talking on the phone?

Now do the experiment again, and this time do your best to extend your listening past the surface noise, past the distractions of your mind. Spend a moment in silence, and you just might hear—no, feel—the presence of God's Spirit. Because despite what they show in movies, God doesn't tend to speak with a booming voice blaring out of the sky. More often, he speaks in the stillness of the heart, in the calmness of the mind.

In the silence.

What's more, it's in the silence that God brings rest for the soul. As William Penn remarked, "True silence is the rest of the mind; and it is to the spirit what sleep is to the body, nourishment and refreshment."[10]

Our trouble is that we tend to allow the noise of our busy world to crowd out the whisper of God! We need to learn to revel in the silence, to shut out every distraction and let God lead our thoughts and hearing in new directions. We need to learn to approach Jesus with words—and then listen, silently, expectantly, with everything we have in us.

Of course, this is easier to say than to do! We Americans aren't conditioned for silence; we're trained by our society to expect an assault on the senses at every moment, to live our lives with constant "background noise." The idea of being Christian while we are alone, then, must include an almost un-American concept: the pursuit of silence and peace in our hearts and minds so that we can, in those intimate moments, bring our very being into the presence of a whispering Savior.

I read a story once about a man who worked in an old icehouse. Before the invention of refrigerators, icehouses were quite common; they were like small barns with thick walls, no windows, and tightly sealed doors. In wintertime, blocks of ice would be cut out of frozen lakes and streams and stored in an icehouse, where they would be covered with sawdust to help keep them from melting. The ice would often stay frozen well into the summer months, thus allowing people to preserve perishable food.

At any rate, this man lost a very valuable watch while working at the icehouse one day. He quickly began searching for it, combing carefully through the sawdust. When he could not find it, he recruited his fellow laborers, and they all gave the place a thorough investigation. But in spite of their efforts, the watch remained hidden. At noon they gave up and went outside to have lunch.

While they were eating, a small boy slipped into the icehouse and emerged moments later, proudly carrying the lost watch. The astonished laborers asked how the boy had been able to find it.

"I closed the door, lay down in the sawdust, and kept very still," he replied. "Soon I heard the watch ticking."[11]

It was only in the silence that the watch could be heard—and the treasure found! Friend, sometimes the treasure of spiritual passion is found in the same way, in silence and stillness, listening for the heartbeat of God. But that silence doesn't just happen. It must be planned for and sought after.

We would be wise to follow the example of that boy—and of the father who took his family on a cross-country car trip. To keep things fair, the family members took turns choosing a cassette tape to play on the car stereo. The mother almost always chose hymns. The teenage daughter selected contemporary Christian music. Her little brother liked rock-and-roll. And the dad? When it was his turn he chose his favorite thing: a ninety-minute cassette that was blank![12]

Friend, God can be found in the silence. Let's you and I muster the courage to listen for him there.

DILIGENCE TO GUARD AGAINST TEMPTATION

There's one last aspect of Christian aloneness we need to talk about—temptation. If we are honest, we must admit that temptation is sometimes the strongest when it seems that no one is watching.

Sociologists report that the majority of Americans are really hypocrites on one level or another. For instance, two-thirds of Americans admit that given the chance to have a "one-night-stand" sexual encounter without being caught, they would do so and keep it a secret from their spouses. More than half of Americans say that if they were hooked up to a lie detector machine, they wouldn't let their spouses question them. In addition, nearly half of all Americans (42 percent) say they "don't stand up for what [they] really believe," and 29 percent say they "feel like a fake, phony, or hypocrite most of the time."[13]

> Only those who try to resist temptation know how strong it is…. We never find out the strength of the evil impulse within us until we try to fight it: and Christ, because He was the only man who never yielded to temptation, is also the only man who knows to the full what temptation means.
>
> —*C. S. Lewis*[16]

"We are as sick as our secrets," Kitty Dukakis once said[14]—and she's right. It's the person we are when we're alone that is often most susceptible to temptation.

I have a friend we'll call Dave.[15] Dave is a well-respected business professional, a proud husband and father, and a committed Christian. One Sunday morning during church, I was surprised to see Dave move forward to the altar to pray. Since he was my friend, I decided to join him in prayer and went to kneel by his side. "What are we praying about, Dave?" I asked.

Dave responded, "Well, I'm going on a business trip this week, and I'm going to be all alone in my hotel room in the evenings. In the past, that kind of situation has been unhealthy for me because too often I have given in to the temptation to watch pornographic movies. But I don't want to do that anymore. I'm praying for God to give me strength to remain mentally pure on this trip."

So Dave and I prayed, asking God to do just that—and I continued to pray for him each day that week. The next Sunday I saw Dave at church again. He was back home from his trip. As we passed in the hall, he gave me a big grin, flashed a thumbs-up, and said, "Complete victory! Thanks for praying for me!"

Through this little episode, I came to admire Dave greatly. Not only did he exhibit courage in sharing his struggle with me, he showed me by example how important it is to remain diligent in guarding against temptation when you are by yourself. And from watching him, I learned three principles for being Christian when you're alone:

Principle #1: Be willing to admit your weaknesses to God and others. It would have been easy for Dave to keep this little secret temptation to himself. His wife would never have known; I would never have known. As long as he didn't spill his guts, his secret sin would be safe, right? Wrong. Because no matter what sin we indulge in privately, God knows about it. To hide the sin doesn't blank out God's vision or his presence. It only allows that sinful desire and the accompanying guilt to fester unforgiven within our own hearts. Dave knew he had to be honest with God about his struggle, and for him that started at the altar of our church.

Principle #2: Seek accountability. Dave knew I would question him about his trip when he returned. Knowing that someone at home was aware of the problem and interested in his response gave him a little more edge in overcoming temptation. It also gave him a human part-ner in the struggle for self-control, someone he knew he could trust to cheer him on to victory.

We need this kind of accountability in our lives. We need to find friends and family with whom we can share our deepest secrets and to whom we can turn for added strength. God places us in churches, in his *family*, for a reason. As Christian brothers and sisters, we need each other. We need to help each other. We need to keep each other accountable in our attempts to live by God's standards.

Principle #3: Make prayer your backbone. Truth is, there's no way we can live this Christian life by ourselves. Unless the Spirit of Jesus empowers and protects us, all our attempts at righteousness will add up to just a heap of filthy rags. Dave knew that on his own he was too weak to withstand his temptation. He needed an inner strength that can only come from God. So he did what we often forget to do: He prayed. And he recruited me to pray. Together we approached our loving Father about the problem, and in doing so we helped Dave to access the awesome power of God's Spirit in his life.

It may be easier to behave as a Christian when others are around, watching us. But true courage reveals itself in a desire to live a passionate Christian life when we are all alone, in solitude and silence, facing private temptations—yet knowing that we're wrapped in the protective arms of God. May God give us strength to be that kind of courageous Christian!

And may we never be afraid of being alone again.

WHAT DOES SILENCE CREATE?

It makes room for listening.
It gives us freedom to observe.
It allows time to think.
It provides space in which to feel.
It lets us broaden our awareness.
It opens us to the entry of peace.
It invites us to know our limitations and God's vastness.
—Charles R. Swindoll[17]

Part Four

WEAKNESS
AND
STRENGTH

And He said to me, "My grace is sufficient for you,
for My strength is made perfect in weakness."
—2 Corinthians 12:9 NKJV

When Martha heard that Jesus was coming, she went out to meet him, but Mary stayed at home.

"Lord," Martha said to Jesus, "if you had been here, my brother would not have died. But I know that even now God will give you whatever you ask."

Jesus said to her, "Your brother will rise again."

Martha answered, "I know he will rise again in the resurrection at the last day."

Jesus said to her, "I am the resurrection and the life. He who believes in me will live, even though he dies; and whoever lives and believes in me will never die. Do you believe this?"

"Yes, Lord," she told him, "I believe that you are the Christ, the Son of God, who was to come into the world."

And after she had said this, she went back and called her sister Mary aside. "The Teacher is here," she said, "and is asking for you." When Mary heard this, she got up quickly and went to him. . . .

When Mary reached the place where Jesus was and saw him, she fell at his feet and said, "Lord, if you had been here, my brother would not have died."

When Jesus saw her weeping, and the Jews who had come along with her also weeping, he was deeply moved in spirit and troubled. "Where have you laid him?" he asked.

"Come and see, Lord," they replied.

Jesus wept.

Then the Jews said, "See how he loved him!"

But some of them said, "Could not he who opened the eyes of the blind man have kept this man from dying?"

Jesus, once more deeply moved, came to the tomb. It was a cave with a stone laid across the entrance. "Take away the stone," he said. . . .

So they took away the stone. Then Jesus looked up and said, "Father, I thank you that you have heard me. I knew that you always hear me, but I said this for the benefit of the people standing here, that they may believe that you sent me."

When he had said this, Jesus called in a loud voice, "Lazarus, come out!" The dead man came out, his hands and feet wrapped with strips of linen, and a cloth around his face.

Jesus said to them, "Take off the grave clothes and let him go."

—John 11:20–44 NIV

13

COURAGE TO RELY ON GOD

Trusting God in Everything

Lazarus is sick, terribly sick. No, worse. Lazarus, the beloved brother of Mary and Martha, the friend of the Son of God himself, is dying. He knows it, and his sisters know it, yet they can do nothing to stop it. They have only one hope: Jesus.

In desperation, Mary and Martha send a message to the Messiah. "Lord!" they cry. "The one you love is sick!"

Can you hear their deep concern? Do you sense their fear? They're begging for God to come and help them. And now they wait.

A day passes, then two. Jesus does not come. And Lazarus, at last, dies. The home of Mary and Martha becomes the meeting place of many mourners. Friends and family gather to shed tears, to bury the dead man, and to share the aching hollowness that now consumes the two sisters' hearts.

Another day passes, and still Jesus does not come. Finally, four days after Lazarus has been placed in the tomb, the Messiah dares to arrive on the scene.

Martha rushes out to meet him. "Lord," she cries, "if you had been here, my brother would not have died."

Can you hear her sorrow? Do you feel her disappointment? She had begged for Jesus to come, but he had delayed. She had trusted him for yet another miracle; she had believed in Christ and his love for her family. Maybe she shouldn't have. God was untrustworthy. God was too late.

Jesus joins the party of mourners. He soon sees Mary, who falls at his feet, weeping. "Lord," she chokes out, "if you had been here, my brother would not have died."

Do you hear her pain? She had trusted this Messiah, depended on him. She had needed him more than ever before. But she, like her sister, had been foolish. God had failed even to show up on time.

Seeing her sorrow, Jesus weeps.

Then, drying his tears, Jesus goes to the cave where Lazarus has been wrapped in graveclothes and laid to rest. The entrance to the tomb is blocked by a massive stone. "Take away the stone," Jesus says.

Martha can't believe her hero's ignorance. It has been four days! Surely by now the decaying body of her brother reeks to high heaven. Still, the stone is moved. Jesus speaks again.

"Lazarus, come out!"

The gathered mourners catch their breath in silent disbelief. Something stirs. The dead man walks! The rotting corpse moves, breathes, opens its eyes. Lazarus is alive once more!

Now Mary and Martha weep with joy—and with awe at their Savior. Not even death is powerful enough to withstand Jesus! Their souls leap as they realize the truth: *One is never a fool to rely on God.*

I love this story of the resurrection of Lazarus (originally told in John 11:1–45) because I can relate so well to Mary and Martha. Too many times in my life I've found myself in unhappy circumstances and have cried out to God for help—yet he hasn't come. At such times I'm tempted to believe that God doesn't care or that he has run late and has missed my need. Then I read the story of Lazarus and take courage. I realize that it's never too late for God's love to intervene. It's never too late for God to lead me through the rough times, to fill me with the courage that comes from complete reliance on him.

What about you? Do the difficult times in life tempt you to disbelieve that God is reliable? That he can be trusted to accomplish what he desires in your life? That's OK. It happens to all of us from time to time. But we don't have to give in to that kind of faithless thinking. Want to know why? Read on, friend. Read on!

COURAGE TO FACE YOUR FEARS

It is no easy task to rely on God. Sometimes he insists on taking you to the extreme limits of your faith, like he did with Mary, Martha, and Lazarus. Sometimes he seems to disappear for days, weeks, months, even years.

It's a fearful thing to throw yourself into the hands of God and let him lead you blindfolded through the doors and hallways of life. But it is also the most secure, most rewarding way to live life in any age.

Make no mistake though. Reliance on God doesn't mean you will always be safe. It certainly didn't keep Lazarus safe—he got sick and died! And even after he had been miraculously returned to life, he had to face a murder plot against him (see John 12:9–11). No, friend, reliance on God is often downright dangerous.

> Faith is believing when common sense tells you not to.
>
> —Fred Gailey (as portrayed by John Payne) in *Miracle on 34th Street*[1]

But reliance on God does mean that as courageous Christians we cannot let fear rule our lives. We can't let panic cause us to abandon our trust in God's provision and promises for us. Listen to what noted pastor and author Chuck Swindoll says about this:

> Did you know that you operate at your poorest when you are scared? A little fear is good for us when danger is present, but a lot of it is demoralizing. It takes away the hope, the dream, the vision, the possibility of overcoming. Jesus speaks with a gentle voice and says, "Don't be afraid! If I can't meet your need, what kind of a Savior would I be? Trust me. Quietly trust me."[2]

I want to tell you about a lesson I learned from my son, Tony. This is probably a terrible thing for a parent to say, but when Tony was four years old, he was an adorable crier. Don't get me wrong; whenever tears began to trickle from his sparkly green eyes and stream down his chubby little face, part of me immediately wanted to reach out and comfort him. But another part always wanted to pause for just a moment and take in the precious sight. Invariably, the thought that would run through my mind was, *He's just soooo cute!*—and then finally I'd reach down and hold him close until the tears dried up and a smile returned to his innocent little face.

But one day in 1994, my little Tony was fighting back the tears (doing admirably, I must say, but losing the battle nonetheless), and I stood before him determined to be firm.

"But Dad," he was saying, "I-I-I want my b-ball…" The tiny voice choked down a sob.

"Fine," I said. "You can play with your ball, but you have to go downstairs to get it."

Now the tears came without restraint. He plopped right down on the floor in front of me, crying his heart out.

You see, in our home we have a long stairway leading down to a finished basement. In the basement was Tony's playroom—and thus it held all of Tony's treasures: stuffed animals, Nerf balls, action figures, and lots of other toys and games that four-year-olds love. Tony spent hours down there, playing, imagining, laughing (and occasionally breaking something by accident!). The playroom was Tony's place, the one part of the house where a four-year-old ruled supreme.

Except for one thing. In order to turn on the light in the basement, you first had to descend through the darkened stairway, step into the shadowy playroom, *then* reach for the light switch. And that was Tony's dilemma. He desperately wanted to play with his toys. But like most preschoolers, he also was desperately frightened of the dark that cloaked his personal little heaven.

"Tony," I said, trying to be heard through his sniffles. "You're going to have to learn how to deal with the dark. You *know* what's in the playroom. Everything in there is just the same in the dark as it is in the light. I'm sorry, but if you want your ball, you will have to go down and get it yourself."

The sobs softened some, and he looked up at me with those irresistible, tear-stained eyes. "B-b-but Dad," he sniffed, "I'm *s-s-scared* of the dark."

Don't give in, I thought to myself. *Help him be strong. Teach him by experience that he is more powerful than a silly light switch on a wall.*

"OK, here's the deal," I said. "I'll walk with you to the top of the stairs. Then I'll stand at the landing while you go down into the dark and switch on the light. I'll stay where you can hear my voice until the light comes on in the playroom. How's that sound?"

If smiles were sunshine, I'd have needed SPF-30 sunscreen to protect myself from the grin that replaced Tony's tears. His confidence restored, he got up and walked bravely to the top of the stairs. I stopped there, but Tony continued without hesitation. Then, when he was partway down into the darkness, I heard him hesitate.

"Dad?" he called out.

"Yes, Tony?"

"Nothing."

Seconds later the light was on, and Tony was happily throwing a Nerf basketball through a miniature hoop, back in his own little heaven of a playroom. Simply knowing that his father was nearby was enough to give him courage to face—and overcome—his fear of the darkness.

I'm a grown man, and, unlike Tony, I don't find much in darkness to cause me to be afraid. But because I'm a grown man, I do have other fears—ones I'm betting you have too: financial fears, health concerns, family worries, political apprehensions, cultural and criminal frights,

> Any fear is an illusion. You think something is standing in your way, but nothing is really there. What *is* there is an opportunity to do your best and gain some success. If you run into a wall, don't turn around and give up. Figure out how to climb it, go through it, or work around it.
>
> —*basketball great Michael Jordan*[3]

relational and emotional panics, and the list goes on. If I let these fears run rampant, before long I become paralyzed, like a four-year-old boy who is afraid of the dark.

When fear threatens to darken my world, in my mind's eye I see the tears on Tony's face become tears on my own. And looking down on me through the gloom is God, my heavenly Father, letting me know he's still near. Despite the circumstances, nothing about our relationship has changed. It's time for me to trust in the darkness what I know in the light—to rely on God to bring me through any and every situation. In those times of inky blackness, when darkness covers my heart, I call out silently, "Father?"

And he always answers, "Yes, my son?"

"Nothing."

Just knowing he's near is enough comfort for me. I know that in the end I'll be all right, that I *will* fight through this fearful darkness and into the light of heaven. Until that day I won't be afraid, because I know one very important truth: God is waiting for me at the top of the stairs.

He's waiting for you too.

GOD IS IN THE SMALL STUFF

One interesting thing I've discovered among Christians is that many of us are more than willing to trust God for the situations that are out of our control.

"It's cancer," a doctor says.

"We'll just have to pray and trust God," the Christian naturally responds. And in every instance, that's a good thing to do. Sometimes it can even result in physical healing.

But what about when the doctor says, "It's just a common cold"? Or, "It's only dry skin causing a rash"? Or, "It's just a headache"? Those same Christians who rush to God's throne to pray about cancer can quickly forget God's address when the problem is something minor like a cold or a rash or a headache.

Why? Because cancer, to a large degree, is out of our control. A cold? We can take care of that with a little rest, vitamin C, and a bottle of nasal spray. We don't need God to care about a rash on an arm— we've got medicated lotion that'll heal that right up. And a headache? Take two Tylenol, and an hour later we'll forget we had it.

In our own self-sufficiency, we perceive no need for reliance on God.[4]

Let me explain this another way. A few years ago, Amy and I received an unusual phone call. A young, college-aged girl we had met only once (but who was a friend of relatives) had learned she was unex-pectedly pregnant. The father had ended his relationship with her before this discovery and was completely uninterested in parenting the child to come. The girl sent word to us of her pregnancy through fam-ily members and asked us to adopt her child.

So began our adoption adventure. We soon found out that in order to pay all the legal fees, hospital costs, adoption agency fees, and such, we'd need a minimum of six thousand dollars within about eight weeks' time. After scraping together all our worldly resources, we found our-selves about five thousand dollars short!

Funny thing is, I had no doubt that God would provide the money. I *knew* he could—and would—make a way. In fact, Amy, Tony, and I decided not to ask anyone for help in raising the money. Instead, we prayed each day for God to provide. If people asked, we told them we were planning to adopt but stopped short of asking for funds.

Amazingly, over the next few weeks, money came pouring in. Distant friends would call and say, "God's really placed you guys on my heart lately. Is there something I can help you with?" We got letters from people that said, "I don't know why, but I feel God telling me to send you this money," and a check would be enclosed—fifty dollars here, a hundred dollars there, a thousand dollars from someplace else. To make a long story short, a miracle occurred, and at the end of four weeks, we suddenly had six thousand dollars in our bank account to use for adoption expenses! (There is a "part 2" to this story, but I'll share that with you later in this chapter.)

My point is this: It didn't take much effort for me to rely on God to provide that money. The amount was greater than anything I could pull together myself. I knew that on my own I fell far short, but I also felt strongly that the adoption process was God's will. God *had* to do something, or it wouldn't get done.

Fast-forward with me to a more recent time just a few months ago. If you know anything about a writer's life, you know that regular paychecks are only a dream. Publishers pay when they're ready to pay—not when you want them to! Such was the case earlier this year. Several publishers owed us money, but none had gotten around to cutting checks for us.

During this time I needed to purchase a thirty-dollar prescription of medicine for my stomach, but I didn't have enough cash on hand to cover it. I'm embarrassed to tell you I didn't even consult God on this one. After all, I had a credit card, right? So I just charged my medicine and went on my merry way. Later that day, I opened my mail and found a check from a magazine publisher—payment for a small project I'd actually forgotten I'd done. Guess what? It was enough to pay for my medicine with a few bucks to spare.

You see, God had planned all along to meet my need—and to meet it on time. But it was easier for me to trust God to bring in six thousand dollars than it was for me to trust him to bring in thirty dollars! I left him out of that situation, and I missed a blessing because of it.

Friend, perhaps you are like me. You can trust God for something "big," like the six thousand dollars. But can you also trust him for six bucks to take your child out to a matinee movie? To give you a good night's sleep? To be your recognized, sovereign Lord over even the most mundane moments of your life?

Maybe you, like me, need to remember what authors Bruce Bickel and Stan Jantz once said: "God is in the small stuff—and it all matters!"[5] Or, as Abraham Kuyper eloquently put it, "In the total expanse of human life there is not a single square inch of which the Christ, who alone is sovereign, does not declare, 'That is mine!' "[6]

A STUBBORN INSISTENCE THAT GOD IS SOVEREIGN

I told you that there was a "part 2" to our adoption adventure, and here it is.

After we formalized proceedings for adopting this new child, another miracle happened. My wife, who had previously been diagnosed with secondary infertility (meaning she was able to bear our first child without any problems but unable to conceive afterward), miraculously became pregnant. This child, it appeared, would be born within a few months of the one we were to adopt.

We were very excited. We figured that it would be almost like having twins, and we continued with the adoption process even as Amy went through her prenatal doctor visits and bouts of morning sickness.

Then, during her eleventh week of pregnancy, Amy suffered a miscarriage. A few months after that (about a month before our soon-to-be-adopted child was to be born), the birth mother changed her mind and decided to keep her child rather than put it up for adoption.

I would never fault a woman for keeping her child, and I applaud this young mother for being willing to follow through on her responsibility to the child she bore. But suddenly we found ourselves back at square one, even after all the miracles we had witnessed to that point (that is, the six thousand dollars and Amy's conception).

Since we still had a good portion of the money that had been donated to us for the adoption, we decided to pursue the

> Either not a sparrow falls to the ground without Him, or there is no God, and we are fatherless children.
>
> —George MacDonald[7]

adoption of another child. Several months and three failed adoption attempts later, we finally ended our adoption adventure and returned as much of the money to our benefactors as possible.

So what happened? Was God in charge for the miracles and then out of control afterward? Did he lose his place, get distracted, and forget to follow through? Of course not! I don't dare to suggest that I know all the reasons God allowed our adoption efforts to end this way—but I am stubbornly insistent that he is still in control of my life and the lives of my family members.

Who knows? Perhaps the first birth mother would have had an abortion if she had not been confident that we would adopt her baby. Or perhaps we would never have dealt in full with the fact that we are parents of an only child. Or perhaps we might not have realized until it was too late how extremely wonderful a gift our son really is. Or perhaps we would have missed out on a valuable lesson of faith.

Whatever God's reasons, the truth remains that he is sovereign. Jesus is Lord when good things happen in my life, and he is still Lord when he allows uncomfortable things to happen in my life. My responsibility is not to tell God *how* to do his job concerning me; it's to trust that God *is* doing his job concerning me with the utmost love and patience.

And that, my friend, is what it really means to courageously rely on God—come hell or high water. Our God is awesome, powerful, and, most of all, loving. We are never fools when we trust in him.

Where a God who is totally purposive and totally foreseeing acts upon a Nature which is totally interlocked, there can be no accidents or loose ends, nothing whatever of which we can safely use the word merely. Nothing is "merely a byproduct" of anything else.

—C. S. Lewis[8]

When Jesus looked up and saw a great crowd coming toward him, he said to Philip, "Where shall we buy bread for these people to eat?" He asked this only to test him, for he already had in mind what he was going to do.

Philip answered him, "Eight months' wages would not buy enough bread for each one to have a bite!"

Another of his disciples, Andrew, Simon Peter's brother, spoke up, "Here is a boy with five small barley loaves and two small fish, but how far will they go among so many?"

Jesus said, "Have the people sit down." There was plenty of grass in that place, and the men sat down, about five thousand of them. Jesus then took the loaves, gave thanks, and distributed to those who were seated as much as they wanted. He did the same with the fish.

When they had all had enough to eat, he said to his disciples, "Gather the pieces that are left over. Let nothing be wasted." So they gathered them and filled twelve baskets with the pieces of the five barley loaves left over by those who had eaten.

—John 6:5–13 NIV

14

COURAGE TO MULTIPLY YOUR GIFTS AND TALENTS

Assessing and Using Your Spiritual Gifts and Physical Talents

I was in fifth grade when I learned the real power of multiplication. Oh sure, I'd memorized the multiplication tables years before and had been a decent student in math up to that point. But it wasn't until Mr. Webster (I think that was his name!) issued a challenge to a classmate that the true limitlessness of multiplication finally penetrated my dull little brain.

"Let's suppose," Mr. Webster said, "that I hire you to work for me for one month. And for your wages, I give you a choice. I'll either pay you one million dollars for your month of work, or I'll pay you a penny on your first day and then double that wage every day until the end of the month."

Looking around the room, Mr. Webster picked one of my friends (I think his name was Trey). "Trey," he said, "which deal would you take?"

Trey didn't hesitate: "I'll take the million!" Many of us in the class nodded our heads in agreement. After all, who in his right mind would turn down a *million* dollars for one month of work?

Mr. Webster smiled and shook his head. "Bad choice, Trey. Let me show you why."

On the chalkboard, he wrote "$1,000,000" and labeled it as option one. Then he started a new column labeled option two. In that column he numbered from one to thirty—the days of the month. Next to day one, he wrote "$0.01." We all snickered. Then he said, "Let's see what happens if we multiply this by two."

In the day two space, he wrote "$0.02." We all chuckled some more. Mr. Webster simply grinned and continued multiplying each number by two. By day fifteen, he'd finally broken a hundred dollars. The laughter started to quiet down. By day twenty, he'd amassed a daily wage of more than five thousand dollars. Now we were all paying attention. When he finished his multiplication for day thirty, he added up the wages for each day of the month. The total was more than ten million dollars!

> The greatest mathematical discovery of all time is compound interest.
>
> —Albert Einstein [1]

Mr. Webster turned back to the class. "What do you think now, Trey?" he said. "Would you rather have option one or option two?"

Of course Trey chose option two! Ten million dollars is ten times better than one million for the same amount of work.

And that's the beauty of multiplication. Something as miniscule as a penny can be miraculously transformed into millions and millions of dollars if only we allow it to be multiplied. In fact, that's the whole basis behind the concept of compound interest, the key ingredient of savings accounts and stock investments. The idea is to put a certain amount of money in a bank or stock or mutual fund where it will be multiplied by a certain percentage over and over again until the final sum of money is significantly higher than the original amount.

As a Christian, you have extra reason to appreciate the principle of multiplication. God is the Master Multiplier, the only one ever to take nothing and multiply a universe out of it! If he can do that with nothing, imagine what he can do with the gifts and talents he's stored within you!

"But Mike," you say, "I'm not all that great at anything. I'm average at best."

Excellent! Then you're already way ahead of the place God started from at the beginning. Even if you feel you've only got a few pennies' worth of abilities, the use of those abilities—and a little multiplication on God's part—can bring about millions of dollars' worth of results. Fact is, without God you'll never be able to fully maximize your talents —even if you're the best in the world at something. But with God, all things become possible, and your meager gifts and abilities can be transformed into limitless possibilities.

Curious to know more? Then read on!

AVAILABILITY IS MORE IMPORTANT THAN ABILITY

When I was a kid I used to mock the fact that my parents listened to "old fogy" music like Nat King Cole and Louis Armstrong. Now that I'm grown, I still like to listen to current popular tunes—but I've gained a new appreciation for classic artists like Cole and Armstrong. In fact, just last week I added yet another Nat King Cole album to my collection. (Got it for twenty-five cents at a garage sale—am I a bargain hunter or what?)

One of the added bonuses of this thrifty purchase was that it came with a little biographical booklet about the singer and his rise to fame. Seems that young Nat moved to Los Angeles in the latter half of the 1930s to seek fame and fortune as a singer. When an employee of Nat's band absconded with the group's payroll, the band went bust, and Nat found himself hustling to get work—any work—just to keep himself fed.

Six months later, Nat auditioned for a man named Bob Lewis, who was the owner of the Swanee Inn in Hollywood. Lewis was impressed and invited the singer to perform at his inn—provided Nat recruit three others and form a quartet.

Nat King Cole dutifully rounded up three friends, including guitarist Oscar Moore, bassist Wesley Prince, and a now nameless drummer. After several practices, they were ready to roll. On opening night, all the band members showed up except the drummer! So Nat, Oscar, and Wesley went onstage as a makeshift trio instead.

The trio was an immediate hit, and before long the three men had signed a recording contract with Decca Records. That in turn led to a show at the prestigious 311 Club, where record company executive Johnny Mercer heard Nat and his two friends. Impressed, he signed the trio to record for Capitol Records—and the rest, as they say, is history. Over the next several decades, Nat King Cole became a musical legend. The other members of his trio often recorded with him and benefited from his fame and fortune.[2]

That drummer? No one knows what happened to him. Certainly he had the ability to play with Nat King Cole, but because he was unavailable when it came time to use that ability, his name and talent have disappeared into the annals of obscurity.

Ah, the fortunes we miss simply by not being available! And the same is true for us as Christians. The greatest, most gifted people are useless if they don't make themselves available to be used by God. In short, *availability* is more important than *ability*.

Think of it like this: Suppose you own a professional football team, and on your roster is the league's highest-rated quarterback. You're in good shape, right? Only if your quarterback can play! If he is injured, or ill, or holding out for a better contract, or stuck in traffic on the freeway on the way to the stadium, all his talents become useless to your team. His value is not just in his ability, it's in his availability to use that talent for your team during a game.

> Eighty percent of success is showing up.
>
> —Woody Allen[3]

Now let's say you aren't the owner of the team anymore. Let's say you are the second-string quarterback—but with the starting QB stuck in traffic, you are suddenly the most important player on the team. Will you be ready to play? Have you made yourself available during practices and team meetings? Now that your time has come, are you available to go onto the field and lead your team to victory? Or are you as useless as that high-talent guy stuck on the freeway?

You see, in the economy of God's kingdom, your willingness to let your talents be used—no matter how meager you may think they are—makes all the difference.

Perhaps you've heard of Christian singer and songwriter Cindy Morgan. In 1996, Cindy went to Los Angeles to perform a series of concerts. Arriving at a church where she would be singing, she unpacked the dress she planned to wear for the show and was dismayed to discover it was covered with wrinkles.

That's when a woman involved with the production stepped forward and made herself available to do the mundane job of ironing the singing star's dress. No big talent required there, right? So the woman took the dress to the home of a nearby staff member, along with a house key and instructions for where to find the iron. After entering the house, the woman headed toward the laundry room. But when she passed a bedroom, she saw a shocking sight.

The fifteen-year-old daughter of the staff member stood with a gun to her head, preparing to commit suicide.

This story has a happy ending. The "ironing lady" put the dress aside and quietly talked to the distraught girl. Eventually she convinced her to relinquish the gun and go back to the church for help.[4]

As I think about the miraculous way God used this woman to save that teenager's life, one thought sticks out in my mind: What if she hadn't been available? What if she had figured someone else would get around to ironing that dress sooner or later? What would have happened?

And that's the question we must ask ourselves when given opportunities to use our gifts and talents for God. What if we don't make ourselves available? What will happen then?

I'm not suggesting you should stretch yourself to extremes and never say no to an opportunity (reread chapter 7 if you don't believe me!), but I am suggesting that the passionate Christian must be willing to be used by God at any time, in any place, whether on the spur of the moment or planned months ahead. What's really important isn't your ability; it's your availability.

Take Time to Open the Package

Of course, before you can make yourself available to be used, you need to take time to assess what gifts, talents, and resources you have at your disposal. I heard a story once about a father whose son learned this truth the hard way. The son was approaching his high school graduation and had only one thing on his mind: a brand-new car. At every opportunity, the boy let his father know exactly which car he wanted to receive for a graduation present. The two even went out together one day to price the car and go over details about extras the son wanted included on his dream vehicle.

Finally graduation day came, and after the ceremony, family and friends gathered at the boy's home to celebrate. Arrangements had already been made for the son to leave the very next morning to begin college early, during the summer, at a university several states away.

One by one the boy opened his gifts, thanking the appropriate person for each new item. But in his heart, he really wanted to open only one package—the one from his dad. That box was smaller than most of the others, but not too small to hold a set of car keys to a certain sought-after automobile.

Finally he opened the last present. The father stood by smiling as the young man tore the paper off the package and peeked inside. Suddenly the boy's face fell. The disappointment in his expression turned to anger, and he disgustedly pushed the package away only half-opened. Inside was a beautifully covered, leather-bound Bible.

"I can't believe you did this to me," the young man seethed. "You knew I really wanted that car. I can't believe you'd be so cheap, so callous, to even go car shopping with me when you knew you weren't going to buy it!"

Without another word, the boy stormed off to his room. He left early the next morning for school, vowing never to return home.

At college, he discovered that his mother had secretly packed the father's still half-wrapped present among his things. He stored the box in a closet and soon forgot all about it.

Four years later, the young man received an urgent call. The father was ill, dying. Wouldn't he please come home to say good-bye? But the boy refused, using final exams as his excuse but still holding ill will toward the man he felt had betrayed him. A few days later, the father died, and the son began to feel twinges of remorse. Remembering the graduation package, he somberly fished it out of storage.

The paper was faded now, the box weathered but firm. Silently he tore the rest of the wrapping paper off and opened the lid all the way. He sighed and pulled the Bible out of the package. As he did, a note fell out from under the front cover.

"Dear son," the note said, "as you prepare to go out into the world, I can think of only one lasting gift to give you—this Bible. In it I pray you'll find everything you need for living out the rest of your life. Faithfully reading this book will make your dreams come true in more ways than you can imagine. Love, Dad."

The boy tossed the note on his bed and began flipping through the pages of the Bible. Suddenly he felt something. Turning to the inside of the back cover, he found another present from his father: a check, made out to him, for exactly the amount of the brand-new car he'd wanted four years before. As the tears began streaming down the young man's face, his only thought was, *If only I'd opened the package sooner!*

The life you now live is a package, a gift from God to you. At first glance, you may not see everything you wanted in your package. Maybe there are other people who are prettier, who are wealthier, who can sing better, who can do any of a number of things better than you. But like that father, God himself has loaded your human package full of surprises. Now it's up to you to open that gift to the full and discover what's inside—to seek to understand and master the gifts, talents, and abilities God has placed at your fingertips. When you do that, then you can be used fully for God's purposes.

How do you open that package? Begin by assessing yourself—your talents, your resources, your interests. What do you like to do? What are you good at? What do others always seem to look to you for? What resources are at your disposal?

Perhaps some of these things are surprises God has put in your package. Find the ones that seem to draw you and invest in improving those skills. Take classes. Practice. Get advice from people you respect. Practice some more. Look for opportunities to use your talents. If using that ability somehow energizes you, chances are you've found a special surprise from God.

It would also be wise for you to study scriptures that teach about the gifts of the Holy Spirit. If the Bible is to be believed (and it is), God has placed within you one or more spiritual gifts that he desires you to "open up" and use. Read Romans 12:6–8; 1 Corinthians 12:4–11, 27–31; Ephesians 4:7–13; and 1 Peter 4:10–11. These scriptures are great starting points for understanding God's special gifts to you.

LET GOD DO HIS THING

There's one last aspect of multiplying your gifts and talents that you need to consider, and it's really the most important truth of all. (I suppose I should have written this section first, but I wanted to save the best for last!)

After you have determined to make yourself available to God, and after you've "opened the package" to discover the gifts and talents God has blessed you with, you must now let God do his thing. He alone is the Great Multiplier, and he alone can bring true fruit from your efforts.

Yes, you're responsible for assessing your abilities. Yes, you're responsible for making those gifts and talents available and for putting them to use to the best of your ability. But the results—well, they're up to God.

Through my work at Nappaland Communications, Inc., I've come into contact with many authors of great skill. Some of equal skill have achieved greatly disparate levels of success. I know a phenomenal novelist, for example, who's written three books—and sold meager amounts of them. I know another novelist of equal talent who has sold more than a million books.

Does that mean the second novelist is God's favorite? Of course not. Does that mean the first novelist should get out of the writing business altogether? Of course not! It means that both men are using their God-given talents to the best of their ability, and they're leaving the results up to God. Both men are successful in God's eyes. You see, they aren't responsible for God's part of the equation; they're only responsible for using the gifts he has given them to the fullest. It's up to God to decide which multiplication factor to apply to their work.

I think the Reverend Billy Graham has probably illustrated this point best. As I'm sure you are aware, Billy Graham has been the world's premiere evangelist for most of the twentieth century, and at the time of this writing, he shows no signs of slowing down. At the same time (and with all due respect), there are thousands of preachers of equal skill to Reverend Graham who will never witness the millions of people brought to Christ through their ministry that he has. Does that mean that Billy Graham is better than they are or that he has some special secret that others don't have?

I'll let Reverend Graham answer that question for you. He says:

> So many people think that somehow I carry a revival around in a suitcase, and they just announce me and something happens— but that's not true. This is the work of God, and the Bible warns that God will not share his glory with another. All the publicity [the crusades] receive sometimes frightens me because I feel that therein lies great danger. If God should take his hand off me, I would have no more spiritual power. The whole secret of the success of our meetings is spiritual—it's God answering prayer. I cannot take credit for any of it.[5]

I'd like to end this chapter with one last story of God's multiplying power—one last example of what can happen when we determine to let God do his thing with the resources we offer him. (If you want to read the original account of this story, you'll find it in John 6:5–13.)

It was the height of Jesus' public ministry. Everywhere he went, great crowds followed. Finally Jesus decided to take his disciples and retreat to a mountainside to get some "alone time." But the plan didn't work. Soon he noticed a great crowd of people rushing toward him. How many people were there? No one knows for sure, but the Bible says that the men in the crowd numbered around five thousand—and that's not counting the women and children who were with them!

I imagine Jesus had a glint in his eye when he turned to his disciples and casually asked, "Where shall we buy bread for these people to eat?"

The disciples were flabbergasted—as I'm sure you and I would have been—as they quickly calculated the fortune it would take to buy food for this multitude of unexpected dinner guests. Philip was apparently the one who was the quickest at math because he spoke up first. "Eight months' wages would not buy enough bread for each one to have a bite!" he said in shock.

> No eye has seen, no ear has heard, and no mind has imagined what God has prepared for those who love him.
>
> —The apostle Paul in 1 Corinthians 2:9 NLT

I don't know exactly what happened next, but I imagine Jesus just smiled. He probably looked from one disciple to another, then turned his face toward the crowd. Finally, his gaze lighted on one little boy hidden among the ranks. We don't know the boy's name. We don't know where he came from or even what he was doing at this adult-oriented gathering. But we do know he was the only one who thought to bring a little lunch along—two fish and five small loaves of bread.

I picture that lad suddenly realizing he had something Jesus could use, then stepping shyly forward. He nudged Andrew, who was still puzzling over how to get a huge amount of food in a short amount of time.

Of course, Andrew knew right away that the boy's five loaves and two fish would never come close to feeding the entire crowd. And I'm certain the boy had no idea how God was going to multiply the gift he made available when he offered his lunch. But that doesn't matter. What does matter is that Andrew turned back to Jesus and said, "Here is a boy with five small barley loaves and two small fish." Perhaps Andrew scratched his head at this point, because he asked, " But how far will they go among so many?"

In human terms, Andrew? Not very far. But when God decides to do his thing? Farther than any of us could ever imagine.

And so the heavenly multiplication began. Two fish and five barley loaves, touched by the hands of the Master, soon became a feast for thousands—with enough left over to feed a few thousand more!

Friend, what are the "fish and loaves" you have in your life? Your time? Your talents? Your gifts? Your friends and family? Your financial resources? Your home? Your car? Your intelligence? Your sense of humor? What? Perhaps today is the day for you to finally lay those simple things at the feet of the Master, to follow his direction and allow him to use whatever he wants.

Then get ready for God to do his thing with your offering. The results, I promise, will be more than you could ever imagine.

SPIRITUAL-GIFTS INDICATOR[6]

This spiritual-gifts indicator is based on the gifts listed in Romans 12:6–8. Other spiritual gifts are listed in 1 Corinthians 12:4–11, 27–31; Ephesians 4:7–13; and 1 Peter 4:10–11.

Read each of the following statements and determine how well it describes you. Mark the statements according to the following scale:

M=This describes me most of the time
S=This describes me sometimes.
N=This does not really describe me.

____ 1. *I look for creative ways to meet others' needs.*

____ 2. *People generally look to me to make the first move.*

____ 3. *I try hard to help others feel good about themselves.*

____ 4. *Teaching a Sunday school class or Bible study interests me.*

_____ 5. I'm likely to mow a neighbor's lawn or take a meal to someone who's been sick.

_____ 6. I'm drawn to people others might consider "outcasts."

_____ 7. I'm likely to notice when those around me are feeling down.

_____ 8. I like the idea of sharing what God has told me with others.

_____ 9. Giving is an important part of my financial plan.

_____10. I'm likely to generate enthusiasm among others.

_____11. When I lend things, I don't worry about getting them back.

_____12. Others tell me I explain things in a clear, easy-to-understand way.

_____13. I appreciate what others do, and I tell them so.

_____14. I feel called to tell others what God reveals to me.

_____15. I'm not bothered when my work goes unnoticed.

_____16. People who need help solving problems often ask for my opinion.

_____17. I think everyone deserves second and third chances.

_____18. I enjoy preparing lessons because I like sharing what I learn with others.

_____19. I'm interested in ministering to prisoners, the homeless, the disabled, and people in similar situations.

_____20. People tell me I present biblical messages in a clear, compelling way.

_____21. I'm likely to volunteer for tasks others my have neglected.

Each statement describes a possible demonstration of a spiritual gift. Statements you marked with an M could indicate giftedness in the corresponding spiritual gift. Two or more related statements marked with an S could also indicate giftedness.

Match your responses with the gifts below by circling the statement numbers that you ranked with an M. Those qualities with the most M rankings are probably your spiritual gifts.

- *prophecy: 8, 14, 20*
- *serving: 5, 15, 21*
- *teaching: 4, 12, 18*
- *showing mercy: 6, 17, 19*

- *encouraging: 3, 7, 13*
- *giving: 1, 9, 11*
- *leading: 2, 10, 16*

Meanwhile, the disciples were in trouble far away from land, for a strong wind had risen, and they were fighting heavy waves.

About three o'clock in the morning Jesus came to them, walking on the water. When the disciples saw him, they screamed in terror, thinking he was a ghost. But Jesus spoke to them at once. "It's all right," he said. "I am here! Don't be afraid."

Then Peter called to him, "Lord, if it's really you, tell me to come to you by walking on water."

"All right, come," Jesus said.

So Peter went over the side of the boat and walked on the water toward Jesus. But when he looked around at the high waves, he was terrified and began to sink. "Save me, Lord!" he shouted.

Instantly Jesus reached out his hand and grabbed him. "You don't have much faith," Jesus said. "Why did you doubt me?" And when they climbed back into the boat, the wind stopped.

—Matthew 14:24–32 NLT

15

COURAGE TO GO IN OVER YOUR HEAD—AND RISK IT ALL

Stretching Your Potential for Christ to Its Fullest Limit

Steven Curtis Chapman is probably one of my top three, all-time-favorite musicians. This guy has won a zillion awards and sold millions of albums, but I don't really care about that. What I care about is the musical artistry and lyrical depth he displays in song after song.

One of our family's favorite SC^2 songs illustrates well what I'm talking about. It's the tune "Dive" from his 1999 *Speechless* album. In this pulsing melody, the artist sings about a rushing river and being faced with the decision of whether or not to enter into its powerful flow. Finally he reaches the chorus, where he practically shouts with enthusiastic determination: "The river's deep, the river's wide, the river's water is alive, so sink or swim, I'm diving in!"[1]

Very cool song! But what's even cooler is the message behind the words. Listen to how Steven explains it:

> ["Dive"] was inspired by a story Pastor Scotty Smith told during one of his sermons. He had an awesome fishing trip with fellow Pastor Scott Roley. They had gone trout fishing and found a stream that produced a day of fishing that was a dream come true. They were standing chest deep in this stream catching trout left and right and at the day's end had caught two hundred fish. It was just unbelievable. He said the interesting thing was all the people

standing on the shore watching them. Nobody was catching fish from the shore because you had to be out in the deep water where the fish were.

Scotty related this story to the Christian life by saying it's not a spectator sport, it's not something we just sit on the side [for]; we've got to get deep into the living water to experience what it is. It's dangerous, it's scary, it's frightening, and it's all those things, but that's where we are called to live our lives.... If we're really going to do it and really dive in deep to what it means to get lost and lose ourselves in the flow of the living water, it's a scary thing; you stand there with your knees knocking, you're excited, you're speechless, and you almost can't catch your breath. Your heart's racing, and you know once you take that step, there isn't any turning back.[2]

Wow, doesn't that sound like a thrill ride? Like a huge, spiritual adrenaline rush? That kind of joyful abandon into the plans and power of God in our lives is a beautiful picture of what it means to live with passion and courage for Christ. It's a call for each of us to let Jesus lead us out into the world—in "over our heads" if need be—to relish the awesomeness and excitement of serving a mighty Savior. It's an invitation to step out of our comfort zones and to be willing to risk it all for God—no matter what.

CHRISTIANITY IS RISKY BUSINESS

In case I haven't made this clear before, I want to say it plainly here: This Christian life we are endeavoring to live is no safe path. Christianity is risky business! If this life of faith were a sport, it wouldn't be something safe and predictable like baseball or bowling. No, the Christianity that Jesus calls us to is more like an extreme sport—rock climbing without a safety line, hang gliding over an open sea, bungee jumping off a tall bridge.

Earlier in this book we talked about what it means to give your all to God. Now let's explore what it means to *risk* all you've been given for God. You see, God has placed within you a wellspring of gifts, talents, and resources (as we talked about in the last chapter). Those gifts and resources are like investment capital God has put in your little "life brokerage." God has given you his checkbook, added your name to his signature card, and said, "Get to work! Here's the seed money you need to impact your world for Christ—now get out there and invest it!"

So what are you going to do with that checkbook? Hoard most of the resources away under your mattress at home? Or start spreading your seed money around in hopes of doubling, tripling, even generating a hundredfold return on God's investment? This is the exciting stuff of the Christian life, friend. Don't miss out on this awesome experience simply because you're unwilling to take risks in your pursuit of God's will for your life.

I'm reminded of the seventy-one-year-old widow who died in West Palm Beach, Florida, sometime ago. For years she had gotten all her clothes from the Salvation Army and begged for food at her neighbors' back doors. Eventually she wasted away to a mere fifty pounds and finally died of malnutrition.

> We need to make an investigation of our possessiveness, our tendency to hoard, to hold on to, rather than investing in the lives of others.
> —*Charles R. Swindoll*[3]

When investigators examined her home, they found a huge mess of secondhand junk and, to their surprise, two keys. Further investigation revealed that the keys were to safe-deposit boxes at two local banks. In one box officials found hundreds of stock certificates in the deceased woman's name valued at more than a quarter of a million dollars. Mixed in with those certificates was more than $200,000 in cash. When they opened the second box they found more cash—more than $600,000, to be exact! In all, that seemingly penniless recluse who died for lack of food held more than *a million dollars* in assets. But because she was unwilling to risk spending any of it, she lived out her life in pitiful condition.[4]

You may not have a million dollars lying around, but you do have spiritual riches waiting to be invested in your everyday life and in the lives of others. Take a chance. Risk a little for God. Loosen your grasp on the things that fill up your life. As the old saying goes, we are wisest when we hold God tightly—and everything else loosely!

Are you ready to take the plunge? Then let me share with you four principles for risky Christian living:

Principle #1: God owns it—you're just managing it. All of the resources in your life—your gifts, your talents, your time, your finances, your intelligence, your creativity, your home, your car, and anything else you call your own—are only yours on loan. The true owner is God, and he, in his infinite wisdom, has given these things to you to use and to manage. You are his investment counselor. What kind of portfolio are you building for the kingdom of heaven?

Principle #2: The only eternal investments are the ones you make in people. The only things you can take with you to heaven are other people. Everything else stays behind. You see, God doesn't care if you own a fortune in cattle futures; he does care if you are helping draw others closer to him. So when you are weighing the risks and rewards of a course of action, be sure to factor in the "people interest"—that is, whether or not people are benefiting from your risk and to what extent they benefit.

Principle #3: Don't risk God's capital in your life foolishly. It isn't admirable to throw money over the edge of Niagara Falls and hope it will somehow reach a needy person somewhere below. Likewise simply taking a risk—any risk that comes along—for God's sake isn't a godly endeavor. You need to manage God's resources in your life like you would your money. Carefully explore possibilities in your life; prayerfully seek God's direction. Then, when you feel certain God is leading you in a particular direction, follow through with a firm commitment to strive toward the goal God has set.

Principle #4: Let go and let God work. Do the best you can with what you have. Act faithfully and responsibly with the resources God has given you. Then let him be in charge of the results. Maybe you'll reach your goal; maybe you won't. Doesn't matter! What does matter is that you were obedient and faithful to follow God's leading as best you knew how.

DARE THE IMPOSSIBLE—OR AT LEAST THE IMPROBABLE

I read recently about an underwater platform that's under construction in the Middle East. The plan is to build a walkway that rises almost—but not quite—to the surface of the Sea of Galilee. The thinking is that tourists will pay for the chance to discover how it feels to walk on water! (I'm told lifeguards will be nearby to catch the "faint of faith.")[5]

We chuckle at this kind of ingenious commercialization of Christ's history. But there is one other person besides Jesus who dared this kind of impossible task—and succeeded! Let's go back for a moment to that incredible night.

Jesus and his disciples have separated for a short time. Christ, needing time alone, has sent them by boat across a lake while he takes time to pray in the mountains.

It's the dead of night—3:00 A.M. to be exact—and the disciples are having a difficult time rowing across the lake. Wind whips at their faces, and waves tower and threaten to capsize them. Suddenly in the darkness of the night, one of the disciples chokes out a scream, pointing into the mist.

> You miss one hundred percent of the shots you never take.
>
> —hockey legend Wayne Gretzky[6]

There, walking across the choppy lake as if out on a Sunday stroll, is the image of Jesus Christ. Terror ripples through each man on the boat—they think they're seeing a ghost! Immediately Christ calms them: "It's all right. I am here! Don't be afraid."

Then Peter musters the courage to ask to do the impossible. "Lord," he calls out, "if it's really you, tell me to come to you by walking on the water."

"All right, come," Jesus replies with no hesitation.

You see, miracles are no big deal to the Creator of time and space. The laws of physics are rules he put into place; and as the maker of life's game, he can suspend those rules at will.

That's when Peter does it. He dares what no other human (besides Christ) has ever done before or since. I picture him looking nervously at his fellow disciples then gingerly leaning one foot out of the boat. To his great surprise, the water holds! Leaning further, he brings the second foot out of the boat—and now he's doing it! He's actually walking on the water!

I imagine him wearing a face of open-mouthed glee as, like a toddler going for the first time from couch to chair, he baby-steps his way toward the God-Man who is making this miracle possible. Then, unexpectedly, a wave cascades down next to him. Distracted, Peter's eyes widen as he sees once again the turbulence of the sea on every side. You can almost hear him thinking at this point: *What am I doing? This is...impossible!*

And so the miracle ends. His faith shaken, the water-walker begins to sink down into the raging waves, where he must be rescued by the Son of God. When they are safely in the boat, Jesus shakes his head and says to Peter, with a trace of sadness, "You don't have much faith. Why did you doubt me?"

What about you? What's the dream, the vision God has placed in your heart? Surely it's easier than walking on water! Are you willing to step out of the boat, to escape the things that confine you, and trust God to work a miracle on your behalf? If you're not sure Jesus is out there, then by all means stay in the boat. But if in your heart of hearts you hear the voice of God beckoning, saying to you, "All right, come," then *what are you waiting for?* Perhaps now is the time for your miracle; maybe this is when you, like Peter, get to do what everyone else says is impossible.

> I think that no idea is so outlandish that it should not be considered with a searching, but at the same time with a steady, eye.
>
> —Sir Winston Churchill[7]

Will you dare it? Do you have the passion, the courage to step out on faith? I hope so. But I also know that we're all human, and sometimes the impossible can seem, well, *impossible*. In that case, friend, let me make a suggestion. Perhaps you're not ready to take the risk to do the impossible. Will you at least meet God halfway? Will you at least dare to do the *improbable*? Will you at least attempt the first step toward the impossible and try that which isn't likely—but possible?

Perhaps you'll fail miserably. So what? At least you'll know you tried. Or perhaps you'll succeed beyond your wildest dreams! It's all up to you and God. Will you risk it? Will you take a chance on God's dreams for you? The choice is yours, my friend. May God give you the courage to answer yes.

Enjoy the Adventure As Much As the Destination

Mike, I hear you thinking, *this is all well and good. But what if I risk it all, go in over my head, get swamped, and fall far short of my goal?*

I have to be honest with you: That outcome is a distinct possibility. After all, isn't that what happened to Peter? He risked his reputation and his life on the invitation of God—and got a good dunking as a result. But which do you think would have filled him with more regret later in life: responding to the call of God and getting wet? Or hearing God's voice and being too fearful to respond?

My wife and I have a theme in our lives, and it's two simple words: *no regrets*. Truth is, we're always going to make stupid decisions; we're always going to fall short of our goals. Therefore, before we take any new course of action, Amy and I make a deal with ourselves. We will do our best to follow where we think God is leading—and once we move ahead, we won't second-guess ourselves and play the "if only" game: "If only I hadn't bought that car"; "If only I had taken that higher-paying job"; "If only we'd invested in Microsoft ten years ago"; and so on.

We also agree ahead of time that the destination we aim for— though important—won't be our only measure of success. What really matters is that we enjoy the ride as much as we enjoy getting to the end of the ride. We want to glean joy and enthusiasm and satisfaction from simply being in the race, regardless of where we finish it.

You see, if you live only for what's at the end of the adventure, you get to enjoy only one good day—the last one. And that's only if you succeed! But when you live for the adventure, each day is a success of its own. Each day you get to stretch yourself to the fullest, breathe in the stuff of life, and swim in the stream of possibilities. And that's exciting!

Sometime ago I began writing a book for fathers. To be honest, I thought it was a really good book—one of my best. In my research, I found life-changing principles of fatherhood that I couldn't wait to share. I felt truly inspired by God each time I sat down to write a few more pages.

When I had enough material, I started sending the manuscript around to publishers. I eagerly awaited the day when I would sign the contract that would get that book into stores nationwide. Then I got my first rejection letter. And the second. And the third. In the end, I'd heard from about fifteen different publishers, and not one thought the book was worthy to print! I was devastated.

Why, God? I prayed. *Why did you give me this life-changing vision for fathers, only to make it useless in the end because I can't find a publisher for it?*

There was no answer. Finally, after about two years—with the book sitting undisturbed in my file cabinet—I realized the source of my dissatisfaction. I'd been so focused on getting my book published (the "end of the race" for me), that I'd missed out on the joy of the adventure up to that point. I finally reached a place where my prayer became: *Lord, even if I'm the only person who ever benefits from this book, it's been worth it because the things I've discovered make each day I live as a parent that much better. And they make each day my son lives with me as his dad a priceless memory he will have for the rest of his life.*

I finally learned to enjoy the process of making that book and the results it manifested in my family. After that, it didn't matter whether or not the book was ever published. What mattered was that I'd been obedient to God's call to create it, and my family and I were blessed because of it.[8]

If you've never been on the Star Tours ride at Disneyland, I encourage you to check it out because it illustrates exactly what I'm talking about here. The actual ride—a simulation of being inside a futuristic starship—is only about five minutes long. On a good day you'll spend about six times that length just waiting in line!

But if all you want to enjoy is the five-minute ride, you'll waste a good thirty minutes of fun. That's because every step of the way leading up to the ride is filled with wondrous "animatronics," humorous sounds, technological sights, and more. Disney has created a veritable cornucopia of entertainment to keep you interested from the beginning of the line to the end of it. All you have to do is sit back and enjoy the show as you move slowly from the start to the finish.

Friend, that's what this adventurous Christian life is like. God has planted within your heart a vision that he wants you to pursue with passion. But all along the way he's placed people and events in your life to bring you joy as you continue on toward his great goal. Now it's up to you to enjoy the adventure as much as you'll enjoy its destination.

Why not start today?

Any road you travel in life is made infinitely better if you remember to pack a smile in your luggage and take it out frequently on your trip.

—Anthony Vespugio[9]

Part Five

FAILURE IS AN EVENT, NOT A PERSON

And I am sure that God, who began the good work within you,
will continue his work until it is finally
finished on that day when Christ Jesus comes back again.
—Philippians 1:6 NLT

Jesus appeared again to his disciples, by the Sea of Tiberias. It happened this way: Simon Peter, Thomas (called Didymus), Nathanael from Cana in Galilee, the sons of Zebedee, and two other disciples were together. "I'm going out to fish," Simon Peter told them, and they said, "We'll go with you." So they went out and got into the boat, but that night they caught nothing.

Early in the morning, Jesus stood on the shore, but the disciples did not realize that it was Jesus.

He called out to them, "Friends, haven't you any fish?"

"No," they answered.

He said, "Throw your net on the right side of the boat and you will find some." When they did, they were unable to haul the net in because of the large number of fish...

When they landed, they saw a fire of burning coals there with fish on it, and some bread.

Jesus said to them, "Bring some of the fish you have just caught."

Simon Peter climbed aboard and dragged the net ashore. It was full of large fish, 153, but even with so many the net was not torn. Jesus said to the, "Come and have breakfast." Non of the disciples dared as him, "Who are you?" They knew it was the Lord...

When they had finished eating, Jesus said to Simon Peter, "Simon son of John, do you truly love me more than these?"

"Yes, Lord," he said, "you know that I love you."

Jesus said, "Feed my lambs."

Again Jesus said, "Simon son of John, do you truly love me?"

He answered, "Yes, Lord, you know that I love you."

Jesus said, "Take care of my sheep."

The third time he said to him, "Simon son of John, do you love me?"

Peter was hurt because Jesus asked him the third time, "Do you love me?" He said, "Lord, you know all things; you know that I love you."

Jesus said, "Feed my sheep."

—John 21:15–17 NIV

16

COURAGE TO RISK IT ALL...AGAIN

Picking Up the Pieces and Trying Again When You Fail

Of all the chapters in this book, this is the one I feel most qualified to write! You see, the one constant about being willing to risk it all for God is the possibility of failure—and thus the need to risk it all again. And failure is something at which I've become something of an expert.

I could regale you for hours with all the ways I've managed to fail—from all the rejection letters I've gotten for my books (hundreds and hundreds), to all the old girlfriends who dumped me for another guy (more than I care to mention), to business endeavors (always lost money), to parenting moments (did I tell you I once accused my son of stealing something that was already his?), to public speaking (yes, I've managed to put a few people to sleep in my time), to disappointing God (sin does seem to follow me around), to books that just didn't sell, to being fired from two jobs, to...well, I think you get the idea.

And yet, God has never said to me, "Mike, follow me until you fail. Then you're off the hook." Funny thing about God. He still demands my all, even when my all really amounts to nothing!

I've had times when I've screwed up royally and made a complete mess of the task God placed before me. Other times, I've been so embarrassed by my failure that I've been afraid to show my face in public. Yet God still asks, "Mike, are you willing to risk it all...again?"

> Learn how to fail intelligently, for failing is one of the greatest arts in the world.
>
> —*Charles Kettering*[1]

What about you? Ever experience failure, big or small? How did you respond? Truth is, failure is a big part of every person's life—but it never relieves us of the obligation to give everything we've got in service to our Savior. That means we have two choices: (1) we can experience failure, call "game over," and let that disappointment continue for the rest of our lives; or (2) we can experience failure, call "do-over," and let that failure motivate us to risk again on new success.

As I said before, I am an old pro at this failure thing. Let me share with you a few things I've learned about failure—and the courage to try again—from my vast experience in this great art.

REMEMBER—FAILURE IS AN EVENT, NOT A PERSON

Reread the title of this section once more.

That truth is the most important thing you'll ever learn about success and failure. It changes the weight of failure from a personal assessment ("I'm a failure") to a situational outcome ("I failed"). And that's just the way it ought to be.

I read recently that in a poll rating past presidents, Abraham Lincoln was picked by the majority of people as America's number one leader of all time. Even if you disagree with that ranking, you'd be hard-pressed to label Honest Abe a failure.

Yet, interestingly enough, Abraham Lincoln's road to the Oval Office was filled with failures! Here are just a few:

- Ran for state legislature. Lost convincingly.

- Entered into business with a partner. Business soon failed; spent the next seventeen years paying off his partner's bad debts.

- Became engaged to a beautiful woman whom he loved deeply. She died before they could marry.

- Ran for a seat in the United States Congress. Lost convincingly.

- Lobbied for an appointment in the United States Land Office. Was denied.

- Ran for a seat in the United States Senate. Lost convincingly.

- Defeated in another run for the Senate two years later.[2]

Finally, in 1861, Abraham Lincoln was voted into the office of president of the United States—and the rest is history. Yes, Abraham Lincoln failed many times during his life, but the man certainly was not a failure. Why? Because *failure is an event, not a person.*

Jesus brought this point home in John 21:15–17 (for the complete story read verses 1–17). Picture the scene with me, if you will. It is after the time of Jesus' resurrection from the dead, and he has appeared sporadically to his disciples—including Simon Peter. This day, though, he's nowhere in sight, so Peter and a few of the other disciples do what they know best. They go fishing.

All morning they fish—but they don't get a bite. Remember, these are commercial fisherman; they fish for a living. But each time they check their nets they find them empty. It appears as though it will be a wasted morning.

On the shore a stranger appears. "Throw your net on the right side of the boat," he says to the fishermen. They obey, and *voila!* All the fish in the area seem to swim into their net. That's when Peter recognizes the stranger. It's Jesus.

Peter has a secret—a secret he knows that only Jesus knows. Days earlier, Simon Peter had failed his Messiah miserably, just as Jesus had predicted. At the time when Jesus needed Peter most—during his illegal trial and condemnation to

> Well, we are whipped again, I am afraid. What shall we do? The bottom is out of the tub, the bottom is out of the tub!
>
> —*Abraham Lincoln, responding to a Union army defeat at the hands of the southern Confederate army, August, 1862.*[3]

death on a cross—Peter had abandoned him. Earlier Peter had declared that he would die for Jesus. But on the night before Christ's crucifixion, when placed on the spot, Peter had denied even knowing Jesus. Three times. And with a curse thrown in for good measure!

Now Peter sits on the shore with the resurrected Lord and waits for the shoe to drop. During a breakfast meal, Jesus turns to confront him. Will Peter's cowardice now be made known to all? Will Christ proclaim Peter a failure and pass his mantle of leadership to one of the other disciples? Let's listen in.

"Simon son of John, do you truly love me more than these?" Jesus asks.

"Yes, Lord," Peter replies. "You know that I love you."

Jesus responds, "Feed my lambs."

Then again Jesus asks, "Simon son of John, do you truly love me?"

Peter answers a second time, "Yes, Lord, you know that I love you."

Jesus responds, "Take care of my sheep."

A *third* time Jesus says to him, "Simon son of John, do you love me?"

Peter is hurt because Jesus has asked him the same question a third time. With everything within him, he replies, "Lord, you know all things; you know that I love you."

Jesus says, "Feed my sheep."

And then it's done. Three times Peter had denied his Christ. Now Jesus has given him three opportunities to reverse his denial. The understanding dawns on him: His failure has been erased! I picture Jesus smiling during this conversation because he knows that while Peter had failed, Peter is not a failure in the sight of God. And history, of course, has proven Christ correct. When the Master finally ascended into heaven, he left Peter in charge—and never once did Peter waver or come close to repeating the failure he'd experienced on the eve of Christ's death.

Friend, you and I and Peter and Abraham Lincoln are all the same. We may fail, but thanks to the grace of our loving God, we need never be *failures*.

GIVE YOURSELF THE FREEDOM TO FAIL

Here's the second thing I've learned about the art of failing: It is a necessary element of any success. I'm not saying you must fail before you can succeed (although that is a likely thing). I'm saying that in order to succeed, you must *give yourself the freedom to risk failing.* You can't let the fear of failure keep you from risking all for God.

Consider the example of John Wesley, renowned preacher of the eighteenth century and founder of the Methodist church. Believe it or not, each time he preached, Wesley exposed himself to the risk of failure. Check out Wesley's diary entries from one month in his life:

Sunday A.M., May 5, preached in St. Ann's, was asked not to come back anymore.

Sunday P.M., May 5, preached at St. John's, deacons said, "Get out and stay out."

Sunday A.M., May 12, preached at St. Jude's, can't go back there either.

Sunday P.M., May 12, preached at St. George's, kicked out again.

Sunday A.M., May 19, preached at St. somebody else's, deacons called special meeting and said I couldn't return.

Sunday P.M., May 19, preached on the street, kicked off the street.

Sunday A.M., May 26, preached in a meadow, chased out of meadow as a bull was turned loose during the services.

Sunday A.M., June 2, preached out at the edge of town, kicked off the highway.

Sunday P.M., June 2, afternoon service, preached in a pasture, 10,000 people came to hear me.[4]

If only we had Wesley's determination and willingness to keep risking our all for God over and again, regardless of the results! We too might change our world for centuries to come.

Robert Allen, millionaire author and speaker, is another example of someone who has failed and been willing to risk again. "I've lost everything twice in my life," he says. "Each time was embarrassing, painful, and just plain 'not smart.'... I've learned a lot from these experiences...[including that] people are simply afraid to fail. Fear blocks our success. Some people would rather do nothing successfully than do what really counts and risk failing. Fear is too expensive a habit. So let's learn to recognize it, face it, tackle it, and move through it."[5]

You see, risking all for God includes a willingness to risk failure. Certainly you want to do all you can to minimize that risk. But you must be willing to risk losing if you want to pursue what God has called you to pursue. Every winner has lost at one time or another; only a loser allows a loss to kick him or her out of the game.

I love the attitude of the boy who loved baseball and decided he would be the best hitter in the entire world. Taking a ball and bat into his backyard, he stopped at his chosen spot then announced to himself, "I'm the greatest hitter in the world!"

Next he tossed the ball in the air and swung a mighty swing. And missed. "Strike one," he said to himself as he bent down to examine his ball and bat for flaws.

A moment later he announced again, "I'm the greatest hitter in the world!" Up went the ball again; *whoosh* went his mighty swing.

"Hmm," he said. "Strike two."

> I would rather fail in a cause that will ultimately succeed than to succeed in a cause that will ultimately fail.
>
> —President Woodrow Wilson [6]

The boy spit on his hands, rubbed them together and declared once again, "I'm the greatest hitter in the world!" He threw the ball in the air and gave his bat a wicked slash. And missed yet a third time.

"Strike three," the boy muttered. Then he smiled. "Well, what do you know? I'm the greatest *pitcher* in the world!"[7]

That, my friend, is the attitude we need to carry with us when we take on a great risk for God. *Whoosh!* Missed the target? Experienced failure? So what? God still chose *you* to do whatever task you are doing; for as long as you are faithful—even in failure—you are "the greatest" at what you have endeavored to do. Perhaps God will use that failure to point you in another direction (for instance, as a pitcher rather than a hitter). Or maybe God will use that failure to expose weaknesses that are limiting you or to teach you a different way to achieve your goal.

And that leads me to the last thing I've learned about failing.

Let Failure Be Your Fertilizer

I'm amazed that there are people who can actually make a career out of selling dung. I mean, think about it. This is the stuff we flush down commodes and avoid like the plague when dogs leave it on the sidewalk. Yet I have to admit that just last week I paid hard-earned money to obtain a large bag of it, and my wife (wonderful woman that she is) spent an entire afternoon carefully spreading it all over our yard.

Why? Because in this fertilizer are the nutrients that make things grow.

You see where I'm going with this, don't you? Already got me figured out, I'm sure! But I'm going to say it anyway: Failure, my friend, is like manure. If you wallow around in it, all you'll get is a serious case of *need-a-shower-itis.* But if you apply it like fertilizer and use it to grow, it will become one of the most valuable resources of your life.

Listen to what others have said about the success of failure:

Failure is not falling down; it is remaining there when you have fallen.

—Anonymous

If you don't get bitter, you've got a chance to get better.
—Curley Hallman, college football coach

Great accomplishments are often attempted but only occasionally reached. Those who reach them are usually those who missed many times before. Failures are only temporary tests to prepare us for permanent triumphs.

—Chuck Swindoll

Winning is overemphasized. The only time it is *really* important is in surgery or in war.

—Al McGuire, college basketball coach

If you've never stubbed your toe, you're probably standing still.

—Anonymous

Jesus Christ's life was an absolute failure from every standpoint but God's.

—Oswald Chambers

Make kindling out of a fallen tree.

—Spanish Proverb

No amount of falls will really undo us if we keep picking ourselves up each time. We shall of course be very muddy and tattered children by the time we reach home.... It is when we notice the dirt that God is most present in us; it is the very sign of his presence.

—C. S. Lewis

If at first you don't succeed, relax; you're just like the rest of us.

—Anonymous

If you're going to lose, lose like champions.

—Red Auerbach, NBA coach[8]

History is littered with "successful failures." Charles M. Schulz flunked eighth grade completely and also later flunked physics, Latin, algebra, and English. But he turned that experience with failure into the beloved character of Charlie Brown in the *Peanuts* comic strip—making himself a multimillionaire and adding Charlie Brown, Linus, and Lucy to the world's common vocabulary.[9] Thomas Edison failed in more than nine hundred attempts to create a light bulb—and used every single failure as a lesson for creating the bulb that finally worked.[10] James Kraft's cheese-selling business finished its first year three thousand dollars in debt because the cheese kept spoiling too fast. So the American immigrant devised a way to preserve cheese longer—and went on to make several fortunes with his now-giant Kraft corporation.[11]

And the list goes on. What do all of these folks have in common? They refused to let failure be a wall that blocked them from pursuing God's plans for their lives. Instead, they turned failure into fertilizer, using it to bring growth and subsequent success.

That, my friend, is what it means to be courageous enough to risk it all for God...again. Are you ready to allow God to work that way in your life? Then brace yourself—it's going to be an exciting ride!

A NEW DEFINITION OF FREEDOM

Failure
Redone, which
Employs
Everything
Done before,
Only adding a little bit
More.

And when they had come to the place called Calvary, there they crucified Him, and the criminals, one on the right hand and the other on the left. Then Jesus said, "Father, forgive them, for they do not know what they do."

—Luke 23:33–34 NKJV

17

COURAGE TO FORGIVE— YOURSELF AND OTHERS

Exercising the Power of Forgiveness in Your Daily Life

The tinkling of silverware and polite conversation silenced almost of its own will and volition. The diners at the restaurant of Chicago's Blackstone Hotel stared open-mouthed, as if waiting for a volcano to erupt.

The year was 1918, and in the doorway stood a man who was hard to miss—all 330 pounds of the nation's former Republican president, William Howard Taft. Democrat Woodrow Wilson was president now, having defeated the incumbent in 1913 after a bitter political dispute split Republican supporters between Taft and his former presidential ally, Theodore Roosevelt.

Roosevelt had ruled America from 1901 to 1909 and then hand-picked Taft to succeed him as president. The two men were best of friends and staunch political allies, and with Roosevelt's support, Taft easily won the office. But once in the White House, Taft made a number of policy decisions that Roosevelt sorely opposed, and each felt betrayed by the other. Soon their friendship deteriorated into a bitter rivalry.

When it came time for reelection, an angry Roosevelt ran against his old friend for the presidency, publicly branding Taft a "weakling," "puzzlewit," and "fathead with the brains of a guinea pig." Taft, for his part, called his old mentor an "egotist" and "demagogue." In the end, they both lost. Wilson took the White House in 1913, and Roosevelt and Taft were left as angry, bitter also-rans who refused to speak to each other. Their relationship was officially over.

Five years later, as Taft was checking into the Blackstone Hotel, the clerk made a surprising announcement. "Theodore Roosevelt," he said, "is upstairs right now, in the restaurant, dining alone."

Taft didn't hesitate, but immediately made his way to the restaurant where he paused at the door to locate his one-time friend. Onlookers held their breath, not knowing how the volatile Roosevelt would react. In his book, *TR and Will*, William Manners reveals what happened next:

> Looking about, Taft finally located TR [Theodore Roosevelt] at a little table across the room and walked quickly toward him. Intent on his meal though TR was, the sudden stillness in the dining room caused him to look up. He immediately threw down his napkin and rose, his hand extended. They shook hands vigorously and slapped each other on the back. Those in the dining hall cheered, and it was not until then that TR and Will Taft realized that they had an audience and bowed and smiled to it. Then they sat down and chatted for half an hour.

Forgiveness had finally come to both men, from both sides. Less than a year after that meeting, Theodore Roosevelt died, and Taft later said that he was eternally grateful that the two had been able to finally forgive—and that they'd done it before Roosevelt's death.[1]

Like many of life's relationships, the pureness of a friendship is easily soiled by words spoken in anger, by actions that unintentionally separate, by human failing and error. When this happens, as it did with Roosevelt and Taft, only the

> I want to say to you how glad I am that Theodore and I came together after that long, painful interval. Had he died in a hostile state of mind toward me, I would have mourned the fact all my life. I loved him always and cherish his memory.
>
> —William Howard Taft [2]

power of forgiveness can restore what once was a beautiful thing. And it's that awesome power we're going to explore in this chapter.

CHRIST IS THE KING OF FORGIVING

The most important thing I could ever tell you about forgiveness is this: Christ is the King of Forgiving. No one, not now, not ever, can even hope to match his incredible act of forgiveness toward all humankind. The four Gospels in the New Testament (Matthew, Mark, Luke, and John) are rife with example after example of Jesus reaching out to touch people with the grace of his forgiveness. In the language of an old country farmer, "You can't hardly throw a rock in the Gospels without hitting a story about Jesus forgiving yet another poor, wretched soul!"

Still, I believe there is one story of Christ that captures beautifully the full extent of his forgiving power. It's recorded in Luke 22 and 23.

It is the end of Jesus' earthly life—and a brutal end indeed. While praying in the garden, Jesus is betrayed by one of his most trusted disciples. Under the cover of darkness, Judas leads a small army of soldiers to the place where Jesus is, identifies him to the others, and watches in silence as the soldiers move in to arrest the Christ.

Now the soldiers get to have their fun. They would soon be taking Jesus before the Jewish ruling council, the Sanhedrin. But while they wait, they begin to mock and beat the Messiah. Roughly, they tie a blindfold over his eyes and place him in the center of a vicious circle.

Whack! One soldier unleashes a bloody blow, knocking Jesus off his feet. Another kicks him on the ground. A third laughs and spits on him, adding a poke of his own. "Prophesy!" Jesus hears someone shout amid the dizzying pain. "Who is the one who hit you?"

But the Prophet can only groan, tasting the blood that is already forming in his mouth.

Suddenly he's dragged to his feet and shoved unceremoniously into the midnight courtroom of the Sanhedrin. There these so-called righteous ones ignore his blood and torn clothing and begin to interrogate him, demanding immediate answers. When he admits the truth—that he is the Son of God—his enemies seize on that as a crime and ship him off to the Roman governor, Pontius Pilate, demanding that he be exe-cuted. Pilate, a coward, sends Jesus to King Herod for judgment instead.

There, in the wee hours of the morning, the Messiah is beaten and mocked again, all the while enduring the venomous accusations of the religious elite, the so-called mouthpieces of God. Herod, taking his turn in the interrogation, is genuinely surprised that the beaten, wounded, half-dead man before him doesn't respond to the questioning.

And so it's back to Pilate, where Jesus is beaten yet again, scourged with a whip until he is only a bloody mass of flesh, too weak to stand or speak. By now it is nearing midday, and the Christ's destiny is sealed. He is led to a hill called Calvary with two other criminals. There, what's left of this once-hailed Messiah is thrown upon rough wooden beams. Cruel spikes are hammered through muscle and tissue in his hands and feet, securing them to the cross, and he is raised up, suspended between heaven and earth in a public dis-play of pain and humiliation.

[After the assassination attempt] my father said he knew his physical healing was directly dependent on his ability to forgive [would-be assassin] John Hinckley. By showing me that for-giveness is the key to everything, including physical health and healing, he gave me an example of Christ-like thinking.

—Patti (Reagan) Davis, recalling the words of her father, President Ronald Reagan, the day after a 1982 attempt on his life.[3]

Now he awaits death, but not by blood loss. His death will come by suffocation, because his body is too heavy to be fully supported by the nails. As Christ's frame sags on the cross, his lungs are crushed and he cannot breathe. His only recourse is to put his entire weight on the spike imbed-ded in his feet, push up on that peg, and gasp for breath. Again and again he does this, his muscles trembling to find the strength to push up just once more.

Then something miraculous happens. He seems only semiconscious, blinded by pain and defeat. Almost mechanically, he groans as he lifts up to gasp at life again, and with that breath Jesus utters these unbelievable words:

"Father, forgive them, for they do not know what they do."

He would die in a few short hours. And a few days later he would return to life, King of All Creation, Lord of the Entire Universe. But it is while he groans and gasps on the cross that he proves what you and I have discovered firsthand: *Jesus Christ is the King of Forgiving.*

Even at the darkest, cruelest moment in his earthly existence, even while wicked humans viciously steal away the life that he himself created, our Savior utters words of forgiveness. His murderers do not want it, don't think they need it. But they get it anyway. At the very end, Jesus forgives—and he's been forgiving ever since.

FORGIVE—EVEN IF YOU CAN'T FORGET

I'm awed by the courage and passion Jesus Christ demonstrated at his death. I'm also immeasurably grateful. You see, it was during those brutal moments of torture and death that Jesus made it possible for me to be forgiven—and made it possible for you too.

Now I stand two thousand years later and realize that I, too, have a portion of the power Christ revealed back then. Of course, I can't forgive sins against God, and I can't single-handedly restore a person into God's favor like Jesus did. But, by God's grace, I can forgive sins against *me.* As a subject of the King of Forgiving, I can imitate my Master and practice forgiveness toward others.

I must tell you, though, this is not my strong point. If you cause me pain, my natural reaction is to want to strike you right back! But as Archibald Hart explains it, "Forgiveness is surrendering my right to hurt you for hurting me."[4]

Do I have the courage to accept such surrender? The passion to forgive in spite of my pain? Do you? That, dear friend, is what we must discover; and when we find ourselves falling short of this great goal, we must turn again to the King of Forgiving and ask him to give us a measure of his strength and power to forgive once more.

Personally, I am often prone toward unforgiveness. When I read of another child abandoned or killed by his or her parents, I do not care to forgive. When I feel the stinging words of others toward my family or myself, it's easier to sting back than to ignore them. When I witness unholiness and hatred in the Christians around me, in the popular media, in churches, in politicians, and in bastions of the world, I want to condemn them all straight to hell. But I know that even if I had that power, I couldn't do it. As Pope John Paul II so succinctly points out, "We should always forgive, remembering that we too are in need of forgiveness."[5]

Strong words considering they come from a man who was once nearly assassinated by a terrorist—and who almost immediately acted out forgiveness toward that same man. Like the Pope, I must forgive. I have no choice. I am in too much need of forgiveness myself. I must do my best to sow seeds of forgiveness, and so must you.

Seeds of unforgiveness are easy to sow. With trivial words and thoughtless actions we can drop these little pellets with very little effort. We can plant them in friends and enemies alike and barely have to tend them in order for them to grow.

Yet when those seeds of unforgiveness bloom, they yield a crop of terrible fruit, such as

bitterness	anger	hatred
mercilessness	theft	insanity
vengeance	war	strife
pain	lies	sorrow
unkindness	precious time lost forever	

But if we just make a little more effort and call on God to help us, we can instead plant seeds of forgiveness in the lives of others. Then, regardless of their response to our forgiveness, we can reap an entirely different kind of crop:

joy	peace	love
mercy	pleasure	kindness
restoration	truth	happiness
cooperation	family unity	clearness of mind
grace	precious time gained forever	

We also can reap forgiveness from others in return. It is no easy task, this forgiveness. But if we are to be men and women of spiritual courage, we must at least be determined to try—day in, day out, hour by hour, minute by minute—to practice forgiveness in our lives.

COURAGE TO INCLUDE YOURSELF IN THE FORGIVING

It's funny how often a writer must put into practice exactly what he or she's writing about just as the writing takes place! Suffice it to say I learned a lesson about forgiving myself just this week.

You see, three days ago, I put the finishing touches on the outline for this very chapter. Then, two days ago, I did some routine maintenance on the subscriber list for our company's monthly "webzine" for families.[6] Being the natural genius that I am, I managed to delete more than seven hundred of our subscribers' e-mail addresses with just one click of the mouse on my computer!

Not the ideal action for a businessman to take with his customers' critical information! I could've kicked myself. Well, actually, I did kick myself mentally about a hundred times.

After about an hour of this self-abuse, my business partner—and wonderful wife—asked me this question: "Mike, if *I* had been the one who had accidentally deleted those names, would you have been this hard on me?"

My answer was immediate. "Of course not," I said. "I'd be disappointed, but I wouldn't be mad at you."

Then she gave me one of those looks she uses when she knows she's right and I'm wrong. "Then quit beating yourself up about this," she said. "Grant yourself forgiveness. Then you can quit wasting time and fix the problem."

Yep. She took all the fun out of me being mad at myself—and I'm glad. After her gentle rebuke, I was able to get past the error and move on to the solution.

So I spent all day yesterday recapturing *all* those e-mail addresses and dutifully logging them—one by one—back into our database. Then today I returned to work on this book and had a good chuckle when I reread the outline for this chapter. I learned through experience once again how important forgiving yourself is to a healthy, passionate Christian life.

Friend, when it comes time to forgive, we must be courageous enough to grant ourselves the same forgiveness that Christ has granted to us.

There is no honor in pledging allegiance to the flag of unforgiveness. God isn't impressed by how much you can beat yourself up over sin or other mistakes. He's impressed when you learn to model his son's actions and forgive—even when it means forgiving yourself.

Sadly the modern mentality among Christians is much more legalistic, even pharisaical. Dare I say Sanhedrin-like? We've got hundreds of little rules of conduct and expectations we try to live by, and failing in only one can often bring about a spiritually crippling kind of guilt that God never intended. I'm not saying it's OK to sin or that God doesn't have standards for his people to follow. But I am saying that when we fall short, it's OK to allow forgiveness to include us. In fact, it's holy—and a first step back onto the right path.

Listen to what renowned worship leader Dennis Jernigan has to say:

> When we come face to face with our sin, we rightly feel *ashamed*. We feel disgrace and dishonor and unworthiness. But if we allow shame to do godly work, it will bring us to the foot of the Cross, the forgiveness of God will fill our hearts with hope, and the imparted righteousness of Jesus Christ will replace our cloak of shame. God never meant shame to stay in our hearts; it is only meant to bring us to him.[7]

We'll talk more about Dennis and his story in chapter 19, but right now I want to finish this chapter with a story about an old friend of mine. Let's call him Trent.[8] I met Trent in high school. He was the older brother of one of my friends in youth group, and soon we, too, became friends. Trent was the son of a notable pastor and an extremely enjoyable guy. He always seemed to have a smile on his face when he greeted you, always enjoyed hanging out with the guys, playing sports, watching movies, whatever. He quickly became a leader in our group, and even after he graduated, he was still a presence in our lives.

As he approached young adulthood, Trent decided to follow in his father's footsteps and train for a career in full-time ministry. He was a great preacher—thoughtful, insightful, funny, challenging, and more. By the time he reached his early twenties, he'd met and fallen in love with a beautiful young woman from our church. They married and began what we all assumed would be a happily-ever-after life together.

In short, Trent was the kind of guy we all secretly hoped to be just like someday. But Trent had a secret sin—a drug addiction that he couldn't kick by himself. Time and time again, we found out later, Trent had tried to rid himself of his habit, and time and time again he failed to master it completely. Still, he told no one outside his family of his problem, and he felt too embarrassed to seek professional help.

> No human sin can erase the mercy of God, or prevent Him from unleashing all His triumphant power, if only we call upon Him.
>
> —Pope John Paul II[9]

Then one day, only a year or two after his wedding, Trent succumbed again to the temptation of a drug-induced high. Almost immediately afterward, he was overcome with guilt and shame. He'd fallen. Again. That day, Trent drove out into the woods, alone. He wrote a note to his family saying that he'd failed too many times and just couldn't forgive himself, even if God could. Then my friend put a gun to his head and killed himself.

It's been nearly two decades since we lost Trent, but I still think of him often. If only he'd had the courage to accept God's forgiveness for himself. If only he'd heard Dennis Jernigan's words about shame and guilt. If only...

Friend, with all my heart, as I close this chapter, I say to you: Forgive yourself. Accept God's forgiveness and move on. Sure you'll fail, but failure isn't the end. Have the courage to let Christ's forgiveness reign in your life as well as in the lives of others. Don't become another reason for me to write, "If only...If only...If only..."[10]

God holds the unforgiving man with His hand, but turns His face away from him.... With our forgiveness to our neighbor, in flows the consciousness of God's forgiveness to us; or even with the effort, we become capable of believing that God can forgive us.

—George MacDonald[11]

Early on the first day of the week, while it was still dark, Mary Magdalene went to the tomb and saw that the stone had been removed from the entrance. So she came running to Simon Peter and the other disciple, the one Jesus loved, and said, "They have taken the Lord out of the tomb, and we don't know where they have put him!"...

Then [after seeing the empty tomb] the disciples went back to their homes, but Mary stood outside the tomb crying. As she wept, she bent over to look into the tomb and saw two angels in white, seated where Jesus' body had been, one at the head and the other at the foot.

They asked her, "Woman, why are you crying?"

"They have taken my Lord away," she said, "and I don't know where they have put him." At this, she turned around and saw Jesus standing there, but she did not realize that it was Jesus.

"Woman," he said, "why are you crying? Who is it you are looking for?"

Thinking he was the gardener, she said, "Sir, if you have carried him away, tell me where you have put him, and I will get him."

Jesus said to her, "Mary."

She turned toward him and cried out in Aramaic, "Rabboni!" (which means Teacher).

Jesus said, "Do not hold on to me, for I have not yet returned to the Father. Go instead to my brothers and tell them, 'I am returning to my Father and your Father, to my God and your God.' "

Mary Magdalene went to the disciples with the news: "I have seen the Lord!" And she told them that he had said these things to her.

—John 20:1–18 NIV

18

COURAGE TO CHOOSE YOUR RESPONSE TO LIFE CIRCUMSTANCES

Choosing Love and Life in the Face of Difficult Circumstances

It's been said that life can be defined by the choices we make—and the consequences we subsequently endure. Sure, we can't control all the circumstances that come into our lives; but no matter how harsh the situation, we always have control over our choice of how to respond.

Consider the case of the United States senator during the 1920s. Engaged in a lengthy and emotional debate with an opposing senator, our hero tried with professional concern to defend his view by sticking to the facts. In spite of his efforts, the argument soon degenerated into personal attacks on both sides. Finally, the opposing senator was so disgusted that he stood up, pointed a finger at our hero, and shouted, "Oh, why don't you just go to hell!"

The first senator was stunned. Sputtering and fuming, he turned to see President Calvin Coolidge at the podium of the senate chamber. The president was carefully studying a document, poring over it page by page.

"Mr. President!" the offended senator appealed. "Did you hear that?"

Silent Cal (as he was known) looked up from his document and peered at our hero over the top of his reading glasses. "You know, sir," the president said in utter seriousness, "I have been reading the rule book, and it says you don't have to go."[1]

We might chuckle at that little story, but it's true! No matter what kind of hellish circumstances your life threatens to drag you into, you don't have to go. You don't have to let your wounded spirit die. You don't have to let your emotions rule you. You don't have to let hardship dictate how you feel. You don't have to let disappointment ruin your spiritual health.

Whatever may happen in this life, good or bad, you are the one who chooses how it will affect you and your relationship with God. Don't believe me? Then read on, my friend, read on.

No Surrender!

I don't have to explain for you the horrors of the World War II Holocaust. You already know about this horrible chapter of human history when Adolf Hitler's Nazi followers targeted Jews and foreigners for mass execution, enslaving and imprisoning millions of these people; murdering millions more; taking their property, their dignity, and even their bodies for unfathomably evil Nazi agendas.

But perhaps you don't know about Dr. Viktor Frankl. Let me take a moment to tell you a bit of his story.

Dr. Frankl was a psychiatrist and one of the few survivors of the infamous Auschwitz death camp. He, like so many others of his time, was arrested by the Nazis simply because he was a Jew. In the ensuing months, Frankl's wife, children, and parents were all murdered by the Nazi regime.

Listen as he describes one day of his existence during this time—a day when he was being marched to forced labor in a Nazi concentration camp. Pay special attention to the choices he made in response to his terrible situation:

> We stumbled on in the darkness, over big stones and through large puddles, along the one road running through the camp. The accompanying guards kept shouting at us and driving us with the butts of their rifles. Anyone with very sore feet supported himself

on his neighbor's arm. Hardly a word was spoken; the icy wind did not encourage talk. Hiding his hand behind his upturned collar, the man marching next to me whispered suddenly: "If our wives could see us now! I do hope they are better off in their camps and don't know what is happening to us."

That brought thoughts of my own wife to mind. And as we stumbled on for miles, slipping on icy spots, supporting each other time and again, dragging one another on and upward, nothing was said, but we both knew: each of us was thinking of his wife. Occasionally I looked at the sky, where the stars were fading and the pink light of the morning was beginning to spread behind a dark bank of clouds. But my mind clung to my wife's image, imagining it with an uncanny acuteness. I heard her answering me, saw her smile, her frank and encouraging look. Real or not, her look then was more luminous than the sun which was beginning to rise....

In front of me a man stumbled, and those following him fell on top of him. The guard rushed over and used his whip on them all. Thus my thoughts were interrupted for a few minutes. But soon my soul found its way back from the prisoners existence to another world, and I resumed talk with my loved one: I asked her questions, and she answered; she questioned me in return, and I answered....

A thought crossed my mind: I didn't even know if she were still alive, and I had no means of finding out (during all my prison life there was no outgoing or incoming mail); but at that moment it ceased to matter. There was no need to know; nothing could touch the strength of my love and the thoughts of my beloved. Had I known then that my wife was dead, I think that I still would have given myself, undisturbed by that knowledge, to the contemplation of that image, and that my mental conversation with her would have been just as vivid and just as satisfying.

Another time, Hitler's Gestapo police held Dr. Frankl in custody. They treated him shamefully, forcing him to strip and stand at attention, totally naked. Then they added the insult of cutting off his wedding ring; they wanted the gold out of which it was made.

As they were cutting off his ring, Frankl stood there, nude, humiliated, powerless to stop them, and powerless to have any say in his own destiny. He reports that at that time he made a decision. Directing his thoughts to his captors, he said to himself:

> You can take away my wife, you can take away my children, you can strip me of my clothes and my freedom, but there is one thing no person can ever take away from me—and that is my freedom to choose how I will react to what happens to me!

From that time forward, Dr. Viktor Frankl endured hardships you and I can only imagine. Yet through it all, he had one thing he would never surrender: his freedom to choose his response to his situation.[2]

Think your life is rough? Not enough paycheck to last the week— or maybe no paycheck at all? Marital troubles? Career downturn? Illness in your family? Cancer? AIDS? Victim of violence? Loss of a loved one?

Friend, no matter what your situation, no matter how hopeless, how angry, how distraught you may feel, God has given you the power to choose your response to life. Never surrender that choice—not to anyone or anything. Take courage from the example of Viktor Frankl. If he can go through a literal hell on earth, you can make it too.

> I know God won't give me anything I can't handle. I just wish He didn't trust me so much.
>
> —Mother Teresa[3]

Please know I don't say these words lightly. Many of those hardships I listed above are things that I too have faced. And I must admit that more than once I gave up my right to choose life and joy and Jesus in the midst of them. Know what? Abdicating that choice never helped, never made me a better man, never made my life better.

However, on those rare occasions when I allowed God's Holy Spirit to invade my consciousness and help me choose a positive response in the face of negative circumstances, he used those situations to bring about unexpected blessings. And he can do the same for you.

DETERMINE TO REMAIN FAITHFUL UNTIL YOU MEET GOD

But what do we do when we're in the midst of pain—when life seems over but for the actual act of dying? How do we choose a positive response while we're waiting for the blessing? I suggest we take a cue from Mary Magdalene in the Scriptures. John 20:1–18 tells some of her story.

First a little background. Mary Magdalene lived much of her life in suffering. Historians believe she was probably a woman of financial means, but she also quite possibly suffered from epilepsy and "periodic insanity" caused by severe demonic possession. Then she met Jesus, and in one fell swoop the Master brought healing—both physical and spiritual—to this troubled woman. Delivered from her demons, Mary became one of Christ's most faithful followers, traveling where he traveled, donating money to his cause, and helping behind the scenes in his ministry. She was with him to the end, standing by the cross that fateful Friday when her Savior was beaten, ridiculed and killed.[4]

It is now the following Sunday, and we find Mary up early in the morning. What is she doing? Doesn't she know everything is over? She saw Jesus die. They won; the bad guys won. Will she still devote her life to this dead man whom both Rome and Israel branded a criminal?

Quietly she makes her way to Jesus' tomb with a few other women. Yes, he's dead. But she will remain faithful, even in his absence. His body needs to be prepared for proper burial, and she's brought the correct spices and supplies for the somber duty.

She arrives at the tomb and is shocked by the sight. The stone has been rolled away. Jesus is gone! Someone has stolen the dead man's body before she could fulfill her service to it! Even though the sun has not yet risen in the sky, she runs to Christ's former disciples to report the theft. They all go to see the empty tomb for themselves; then shaking their heads sadly, everyone leaves in confusion and sorrow.

But not Mary. Still she remains faithful. She sits by the tomb, tears flowing unrestrained from her grief-stricken eyes. Her body racks with sobs. They've taken him away too soon...too soon...

What's that? Is there movement inside the tomb? Through tear-stained eyes, she looks inside once more and sees...two men! What are they doing here?

"Woman, why are you crying?" they ask her.

"They have taken my Lord away," she says, "and I don't know where they have put him."

A noise. She turns and sees behind her the form of the gardener. Of course! The two men in the tomb must work for the gardener. Will he chase her away now? Will he tell her to take her weeping and go some-place else?

"Woman," he says, "why are you crying? Who is it you are looking for?"

Isn't it obvious why she is crying? Why else do women come to grave sites, if not to mourn? But perhaps this man knows where they've taken the body of Jesus. Perhaps he will tell her.

She does her best to choke back the sorrow. "Sir," she pleads, "if you have carried him away, tell me where you have put him, and I will get him."

The gardener is silent for a moment. Is he smiling? There's something familiar about this man. Now he speaks again.

"Mary."

The woman's eyes fly open, blinded no longer by tears of sorrow, but brightened instead by tears of pure, utter, indescribable joy. It's the Lord! And he's alive!

Faithful Mary has been granted the privilege of being the first to witness the event that is to change human history. But she doesn't care about history. All that matters is that once again she has met God.

The moral of this story? Friend, when sorrow threatens to destroy you, when the vagaries of life tempt you to give in to Satan's defeatist lies, resolve to do what Mary did. Choose to remain faithful until you meet God. Remain faithful even at death's door, knowing that if you have to walk through it, it will be a portal to the moment when you, like Mary, will meet the risen Lord face to face.

SHUN SELF-PITY

Never surrender. Remain faithful until you meet God. And last but not least, when troubles overtake you and you must choose joy like a drink hidden in the desert of sorrow, remember this advice: Shun self-pity.

"Why me?" we so easily cry during times of grief or hardship. "Why was I born to suffer like this?"

It's a natural reaction and an honest one. Truthfully God isn't frightened when we cry out to him this way. But if we let that honest expression of pain devolve into a pool of self-pity, we harm ourselves—and those around us.

We would be so much wiser to do what a woman named Linda has chosen to do. Linda is a friend of popular artist and author Joni Eareckson Tada (who herself has chosen to live a happy, productive life as a paraplegic). In her book *Glorious Intruder*, Tada tells about her friend.

Linda is the victim of chemical poison. As a result, she is unable to tolerate many of the common materials and fumes that most of us live with daily. For instance, everyday things like perfume, deodorant, soap, garlic, onions, or anything spicy can trigger a dangerous reaction within her body that can be crippling or even life threatening. Often, when the neighbors are having a barbecue, Linda must confine herself to her bedroom; without this self-imposed imprisonment, she might accidentally catch a whiff of windblown lighter fluid—and that would leave her unconscious.

Linda lives no normal life, but when self-pity comes knocking on her door, she chooses not to answer. "Suffering and sickness and pain don't rank high on my list of best possible options for a happy life," she says. "But God alone can determine what's best for me. Only he sees the beginning and the end. He's the only one who knows what it's going to take to conform me to the image of his son. And he spares no pain in accomplishing his will in my life. I don't need pity; and what I need even less is my own pity."[5]

I wish I could say that I am like Linda, that I'm an old pro at shunning self-pity. Truth is, I'm not. Oh, I try, mind you, I really do. And sometimes I even succeed. But my life is better characterized by that poor old milkman, Tevya, portrayed by the wonderful actor Topol in the classic musical, *Fiddler on the Roof.* Early in the movie Tevya's doing his best to cope with many of his poverty-induced troubles, and at one point he finally sighs and prays this prayer: "Oh Lord, You made many, many poor people. I realize, of course, it's no shame to be poor. But it's no great honor either. So what would have been so terrible if I had a small fortune?"[6]

> God would like us to be joyful even when our hearts lie panting on the floor.... To life! To life! Lacheim!
>
> —*Tevya in* Fiddler on the Roof[7]

I smile at Tevya's sentiments only because I've shared them all too often. In fact, sometimes I feel like both Tevya (with his financial hardships) *and* Linda (with her physical ones). Thankfully my family no longer worries about where our next meal is coming from, but that was the case for many years during my youth.

And my health? You recall earlier in this book I mentioned that I live with a rare stomach disorder that causes me to feel nausea on a daily basis. Medication helps, but nothing is foolproof. Some days I have only mild nausea and can function almost normally. Other days, the nausea is so severe my only real option is to retreat to my bed and wait for it to pass.

It was during one of those severe days that I learned something about self-pity. I lay in my bed hearing life go on around me—but without me. My son was happily playing in the other room. My stereo was playing some of my favorite CDs. My wife was happily chatting on the phone. I was fighting nausea—and wallowing in my sorrows.

While I lay there, I looked at a picture of my son on the wall. He was two years old—and adorable. I started thinking of the time when the picture was taken. I was healthy back then, hardly ever sick, in fact. I was working at a job I loved—and that paid me more money than I'd ever made in my life. We'd just bought our first house, settled into a new church, and were enjoying our life circumstances to the hilt.

And my son, oh my son! He was the joy of every day, the thing I looked forward to seeing most each day after work. Of course I was certain that he was absolutely the most intelligent, most fun, most happy, most loving child in the world. (Well, actually, I still think that!) I treasured days of playing and roughhousing with Tony and (when she was brave) with Tony's mom.

I stared at the picture, and tears began to form in my eyes. I so longed to go back to those days of no worries, good health, and great times. Yep, I had the self-pity bug—and I had it bad. I prayed all the normal prayers: "It's not fair, God! I'm still a young man! Tony deserves a father who can do all the things I used to do with him—not one who gets motion sick riding in a car or who feels like throwing up after a game of basketball in the driveway!"

I ranted. I cried. I whined. I did it all, and I can't say I'm proud of it. And I thought to myself, *Now I know what they mean when they talk about the "good old days."*

At that moment, in the middle of my pity party, I felt as though God whispered one little question in my ear: "Who says the good old days have to be over?"

That's when I realized I had the power of choice, the right to decide how I would respond to any situation in life—including my health.

"Lord," I prayed again, "I refuse to be one of those people whose best days are behind him. By your grace, I will instead be a man who chooses to revel in whatever I can today and who looks forward to new dreams coming true tomorrow!"

I haven't been the same since, and I believe you can have the same experience. If you choose to shun self-pity and pray that kind of prayer for yourself, it will be a decision you'll never regret. Trust me, I know.

A CREED FOR THOSE WHO HAVE SUFFERED

I asked God for strength, that I might achieve.
I was made weak, that I might learn to humbly obey...

I asked for health, that I might do great things.
I was given infirmity, that I might do better things...

I asked for riches, that I might be happy.
I was given poverty, that I might be wise...

I asked for power, that I might have the praise of men.
I was given weakness, that I might feel the need of God...

I asked for all things, that I might enjoy life.
I was given life, that I might enjoy all things...

I got nothing I asked for—but everything I had hoped for.
Almost despite myself, my unspoken prayers were answered.
I am, among men, most richly blessed!
—an unknown Confederate soldier[8]

Part Six

WHEN ALL
IS SAID
AND DONE

Then the King will say to those on the right,
"Come, you who are blessed by my Father,
inherit the Kingdom prepared for you
from the foundation of the world."

—Matthew 25:34 NLT

Let not your heart be troubled; you believe in God, believe also in Me. In My Father's house are many mansions; if it were not so, I would have told you. I go to prepare a place for you. And if I go and prepare a place for you, I will come again and receive you to Myself; that where I am, there you may be also.

—*John 14:1–3* NKJV

19

COURAGE TO HOPE

Focusing on Jesus and Expecting a Miracle

Twenty-one-year-old Dennis Jernigan fidgeted nervously in his chair. It was 1981, and Dennis was a student nearing graduation from Oklahoma Baptist University. But he had a secret—a terrible, sinful secret. He knew he had to do something to break out of his cycle of addiction—even if that meant telling someone his shameful secret. Nothing could be worse than the private hell he was enduring.

As he gazed at the man sitting across from him, new hope rose within. Surely this man could help. *Would* help. He was a well-respected Christian. A leader. A family man with a devoted wife and children. If anyone could be trusted with this secret, he was the one. He had to be! After all, wasn't this man Dennis's last hope for healing?

But how would this Christian leader respond when he discovered that Dennis wasn't really the decent Christian he made himself out to be? When he learned Dennis was caught in the vicious grip of a homosexual lifestyle?

The young man swallowed hard, wondering if this Christian role model would throw him out, disgusted with his amoral behavior—or worse, shake his head and say there was nothing he could do.

Finally Dennis spoke, baring all to this man—his final hope. He confessed to the homosexual desires he had struggled with since boyhood

—desires that consumed him even after he became a Christian. He confessed to his life of lies and to his need for help. Then he waited. Never in his wildest dreams did Dennis expect what happened next.

The man propositioned him. This friend, this confidant, this Christian role model, wanted to have a homosexual encounter with him. Right then, that night.

Dennis felt sick and lost. If hope couldn't be found here, he reasoned, it couldn't be found anywhere. Hours later, the Bible school student lay on the floor of his apartment, disgusted with his lifestyle and ashamed that he'd acquiesced to the Christian leader's advances earlier that evening.

"I just gave up that night," Dennis says while remembering that awful moment in his life. "I lived by myself and I went home, turned on the little gas heater, and just lay down for a long time. I just wanted to die."

NO HOPE?

The book of Dennis Jernigan's life almost ended that night, with only twenty-one chapters and in a pool of hopelessness. Before we learn the rest of Dennis's story, though, let's talk about you for a moment.

Homosexuality may be far from what you struggle with. But even if that's the case, I'm betting that at some time or another, you, like Dennis, reached a point in life when your situation seemed hopeless. When salvation seemed far away. When all the dreams you had stored up in your life came crashing down in a heap.

Perhaps illness or injury robbed you of your hoped-for future. Maybe your spouse left you for another. It could be that your children's choices in the present blinked away their opportunities for the future. Or perhaps your bank account was so overdrawn it seemed more like a credit card's balance than a checkbook's. Possibly your parents divorced and left you to choose which one loved you more. It may be that a little mistake landed you a prison sentence. Perhaps supposed friends lied and hurt you deeply.

And in the end, you felt that hope was a dream other people were granted—and merely a cruel deception for you.

Friend, have you ever felt that way? I know I have—more than once. Let me take a moment now to share with you a truth I learned from Dennis Jernigan: *There's no such thing as no hope*.

No matter the situation, regardless of the circumstance, for the courageous Christian, hope always remains. Don't believe me? Then listen to the rest of Dennis Jernigan's story.

As you recall, we last left the young man feeling used, helpless, and hopeless, lying on the floor of his apartment sucking in deadly gas with the intention of letting it push the very life out of his body.

He lay there, hearing the poisonous gas hiss out the heater and gulping in breathfuls, hoping to end it all. But even in deathlike misery, he wasn't alone. Through a miracle of the Holy Spirit, he found his thoughts turning to what lay beyond death's door.

What's eternity really going to be like? he wondered. *Am I really going to be free?* The thought filled him with fear.

"I couldn't carry it out," he says today. "I was too afraid of eternity." He pauses, then adds, "Thank God."

> There is never a time when we may not hope in God. Whatever our necessities, however great our difficulties, and though to all appearance help is impossible, yet our business is to hope in God, and it will be found that it is not in vain.
>
> —*George Müller*[1]

So the sorrowful young man closed the gas valve and went to bed, wondering how he would manage to make it through another day...

Fast-forward nineteen years, and you discover an entirely different man than the suicidal student of 1981. The Dennis Jernigan you see today is passionate about life, speaking confidently of God's love and power to redeem even the worst of sinners. His explanation is simple: "I'm ashamed of my sin," he reports, "but proud of what God has done."

It was only a few months after he tried to commit suicide that Dennis attended a concert by the popular Christian band Second

Chapter of Acts. Near the end of the concert, the group's lead singer, Annie Herring, spoke to the crowd.

"God just wants me to tell somebody here tonight that you're hiding something that you'd be devastated if you thought anyone knew about it," she said. "But God wants you to know he sees it, and he loves you anyway."

Dennis froze in his seat. Could this really be true? Could God still love a homosexual? A hypocrite? Hope welled up within him, and moments later Dennis found himself in the arms of God's Holy Spirit—and he's been there ever since. Like scales falling away, Dennis felt himself delivered once and for all from the shackles of sin that had blinded him to the hope of God's grace.

From that day on, Dennis never returned to the homosexual lifestyle. He'd been set free, and though there were battles still to fight, he now had the power to win them. He determined to commit his life to telling others about that power—the power that comes from the Holy Spirit through a relationship with Jesus Christ—and to using his musical talents to facilitate worship of the one who set him free.

Today Dennis Jernigan—former homosexual, former suicidal Bible student—is one of the foremost veterans in the rapidly growing praise and worship category of Christian music. Often called "the psalmist of the century," he performs to packed-out audiences fifty weeks each year. He's recorded twenty-two albums, sold more than a million copies, and garnered two prestigious Dove award nominations. He's also authored two well-received devotional books based on his most recent recordings.

> While there's life there's hope, we say, but the deeper truth is that only while there's hope is there life. Take away hope, and life, with all its fascinating variety of opportunities and experiences, reduces to mere existence—uninteresting, ungratifying, bleak, drab and repellent, a burden and a pain.
>
> —J. I. Packer[2]

But God had even more than musical success in store for Dennis. About two years after that life-changing Second Chapter of Acts concert, he met Melinda Hewitt, the woman who would eventually become his wife and the mother of his nine (count 'em, nine!) children.

"To have not known any one of [my wife or children] would break my heart," Dennis says when reflecting on the way his life almost ended. "And to think that I have all ten of them.... It's overwhelming when you put it in that perspective. And that makes me want to worship the Lord that much more. I mean, it just makes me grateful."

You see, even when Dennis felt hopeless, God never gave up hope for his child. Can you imagine what a tragedy it would have been if Dennis had actually committed suicide? He'd never have experienced the dreams that God had for him—and equally as tragic, we'd never have received the hope his story inspires.

"I've had so many people tell me they were saved, and God just met them, through one of my songs," Dennis says. "And I believe that's one of the reasons God has allowed me to go through some of the junk I've had to go through—so I would get desperate enough to cry out to him and write down my pleas. I mean, that's what most of the songs are. Just my prayers."[3]

Friend, are you tempted to give up hope like Dennis Jernigan? Do you feel as though God has forgotten you? Remember the lesson this worship leader learned the hard way: *There's no such thing as no hope!*

COURAGE TO KEEP YOUR EYES ON THE PRIZE

"But Mike," you say. "You don't understand what I've gone through. My whole life has been one disappointment after another! How am I supposed to find hope in a life like that?"

It's all a matter of vision, my friend. Where you look determines where you go and what possibilities you see. Let me explain what I mean by telling you about a scene from one of my favorite comedy movies, *Galaxy Quest*.

As is the custom in high-flying adventures like this one, our gallant heroes face an intergalactic menace that threatens to doom an entire civilization. In fact, this menace—a group of bloodthirsty lizardlike aliens—has taken over the spaceship that our heroes were using to try to rescue the galaxy.

The crew has been sentenced to slow suffocation, and the ship has been programmed for self-destruction. The commanders (actually a group of hilariously inept, out-of-work actors) are the only ones left to save them all. The good news is that the command crew has access to an impressive new weapon called the Omega 13. The bad news is they have never actually seen the Omega 13 and have no idea how to use it.

That's when we find "Commander" Jason Nesmith (portrayed by Tim Allen) and "Lieutenant" Gwen DeMarco (Sigourney Weaver) tearing through the bowels of the ship, intent on stopping the countdown to annihilation. Helped via communicator by a young teen named Brandon (Justin Long), the two press on until they find themselves teetering warily on a bare metal beam high over a dangerous chasm.

Just then the voice link crackles, and Brandon says, "Commander, what I'd give to see what you are seeing!"

"What are you talking about?" the commander responds.

With unrestrained excitement, Brandon announces, "You're deep in the underbelly of the Omega 13! Oh, it must be spectacular!"

"Well, it doesn't look like much to me," says the mystified Gwen. "It's just these few walls and this dumb spinning fan that we have in every single episo—"

Just then the commander taps Gwen on the shoulder and points up. There, whirling above their heads in a breathtaking, DNA-like vortex, is the Omega 13! The majestic power of this great weapon had heretofore been only an absent idea; now Jason and Gwen see it for themselves, and they are awestruck by its beauty and power.

All because they took a moment to look up.[4]

Sure, *Galaxy Quest* is just a funny movie, but that moment of shifted focus is a beautiful picture of how we can live our lives filled with hope. You see, most of us are like Gwen—we keep looking at the obstacles and disappointments of life. We only notice that dumb spinning fan and the bare walls. It's in those moments we must look up and see the awesome, majestic, powerful Savior who reigns supreme.

You see, a Christian's hope doesn't rest in a situation; it rests in the one who holds all situations in the palm of his hand.

Didn't get the promotion you were hoping for? You can still hope in God's abundant provision and sovereign plan for your life. Haven't accomplished what you'd hoped to accomplish? You can still hope in God's grace and strength to accomplish what *he* wants for you. Didn't face down that temptation the way you'd hoped you would? You can still hope in Jesus' forgiving power to give you a second chance.

Scottish theologian George MacDonald once said, "There must be hope while there is existence; for where there is existence there must be God; and God is forever good."[5] I agree and would add that when you are next tempted to give in to hopelessness, look *beyond* your situation. Look up! Seek new hope not in your situation, but in the face of God. Keep your eyes on life's real prize. When God is your hope, you will never be found hopeless, no matter what circumstances you encounter.

REMEMBER, HEAVEN IS OUR GREATEST HOPE

And that leads me to the greatest hope we have in God: heaven, our true home. Even if this world beats you down, batters you into submission, and finally takes your very life, there's one hope it can never take away: Home—God's home that he's prepared just for you. Heaven awaits, no matter what disappointments you encounter here on earth.

Famed evangelist Billy Graham has said, "Some believers are lying on hospital beds today. Some may be suffering from terrible diseases or be in prisons or labor camps. They long for home, where they may find relief from their pain and a new sense of love in their lives. The home and the love that is waiting for them is Jesus Christ himself, and because of him, heaven at last and forever!"[6]

How do we know this great hope is true? Because Jesus himself told us, and it's recorded in John 14:1–3: "Let not your heart be troubled," the Master said to his disciples.

They were all gathered for the Passover meal—a meal which, incidentally, was Jesus' last before his execution. So how could he say this to them? It is obvious that Jesus knew what was about to happen. He knew that in a few short hours he would be torn from his disciples, arrested, beaten, and crucified. He knew the terrible pain that awaited him—and his followers. Still the words of comfort flowed from his lips: "Let not your heart be troubled; you believe in God, believe also in me."

I don't know about you, but if I had been present during the days of Jesus' arrest and crucifixion, my heart would have been troubled—especially if I thought they might be coming after me next!

But Jesus spoke comfort in the face of danger and refocused his disciples not on their present circumstances but on their hope to come: "In my Father's house are many mansions; if it were not so, I would have told you. I go to prepare a place for you. And if I go and prepare a place for you, I will come again and receive you to myself; that where I am, there you may be also."

> One hour of eternity, one moment with the Lord, will make us utterly forget a lifetime of desolations.
>
> —Horatio Bonar[7]

When the darkest days of humanity were descending on Christ's disciples, where did he direct their hopes? Straight to the gates of heaven; right to the promise of eternity with God. Friend, there are three principles you and I can learn about heaven's hope from these words of Jesus:

Principle #1: There is room in heaven for each of us. "In My Father's house are *many* mansions," he said. No room for you on the corporate ladder? That's OK; in heaven there's plenty of space for you. No room for you in your daughter's heart? In your ex-husband's life? In your old circle of friends? In the financial passageways of the rich and famous? Don't despair. There's room for you in the most loving, most loyal, most wealthy place ever created. There's room for you in heaven.

Principle #2: Jesus himself is preparing our places in his Father's house. In a few weeks my family and I will travel to the great vacation spot of Orlando, Florida, where we will spend four glorious days in a posh hotel and at the Universal Studios amusement park. How did we get this opportunity? Believe it or not, my wife won the all-expenses-paid trip in a drawing. I want you to know that we are pretty excited about the preparations the contest company has made for us! We're looking forward to luxuriating in the accommodations they've arranged and in participating in all the entertainment they've set up.

But even their greatest efforts on our behalf pale to nothingness when compared to the preparations the Creator of All is making for you and for me! If we think Universal Studios is going to be good, wait until we see the studios of heaven crafted by the Master Maker himself!

Principle #3: Heaven holds for us the greatest treasure of existence—the very presence of God. "I will come again and receive you to myself," Jesus promised, "that where I am, *there* you may be also." Alone no more, when we stand in heaven, we will embrace the one who holds our hope, the one who promises eternity and guarantees it by his presence. Who cares what disappointments we must endure in this filthy little world? We know that a day will come when Jesus will pluck us from this pit of hope-crushing circumstances and place us squarely in the arms of God forever.

Let me close out this chapter by telling you one last story, this one from the life of the renowned Christian Amy Carmichael. The latter part of Amy's life was spent with physical infirmity that left her a semi-invalid until her death in 1951.

One day before her death, a friend who also struggled with physical disabilities visited Amy. As the two were chatting, the friend commented, "My doctor has warned me not to bend over suddenly, or I might die on the spot!"

Eyes twinkling, Amy responded immediately, "How ever do you resist the temptation?"[8]

Even when she was confined to a wheelchair, Amy Carmichael still held firmly to the hope of heaven—and you can too. Remember, the hopes and dreams of this lifetime can and will disappoint. But the hope of heaven was—and is—God's dream for us, and it will always and evermore be ours. You can count on it.

HOPE AT THE FUNERAL HOME

When the time comes to memorialize this life I've lived,
When my body is dead and my spirit finally free,
Rest assured that I'm finally safe in the arms of my Savior—
And that I have hoped for, longed for this time with all my heart
From my first breath to my last.

With that in mind,
Let there be more laughter than tears,
More joy than sorrow,
More dancing than drooping shoulders,
More smiles than furrowed brows,
More singing than sniffling.

You can smile as you tell everyone,
"He had hoped it would be this way."

[Paul, speaking to King Agrippa, said,] "I used to believe that I ought to do everything I could to oppose the followers of Jesus of Nazareth. Authorized by the leading priests, I caused many of the believers in Jerusalem to be sent to prison. And I cast my vote against them when they were condemned to death. Many times I had them whipped in the synagogues to try to get them to curse Christ. I was so violently opposed to them that I even hounded them in distant cities of foreign lands.

"One day I was on such a mission to Damascus, armed with the authority and commission of the leading priests. About noon, Your Majesty, a light from heaven brighter than the sun shone down on me and my companions. We all fell down, and I heard a voice saying to me in Aramaic, 'Saul, Saul, why are you persecuting me? It is hard for you to fight against my will.'

"'Who are you, sir?' I asked.

"And the Lord replied, 'I am Jesus, the one you are persecuting. Now stand up! For I have appeared to you to appoint you as my servant and my witness. You are to tell the world about this experience and about other times I will appear to you. And I will protect you from both your own people and the Gentiles. Yes, I am going to send you to the Gentiles, to open their eyes so they may turn from darkness to light, and from the power of Satan to God. Then they will receive forgiveness for their sins and be given a place among God's people, who are set apart by faith in me.'

"And so, O King Agrippa, I was not disobedient to that vision from heaven."

—Acts 26:9–19 NLT

20

COURAGE TO PERSEVERE

Hanging in There until Your Miracle Comes

"Ti Chapé!"

That's the name Christian musician Randy Matthews heard over and over when he visited the island nation of Haiti not long ago. He saw lots of young children running and playing in the streets and noticed that parents called many of them by the same name: Ti Chapé. Curious, he asked about the practice.

"I found out the death rate in Haiti is so high among children that many of the parents don't give their children names until they're five years old," Matthews reports. "And up until then they're all called by one name—Ti Chapé—which is a Haitian word that means 'Little Survivor' or 'One Who Has Escaped Death.' If they live to be five, then they're given a name as their fifth birthday present."[1]

Survivor. You might not know it, but that word also describes you. You may not be fighting famine or a high infant mortality rate, but if you are a follower of Christ, then you too are Ti Chapé, one of heaven's Little Survivors. And you don't have to wait five years for your Father to name you—he already has named you after his Son.

It's been said that the Christian life is more like a marathon than a sprint—and that's true. But what's truer is that the Christian life is not much like a race at all; it's more like a hospital where sick people go to be made healthy. And as they gain new vitality, the patients soon become the doctors, teaching others the secrets of survival in a world that hates them because it hates the truth.

Survivor.

Friend, I won't lie to you. Satan hates your guts. He will do anything in his power to end your effectiveness for Christ. He already lost you when you gave your life to Jesus; now he wants to prevent you from exhibiting Christ to the rest of his people—or he might lose them too!

Do you know what that means? The battle lines have been drawn. Each moment of your life you are involved in a war between heaven and hell, whether you like it or not. You have powerful allies—God himself and his Holy Spirit, angels, prayer, Scripture, your church, brothers and sisters in Christ, and more. But only you decide if you will be a casualty in this conflict. Only you decide whether to keep fighting or to give up.

When you feel as if the battle is over and you just want to go home, remember the children in Haiti. Remember that you are Ti Chapé, and by God's sovereign grace, you will survive.

RESOLVE TO NEVER, NEVER, NEVER GIVE UP

With that in mind then, each morning when you wake up, take to heart the first rule of survival: Never give up.

Winston Churchill, prime minister of England during World War II, learned firsthand this principle of perseverance—and taught it to the world—as he rallied his country to thwart the aggression of Germany's Third Reich. Listen to his advice, honed by time and proven by experience:

> Never give in, never give in, never, never, never, never—in nothing great or small, large or petty—never give in except to convictions of honor and good sense. (Spoken in a 1941 speech at Harrow School, his alma mater.)

> We shall not fail or falter; we shall not weaken or tire. Neither the sudden shock of battle nor the long-drawn trials of vigilance and

exertion will wear us down. Give us the tools, and we will finish the job. (Spoken in a 1941 radio broadcast.)

We have not journeyed all this way across the centuries, across the oceans, across the mountains, across the prairies, because we are made of sugar candy.... Neither the length of the struggle nor any form of severity which it may assume shall make us weary or shall make us quit. (Spoken in a 1941 speech to the Canadian Senate and House of Commons.)

We have suffered together and we shall conquer together. (Spoken in the same speech to Canadian officials.)

However tempting it might be to some when much trouble lies ahead to step aside adroitly and put someone else up to take the blows, the heavy and repeated blows which are coming, I do not intend to adopt that cowardly course, but, on the contrary, to stand to my post and persevere in accordance with my duty as I see it. (Spoken in a 1942 speech to the English House of Commons.)

The road upward is stony. There are upon our journey dark and dangerous valleys through which we have to make and fight our way. But it is sure and certain that if we persevere—and we shall persevere—we shall come through these dark and dangerous valleys into a sunlight broader and more genial and more lasting than mankind has ever known. (Spoken in a 1942 speech at Leeds.)

However hard, however long, we shall go forward. (Spoken in a 1943 speech at Harrow School.)

Let us go on then to battle on every front.... Bear with unflinching fortitude whatever evils and blows we may receive. Drive on through the storm, now that it reaches its fury, with the same singleness of purpose and inflexibility of resolve as we showed to the world when we were all alone. (Spoken in a 1944 speech to the House of Commons.)

While God gives me the strength, and the people show me their good will, it is my duty to try, and try I will. (Spoken in a 1950 radio broadcast.)

By our courage, our endurance, and our brains, we have made our way in the world to the lasting benefit of mankind. Let us not lose heart. (Spoken in a 1959 speech at Woodford.)[2]

Friend, I want you to realize that had Winston Churchill failed to persevere during World War II, our world likely would be a vastly different place. I wouldn't be writing this book—and you wouldn't be reading it. And we all might be speaking German, living under the oppressive force of Nazism. Had England fallen—and she was outgunned and outmanned for most of the war—the rest of the world surely would have tumbled along with her, including our beloved United States of America.

Winston Churchill was given an impossible task: to lead his country to victory against the most powerful army in Europe. He took up that fight, determined that no matter what happened, no matter how dark the night or how devastating the trials, he would persevere until the end. And his perseverance literally changed the world.

> Never give up then, for that is just the place and time that the tide will turn.
>
> —Harriet Beecher Stowe[3]

Do you desire to win the spiritual war that Satan wages against us? Then take a lesson from history and resolve to never, never, never give in to the attacks of evil in your life, whether they are physical, mental, emotional, or spiritual. Have the courage to call God to your side; then, when the battle rages, never, never, never give up!

JESUS NEVER GIVES UP ON US

Long before Winston Churchill took charge of England, Jesus Christ practiced the principle of perseverance. In Acts 26:9–19, the apostle Paul (who was formerly named Saul) tells of a remarkable encounter with Jesus that reveals just the kind of stubborn tenacity our Lord has for us.

Paul (or Saul) is on trial, standing before King Agrippa to defend his actions of faith—only this trial quickly turns into a testimonial service! Bound and a prisoner, Paul tells his tale.

"I used to believe that I ought to do everything I could to oppose the followers of Jesus of Nazareth," Paul admits to the king. Then he confesses to specific deeds: falsely imprisoning the followers of Christ; casting his vote for their execution; authorizing their torture; demanding that they curse their Savior; even hunting them down in foreign countries and bringing them back to Jerusalem for punishment.

In short, he had been no friend of God. Just the opposite, in fact. He had created a living hell for Christians—and also made himself a hated enemy of their Christ.

Now let's imagine for a moment that I am Jesus. (It's a stretch, I know; but for the sake of narrative, play along with me on this one!) I have sacrificed my all to redeem my people who were trapped in their sin. I have endured torture and execution and finally proven my deity by returning to life again. Now I sit in heaven watching the events of the world transpire before me. My beloved ones turn from their sin! They accept me and the forgiveness I offer, dedicating their lives to walking more closely with me day by day!

Then a man filled with pure evil, a bloodthirsty religious zealot, shows up and begins a violent crusade against my believers. If I am Christ, do you know what I do then? I snap my fingers and end that evil man's existence. Or maybe I make him suffer first; maybe I afflict him with some painful and socially unacceptable disease like leprosy and then let him die a slow, agonizing death as an outcast from society. Hey, he deserves it! By his

> Success is not measured by what a man accomplishes, but by the opposition he has encountered and the courage with which he has maintained the struggle against overwhelming odds.
>
> —*Charles Lindbergh*[4]

own lips he admits to horrendous acts of violence against Christians. He should be punished, right?

All I can say is, it's a good thing I'm not Christ!

Listen as Paul tells King Agrippa the rest of his story.

He had been on his way to Damascus to hunt down Christians when something amazing occurred. "About noon, Your Majesty, a light from heaven brighter than the sun shone down on me and my companions," he explains. "We all fell down, and I heard a voice saying to me in Aramaic, 'Saul, Saul, why are you persecuting me? It is hard for you to fight against my will.'

"'Who are you, sir?' I asked.

"And the Lord replied, 'I am Jesus, the one you are persecuting. Now stand up! For I have appeared to you to appoint you as my servant and my witness.'"

What a spectacular moment! In one brief instant, the man who hated Christians became a man in love with Christ. The enemy became the friend. History was changed, and we are the benefactors—for Jesus didn't simply halt Saul's deadly rampage; he commanded his service in spreading the good news of Christ around the world. The result was that Saul/Paul became Christianity's first missionary as well as the author of what would later become much of the New Testament canon.

All because Jesus stubbornly refused to give up on Saul—despite all the evil and pain he had caused! Instead, Christ reached out and gave to Saul the same thing he subsequently gave to you and me: forgiveness.

You see, *Jesus never gives up on us.* His persistent love rests with us today as strongly as it rested on Saul almost two thousand years ago.

GOD GIVES STRENGTH TO CARRY ON

We can—and should—take comfort in the fact that Jesus is determined to persevere in our lives, no matter what. But like you, I live each day in this difficult world of ours. And like you, I have days—sometimes weeks or months—when I get tired.

I vote for righteousness, only to find that unrighteousness won by a landslide. I write a book about life, only to find the purveyors of death have outsold me a million to one. I give all I have in ministry service, only to find no one really cares that I had something to give. I plant joy and seem to reap sorrow. I encourage my brothers and sisters to live for God, only to watch them later abandon his standards for the convenience of divorce. I overcome one temptation, only to be felled by a dozen more.

And at the end of the day I lay in the darkness, my wife sleeping contentedly beside me, and I pray, "I'm done, God. It's over. I gave it all I had; now I'm all used up. I'm tired, I'm weak, and I'm worn out from head to toe. It's time for you to use someone else because I'm going on vacation. I wasn't making that much of a difference anyway."

And in the darkness, I really mean what I say. In fact, I think you should know I've quit being a Christian author two dozen times at least! Yet, at the end of my prayer, his gracious voice whispers to me once again, "I'm not done with you yet, Mike. Hold on just another day, just another hour, just another minute. Stick with me, kid, and together we'll make it through this. I promise."

> All I did was stick with it.
>
> —Paul "Bear" Bryant, explaining his legendary success as head football coach at the University of Alabama[5]

So the next morning I get up again, still tired, still weak, still worn out, but determined to persevere just one day more and confident that I will make it because God himself will give me the strength to do so. And he can give you the strength to carry on, too, if only you will let him.

Truth is, we are too weak to live this Christian life on our own. No matter how firm our resolve, no matter how brawny our spiritual muscles, without the enabling power of God's Holy Spirit, we are doomed to fail. So we must give up depending on ourselves and persevere by depending on God's strength to carry us.

One of my favorite stories from the Olympic Games is that of British track star Derek Redmond. Derek represented his home country in the 1992 Summer Olympics in Barcelona, Spain, running in the 400-meter race. Prognosticators picked the fleet-footed runner as a serious threat to win the gold medal for England—or at least to nab a second-place silver.

Derek had trained hard, and it showed. He easily placed in the semifinal heat. But when the medal-winning runners crossed the finish line, Derek was not among them. Partway through the race, Derek's hamstring had ruptured, causing him to fall to the track in agony. While the rest of the athletes raced past him to victory, Derek lay broken on the ground, tears streaming from his face.

Finally the courageous young man rose to his feet. With pain searing through him with every step, he began an awkward hobble toward the finish line. The crowd went silent as they watched Derek's awful struggle to make it to the end.

Suddenly a middle-aged man wearing a T-shirt and a ball cap jumped from the stands, fought his way past the security guards, and ran directly to Derek's side. Jim Redmond, Derek's father, would help his son finish the race. Arm in arm and shoulder to shoulder, Jim carried Derek, supporting the weight that his son's injured leg could not. Together they stayed in Derek's lane all the way to the finish line, which they crossed together. As they took that last step, the crowd in Barcelona rose to its feet in a standing ovation, cheering and crying tears of triumph for Derek—and his father.

Sports Illustrated later reported, "Derek [Redmond] didn't walk away with the gold medal, but he walked away with an incredible memory of a father who, when he saw his son in pain, left his seat in the stands to help him finish the race."[6]

Friend, I've got good news and bad news for you today. The bad news is that sin has already crippled you, and Satan wants you out of the race of spiritual passion for good.

Now the good news: If you persevere in this race, you'll never have to run it alone. God himself has already come down from the audience. He stands beside you day by day, moment by moment, ready for you to lean on him and draw the strength to carry on.

You now have two options: You can give up and lay writhing in pain on the hot asphalt of spiritual mediocrity, or like Derek Redmond, you can resolve to persevere in this race until you finally reach the finish line that Jesus has placed before you.

Have you the courage to keep running, even in your pain? The finish line awaits, my friend. Let's cross it together.

THE PARABLE OF THE GOAT AND THE WELL

Once there was a goat that lived happily on a little farm in the country. Feeling thirsty one day, he went looking for a drink of water and happened upon the farmer's well. He leaned way over the edge to investigate. But alas! The hapless goat fell in and found himself trapped chest-deep in water, unable to climb out.

Shortly thereafter, the farmer went out to the well and discovered his poor little goat, bleating madly and trying futilely to climb to freedom. The farmer tried lowering a rope to get the goat out but failed time and time again. Finally, after several hours, the farmer gave up. The best thing to do, he figured, was to give the goat a mercy killing and put him out of his misery. So the farmer took a shovel and sadly began dumping dirt down the well, intent on burying the goat and closing the well forever.

The goat, however, refused to give up so easily.

Each time another shovel of dirt cascaded down the well, the goat would shake it off his back, then step up onto the newly created mud bank it left inside the well. The farmer kept shoveling; the goat kept shaking. Before long the mud had turned into a mound of hard dirt that sloped from the bottom of the well all the way to the top. At last the goat gave one little jump and was free once more.

Moral of the story: Perseverance can overcome even the greatest obstacles.[7]

[Jesus said,] "Dear children, how brief are these moments before I must go away and leave you! Then, though you search for me, you cannot come to me—just as I told the Jewish leaders. So now I am giving you a new commandment: Love each other. Just as I have loved you, you should love each other. Your love for one another will prove to the world that you are my disciples."

—*John 13:33–35* NLT

21

COURAGE TO LOVE— NO MATTER WHAT

Always Practicing Love—from Here to Eternity

Please forgive me, friend, because I've just now realized that I can't write this last chapter for you. I am horribly inadequate to do so.

Oh, I believe I know what needs to be said on this topic. It's just that I've been rereading this chapter title for the past half-hour or so, and I am now painfully aware that this of all subjects is (1) the most important element of passionate Christian living, and (2) the place of the greatest failure in my own spiritual life.

Truth be told, my lack of the kind of love this chapter proclaims leaves me feeling ashamed to be writing this book at all. So I've decided not to author this chapter for you. Instead, I'm going to write it solely for me and allow you to listen in. Maybe you too need to hear what I need to hear. And maybe the best way to start is with a story.

This one takes place in India, Mike, and it's a true story. It happens in a home for the sick and dying—not a hospital, mind you. But a *home*.

It's a bare-looking place, but one filled with warmth in spite of its many sorrows. They call it *Nirmal Hriday*, the name that the founder of this home, Mother Teresa, first gave it many years ago.

Today there is a new worker in the home, a prospective nun that Mother Teresa calls a "come-and-see"—a newcomer who will work alongside Mother Teresa for several months to try out the ministry and see if it's something she can devote her life to. She steps up to the bed of her first patient, and the first thing she notices is the stench. Withered and emaciated, the dying man before her has been fairly consumed by writhing maggots that crawl in the open sores on his body.

It's worse than a scene from a horror movie, Mike, because this horror is real. But this come-and-see is braver than you are. Stifling the convulsions in her stomach, she approaches the man and reaches at arm's length to begin the disgusting task of plucking maggots from his body with tweezers.

Perhaps her face shows her fear. Maybe her uneven breathing betrays her true revulsion. Whatever it is, she has only just begun when she feels a soft touch on her shoulder. There beside her is Mother Teresa. How tiny this older woman is—only four-foot-eleven and less than a hundred pounds! But she has a strength unmatched by most others and the courage to love.

"Let me show you what you are doing wrong," she says kindly to the come-and-see. Taking a razor, Mother Teresa bends down close to the dying man's wounds and gently scrapes away a group of maggots. She pauses then to look the man in the eye and smile. Then she continues her task, deliberately oblivious to the stench, the mess, the filth, the degrading work. She has chosen to love—no matter what—and nothing she sees today (or tomorrow for that matter) is going to stop her.

The come-and-see learns her lesson that day. She is not simply serving her patients; she is loving them. And by loving them, she is loving Christ.[1]

That, Mike, is what this chapter means when it starts out with the title, "Courage to Love—No Matter What." It means giving more of yourself than you have to give to those who have less of themselves with which to give back. It's what Saint Augustine meant when he said, "What does [love] look like? It has hands to help others, feet to hasten to the poor and needy, eyes to see misery and want, ears to hear the sighs and sorrows of men. That is what love looks like."[2]

And that is what you lack.

LET YOUR LIFE BE GOD'S LOVE LETTER TO YOUR WORLD

Please listen to me, Mike. I'm not trying to tell you that in order to truly love, you must hop on a plane to India tomorrow morning and dedicate yourself to working in Nirmal Hriday for the rest of your life. But I am suggesting that to truly love, you must be *willing* to at least respond if God were to ask you to try. And even more importantly, while you don't have to travel to India to love courageously, you must be willing to love where you are—and let it be seen in your actions. Then, like Mother Teresa, your life can be a love letter from God to the people around you.

There's only one person you've known who has shown truly courageous love like that of Mother Teresa. His name, of course, is Jesus Christ. He is the author of love, and he himself became the first love letter that God ever wrapped in flesh. That love cost him his life—and gained you eternity.

Jesus had some very important words to say on this topic, and the Bible records them in John 13:33–35. It happened like this: The night before his execution, Jesus gathered his disciples into a private room where they observed the Passover meal. Knowing that he would soon be taken from these men who'd been following him for three years now, Jesus began to teach them one last time—final thoughts, so to speak.

As he sat with them, teaching them, encouraging them, these words spilled over the God-Man's lips: "I am giving you a new commandment: Love each other."

That's a crazy thing for a man to say just before hatred and envy kill him, don't you think, Mike? Why didn't he say, "When they take me from you, just go and hide for three days or so, then look for me"? Or, "Avenge me, dear brothers. Wreak havoc on the lives of those who will soon kill me"?

> I have found the paradox that if I love until it hurts, then there is no hurt, but only more love.
>
> —*Mother Teresa*[3]

Ah, but that's not what Jesus is about, is it? He's not about safety or vengeance or any other selfish human craving. He is God; his craving is love. Listen to what he said next: "Your love for one another will prove to the world that you are my disciples."

Think about Mother Teresa again, Mike. She's been gone since 1997, but she's not forgotten. Thousands have followed in her footsteps; millions have become better people because of her example. And what did this little woman do?

Just loved. Just lived out that great new command that Jesus gave to his disciples the night before his death. And by living and loving out in the open as she did, she became for your generation physical proof of Jesus' love. We knew she was Jesus' disciple not by her Nobel Peace Prize, not by her many awards and fame, not by her buildings and institutions, but by her love. That was it, and that was enough.

What prompted her to have such a determined, courageous, no-holds-barred kind of love? Jerry Brown, former governor of California, saw it plainly. After spending three weeks by her side, he came home astonished, summing up the little woman's love this way: "Mother Teresa challenges our whole way of life. She lives as if it were God himself lying there in the streets crying out for help."[4]

That's the secret, Mike. It's not a strong stomach or a high endurance for suffering or a self-abasing life of poverty. It's simply seeing the One you love most of all in the ones you like least in this world. In the eyes of the sick, the criminal, the cranky, the selfish, the rude, the hurtful, the manipulative, the vengeful, the cruel, the disrespectful, the sorrowful, the weak—if you dare to look hard enough—you will catch a glimpse of Christ himself. Then loving him makes loving that person much easier.

> Each person, at the moment of receiving my love, is the only person in the world.
>
> —Mother Teresa[5]

We're talking about an indiscriminate kind of love—a love that requires only an object for its outpouring, that doesn't define the conditions the loved one must obey in order to be worthy of love. It's like the orphan child who threw letters out her window to passersby that read, "Whoever finds this, I love you!"[6]

God is no orphan, but he has written those same words inside you and me. When others read us, we have the opportunity to become his love letter to our world: "Whoever finds this child of mine," he says, "know that I love you!"

THE OPPOSITE OF LOVE ISN'T HATE

Mike, at this point I want you to think back a few weeks and remember what your pastor, Kent Hummel, said. It was during his Sunday sermon. You remember, don't you?

"The opposite of love is not hate," he said. "It is *indifference*."

You need not conquer hate today, Mike. You would be better served to concentrate on conquering your indifference. Once again the best way to explain this to you is with another story about Mother Teresa.

Shh, listen now, Mike. Transport yourself mentally to the streets of Calcutta, India—to the place where Mother Teresa spent most of her life and work.

What do you hear? Cars whizzing by? Pedestrian traffic? Workers laughing and chatting as they head to and from their jobs? Beggars calling for food or money?

Listen more closely. Do you hear it? That pale, whimpering sound? That choked, weakened cry of a baby?

Today it's lying on the hot sidewalk, unattended. Yesterday there was one in the trash bin. Before that there were several left on the doorstep of the police station. This baby has obviously been here awhile. Its body is parched, its throat so dry that is barely cries anymore. It is limp and barely moving. It will probably die—and there are so many just like it, it must be better not to get involved. Just keep walking, right, Mike? Perhaps the mother will soon return. It's an SEP—Somebody Else's Problem, right?

Now look. There is one who is moved beyond the indifference that consumes you. She is Mother Teresa, of course, and she doesn't see a *problem* lying there on the sidewalk; she sees a *child*. And in the eyes of that weak, undersized, dehydrated infant, she sees the face of Jesus—

the face of the One she cannot help but love. She has once again combated indifference with love and rescued a child in the process. She scoops the baby to her chest, strokes its little face, then smiles and whispers, "So beautiful…"

You see, in the country of India, the caste system still rules. Social law dictates that people of different castes—or classes of people—must always stay within the caste to which they are born. Thus, those born poor stay poor as though it is their duty. Those born in middle-class or wealthy families concentrate on other things besides the poor, because to lift a man or woman out of poverty is to change that person's caste—and that, they believe, is wrong. Besides, there are so many who belong to this lower caste—what can one person really do to help them all?

So every day on the streets of Calcutta, rich and middle-class people walk over and past the poor—babies who may or may not have been abandoned; filthy, sickly beggars; homeless, jobless families—without so much as a second thought. It's not that these people are hateful or cruel. They are just *indifferent*.[7]

Easy to shake your head and cluck at those heartless folks in India, isn't it? But look here, in your own hometown, Mike. You are surrounded by hurting people too, and the truth is you carry a persistent indifference toward many—and sometimes all—of them. Sure, they may not be begging in your streets or lying in their own refuse waiting to die. But they are hurting—in poor jobs, in broken families, in grief, in loneliness, and so much more. You know it. So what are you doing about it? Loving them? Or simply labeling them SEP and letting indifference rule?

> We are all pencils in the hand of a writing God, who is sending love letters to the world.
>
> —*Mother Teresa*[8]

Mike, think back to when you interviewed Lisa Bragg of the Christian music group Out of Eden. Remember how her words penetrated that attitude of indifference—however briefly—when she explained why she wrote one certain song? Listen again to what she told you:

I was in a grocery store and I saw somebody with a black eye. A young girl, maybe fifteen or sixteen, something like that. And the whole time I was thinking, "Dang, I wonder why that girl has a black eye?" And I'm sure every single person that was with me was thinking the same thing. But I walked out of the grocery store. I left. I thought about it and then it was pretty much gone....

[Later I realized] that sometimes we get in our comfort zone and we don't notice pain. And when we do notice, we don't take the time to look deeper into it or say or do anything.

And I was guilty of it too.[9]

You see it now, don't you, Mike. Mother Teresa was right when she said, "We can do no great things, only small things with great love."[10] You may not be able to love the leper in Calcutta, but you can love the sick child in your church. You may be inept at loving the homeless on the streets of Denver, but you can love the people in your home. You may not be able to finance a great new orphanage, but you can take a teenager whose parents have divorced out for a Coke and conversation.

Face it; you are not doing great things. But if you take the blinders of indifference off your eyes, you can see the needs of those around you—and then you can do small things with great love. How? It happens one person at a time.

LOVE HAPPENS ONE PERSON AT A TIME

Think about this for a moment, Mike. How do you know about love?

It's from the times your mother came into *your* room and sang *you* to sleep at night. From the mornings when your grandfather took *just you* out for a special breakfast. From the afternoons when the parents of your friends fed *you* dinner because they knew you had no meal waiting for you at home. From the day when your wife left all others and came to stand by *your* side through this life. From the times when she gently wipes a cool rag across *your* forehead and empties *your* bedpan (once again) while *you* are sick. From the happy little hands that your son owns, which he chooses to wrap around *your* neck in a good-night hug. From the arms of Jesus wrapped around *your* heart, from here to eternity.

Do you sense a theme yet, Mike? Each of those people at those times loved only one person—and that person was *you*.

How tragic your life would have been had those lovers in your life opted not to love just this one child, this one boy, this one teen, this one man. If you have trouble believing that loving one person at a time makes any difference in life, then you are blind and ignorant to the person you have now become. You need look no further than your own nose for proof of the power of loving just one.

People loved you—only one, and it changed your life. You, too, hold the power to change lives, and you can make it happen by loving just one person at a time.

Now we must deal with one last issue of your heart, Mike. Your feelings. Yes, sometimes you feel as though you could love the whole world at once, and sometimes you even try to act out that love. But there are other days—too many days, I'm afraid—when that feeling of love simply doesn't get past your fatigue, your disappointment, or your anger. When the idea of loving just one single person tires you beyond measure. Here's what you must do then: *Love anyway.*

Make love your daily choice whether you feel like it or not. Choose first to love the ones in this family of yours (even if one of them did scratch your new CD). Then choose to love the one who lives next-door to you, and the one across the street, and the one on the corner. Then choose to love the ones at your church—both the people you like and the people that annoy you. (Thankfully, there are very few of the annoying kind at your church!) Then choose to love the ones you see today in your city—the cashier at the grocery store, the car mechanic, the teacher at the school, the police officer and anyone else you may come into contact with this day.

> People are unreasonable, illogical, and self-centered. Love them anyway.
>
> —Mother Teresa[11]

It's possible you will next have the

opportunity to choose to love those in your state, your nation, and even the world—but don't worry about that. Concentrate on loving those in your immediate circle, and everything else will take care of itself. When you choose to love this way regardless of how you feel, you are at the beginning of learning the courage to love—no matter what.

Our time is almost done now, Mike. But before we end this chapter and this book, let me leave you with the words of C. S. Lewis on the topic of love:

> It would be quite wrong to think that the way to become charitable is to sit trying to manufacture affectionate feelings. Some people are "cold" by temperament; that may be a misfortune for them, but it is no more a sin than having a bad digestion is a sin; and it does not cut them out from the chance, or excuse them from the duty, of learning charity. The rule for all of us is perfectly simple. Do not waste time bothering whether you "love" your neighbour; act as if you did. As soon as we do this we find one of the great secrets. When you are behaving as if you loved someone, you will presently come to love him. If you injure someone you dislike, you will find yourself disliking him more. If you do him a good turn, you will find yourself disliking him less.... Whenever we do good to another self, just because it is a self, made (like us) by God, and desiring its own happiness as we desire ours, we shall have learned to love it a little more or, at least, to dislike it less.[12]

And now we are done and left with the last question of passionate Christianity. Sure, you don't have the courage yet to love with godly abandon like Mother Teresa did. But, Mike, do you at least have the courage to love some, to love to the limit of your ability right now, and then to trust God to increase that love within you each day from this moment forward?

I hope you do, Mike, I truly hope you do. For only then will you have learned what it really means to have the courage to be Christian.

Epilogue

Is This the End?

I know what you must be thinking right now. "Mike! After writing a book *this long*, how can you possibly have anything left to say?"

Well, what I have left is not much, but it is important: Thanks.

Thank you, friend, for taking the time to go on the journey through this book with me. For listening while I ranted, for understanding when I cried, for sticking with me when you thought I must be crazy, for making me think through every syllable of what I had to say. For being willing to risk living a life of passionate Christianity and letting me play some small part in that.

That's all. Just thanks. And I hope this book has been worthwhile for you. If you'd like to jot me a note, I'd love to hear from you. You can send e-mail to me through my Web site at: www.Nappaland.com.

In the meantime, let's both remember to live with courage, with passion, and holding tightly to the Savior's hand.

DISCUSSION AND STUDY GUIDE

by Michael D. Warden

Use the study questions that follow to further explore each chapter's content in this book. These questions can be used individually or with a group.

INTRODUCTION: CHRISTIANITY ISN'T FOR WIMPS

Think for a moment about the definition for "courageous passion" given in the sidebar on page 3: "Desire, fueled by determination and rewarded by the *pursuit of*—not necessarily the *acquisition of*—the object of desire."

1. As a Christian, what would you say is "the object of your desire"?

2. In what ways specifically are you pursuing that desire in your daily life?

3. Would you describe yourself as "passionate" about your relationship with God? As "courageous"? Why or why not?

4. If your relationship with God were more courageous or passionate, how would your life change?

5. Why does courageous passion require us to focus on the rewards of pursuing God—and not just on acquiring him?

PART ONE: THE PASSIONATE PURSUIT OF GOD
CHAPTER 1: COURAGE TO PRAY

1. Do you agree with the definition of prayer as "practicing intimacy with God"? Why or why not?
2. If those closest to you were to examine your prayer life, do you think they would describe your prayers as intimate? Honest? Committed to seeking God's will? Why or why not?
3. Read the chapter's key passage, Mark 14:32–35, again. In what way are your prayers most similar to Jesus' prayer in this passage? In what way are your prayers most unlike Christ's?
4. Which five adjectives best describe your prayer life?
5. Which five adjectives best describe the kind of prayer life you'd like to have?
6. What obstacles (internal or external) are keeping you from developing the kind of prayer life you'd like to have?

CHAPTER 2: COURAGE TO THINK

1. As Christians, why do we need to have the "courage to think?"
2. Why do you think so many Christians have lost the courage to think critically about matters of faith and truth?
3. Do you believe you should regularly examine your own church's teachings in the light of Scripture? Why or why not?
4. Read again this chapter's key passage, Luke 4:1–13. Why do you think Jesus used God's Word to combat Satan? What does that say about our own need to know God's Word?
5. Think about your own thought life for a moment. What process do you typically go through to discern whether a particular statement, belief, or action is right or wrong?
6. In what ways is your thinking process similar to Jesus' in this passage? In what ways is it different?

CHAPTER 3: COURAGE TO WORSHIP

1. Why does worship matter to you?

2. Can you remember a time when worshiping God impacted you deeply? If so, what happened? If not, why do you think that is?

3. How might your sincere, honest worship impact God?

4. What aspect of biblical worship described in this chapter makes you the most uncomfortable? Explain.

5. What do you think your response to the last question says about you? About your understanding of God?

Part Two: The Cost of Pursuing God

Chapter 4: Courage to Give Your All

1. How do you think American Christians have transformed Christianity into a bland and easygoing way of life?

2. Many Christians around the globe have lost everything because of their faith in Jesus—including their jobs, their health, their civil rights, their freedom, and even their families. If you were in a similar situation, how do you think you would respond?

3. In this chapter you read, "At some point in our lives we need to take a hard look at everything we call our own, both the tangible (possessions, money, time, talents) and the intangible (personality, relationships, hopes, dreams). Then we must ask ourselves: Are we willing to give these to God, regardless of the cost?" Do you think you've reached that point yet? Why or why not?

4. Look again at the key passage in this chapter, Mark 10:17–22. If Jesus were talking to you instead of to the rich young ruler, what do you suspect he might ask you to give up in order to follow him?

5. In what other ways have you not yet summoned the courage to "give your all" for Jesus?

Chapter 5: Courage to Serve

1. Do you think the people closest to you—your family and close

friends—would consider you a good servant of their needs? (If you are at all unsure of the answer, perhaps you should ask them.)

2. In what ways do you serve others faithfully?

3. In what ways do you expect others to serve you in your family? In your workplace? In your church? Are your expectations in line with Jesus' instruction to become the "servant of all"? Explain.

4. What circumstances in your life cause you to feel "taken advantage of"?

5. How can you become a better servant in those difficult situations?

CHAPTER 6: COURAGE TO LEAD—AND FOLLOW

1. Why do you think "the courage to lead begins with a passion to follow"?

2. Think back over the past year. In that time, what evidence shows that you have been a passionate "follower" of Christ?

3. In that same time period, think about those who have looked to you as a leader. Would the evidence suggest that you have led these people "courageously"? Why or why not?

4. How has your leadership led others to encounter Jesus?

5. What is your greatest weakness as a leader?

6. How might God use that weakness for his glory?

CHAPTER 7: COURAGE TO SAY NO—TO YOURSELF AND OTHERS

1. Practically speaking, what does it mean to say yes to the things in life that really matter?

2. What are the things that you consistently say yes to in your life?

3. What circumstances make it hard for you to say no, even when you suspect you should?

4. In this chapter, you read that "in the end it's not what we

accumulate in life that matters but the relationships we cultivate each day." In what ways does your life reflect this value?

5. What steps can you take to make sure your life is prioritized
around eternal matters—God, family, and relationships?

PART THREE: PUTTING YOUR PASSION INTO ACTION

CHAPTER 8: COURAGE TO BE CHRISTIAN AT HOME

1. How would you feel if Jesus walked through your front door
and announced that he was going to live with you?

2. How would the dynamics of home life change among you and
those you live with if Jesus moved in?

3. What does your response say about your relationship with
God? About Christ's role in your family relationships?

4. Is love a priority in your home? On what evidence do you base
that opinion?

5. If your family were continually characterized by joy and peace,
what would it look like?

CHAPTER 9: COURAGE TO BE CHRISTIAN AT WORK

1. Are you happy in your work? Why or why not?

2. What motivates you to do your best at work?

3. How does that compare to what the Bible says should motivate
you to do your best?

4. What's the best way you can display your Christianity in your
workplace?

5. What qualities or behaviors do you think should separate
Christians from non-Christians in the workplace?

6. What qualities or behaviors set you apart from the non-
Christians in your workplace?

CHAPTER 10: COURAGE TO BE CHRISTIAN IN YOUR COMMUNITY

1. What adjectives do people generally use to describe your attitude toward life?

2. In this chapter you read that "each person's life is a story God is telling." If that's so, then what story do you think God wants to share with your community through you?

3. Is the story getting through? What, if anything, is keeping God from sharing his story through you?

4. "The medium is the message." What do you think that means in the context of ministry to your community?

5. Based on that same principle, what "message" about your faith are you communicating to your community?

6. What message would you like to communicate? What would it take for that to happen?

CHAPTER 11: COURAGE TO BE CHRISTIAN AT LEISURE

1. Is your life full of fun times and celebration? Why or why not?

2. Does the way you spend your leisure time inspire others to celebrate God's joy? If so, how? If not, why not?

3. Do you typically view leisure time as an opportunity to run to God or an excuse to escape from him (and everything else)? Why is that so?

4. What's the difference between the Western concept of "leisure" and the biblical principle of "Sabbath rest" (Heb. 3–4)?

5. What do you really want to get out of your leisure time? What do you think God wants you to get out of it?

CHAPTER 12: COURAGE TO BE CHRISTIAN WHEN YOU'RE ALONE

1. When was the last time you genuinely encountered God in solitude? Explain.

2. Do you struggle with seeing the value of spending extended times alone with God? Why or why not?

3. What scares you most about solitude?

4. If you could spend three days away in the country and you knew that Jesus would be physically present with you the entire time, how would you prepare yourself for that encounter?

5. What would you want to talk about? What questions would you ask? What would you want to do together?

6. Since Jesus is fully present within your spirit, why do you think it's so hard to get away and spend extended time alone with him?

PART FOUR: WEAKNESS AND STRENGTH

CHAPTER 13: COURAGE TO RELY ON GOD

1. Do the difficult times in life tempt you to disbelieve that God is reliable? Why or why not?

2. What do you find most frightening about relying on God?

3. In what ways are you good at relying on God?

4. Which idea does your daily life and attitude reflect more: "God is sovereign," or "I am in control"?

5. What's one key area of life in which you need to rely on God more—by letting go of control, trusting him, and resting in his sovereignty? Why don't you?

CHAPTER 14: COURAGE TO MULTIPLY YOUR GIFTS AND TALENTS

1. Think for a moment about what you did yesterday. In what ways were you "unavailable" to God? In what ways did you make yourself available to him?

2. What does the way you spend your time on a typical day say about your commitment to multiply your gifts and talents?

3. What's risky about making your gifts and talents available to God?

4. If you fully committed yourself to multiplying your gifts and talents for God's glory, what would change about your daily life?

5. What's the greatest obstacle you face when it comes to multiplying your gifts and talents? How can you overcome that obstacle?

CHAPTER 15: COURAGE TO GO IN OVER YOUR HEAD— AND RISK IT ALL

1. What are the greatest risks you've taken in following Christ?

2. What does that say about your willingness to "go in over your head" in your relationship with God?

3. Read again this chapter's key passage, Matthew 14:24–32. What was the main difference between Peter's attitude and the attitudes of the disciples who stayed in the boat?

4. Who are you most like in this story—Peter or the other disciples? Explain.

5. Based on Peter's experience, what's the key to success when it comes to "risking it all" for God?

6. What's one specific way you can emulate Peter's risktaking attitude in your own life?

PART FIVE: FAILURE IS AN EVENT, NOT A PERSON

CHAPTER 16: COURAGE TO RISK IT ALL...AGAIN

1. When you fail, are you more likely to say "game over" and walk away or call a "do-over" and try again? Why?

2. In what ways, if any, do you consider yourself a failure?

3. In this chapter, you read that "in order to succeed you must give yourself the freedom to risk failing." In what areas of life do you struggle with giving yourself the freedom to fail? Why?

4. Which quality is more important to you: success or faithful determination? How does your lifestyle reflect that belief?

5. Read again this chapter's key passage, John 21:1–17. How can the power of forgiveness give you the power to succeed?

CHAPTER 17: COURAGE TO FORGIVE—YOURSELF AND OTHERS

1. Outside of Christ's act on the cross, what's the greatest act of forgiveness that has ever been extended to you?

2. What is the most courageous act of forgiveness you have ever extended to another person?

3. How have these two experiences of forgiving and being forgiven impacted your life?
4. Based on your experience, why is forgiveness so powerful?
5. Read again the list of fruit that comes from unforgiveness (page 202). Are any of these fruits present in your heart? If so, whom do you need to forgive?

CHAPTER 18: COURAGE TO CHOOSE YOUR RESPONSE TO LIFE CIRCUMSTANCES

1. Do you believe you have the power to choose how you respond to any circumstance? How does your life reflect that belief?
2. What circumstances do you face that make you feel powerless?
3. What typically rules your responses in those situations—your emotions, other people's attitudes, or your faith? Or something else entirely?
4. Why do you suppose we are so prone to abdicate our power to choose our response to life's circumstances?
5. In what areas of your life do you need to reclaim your power to choose how you'll respond?

PART SIX: WHEN ALL IS SAID AND DONE
CHAPTER 19: COURAGE TO HOPE

1. In what areas of life do you feel hopeless, as if God has forgotten you? What has caused you to lose hope?
2. If you agree with George MacDonald's belief that hope is always present with us because "God is forever good," why do you still sometimes struggle with feelings of hopelessness?
3. Are you ever afraid to hope? Why or why not?
4. Read again this chapter's key passage, John 14:1–3. Why does Jesus encourage us to base our hope on our heavenly inheritance, rather than on earthly things?
5. List three reasons you should commit yourself to "hope in God," regardless of life's circumstances.

CHAPTER 20: COURAGE TO PERSEVERE

1. How does your attitude and daily practices reflect your belief that "Jesus never gives up on you"?

2. When was the last time you gave up when you should have persevered? Why did you give up? What was the result?

3. In what ways are you most tempted to give up on yourself? To believe that Jesus has given up on you?

4. Why do you think God made perseverance a key theme in our relationship with him?

5. How has your willingness or unwillingness to persevere shaped who you are?

CHAPTER 21: COURAGE TO LOVE—NO MATTER WHAT

1. Do you agree with the idea that the opposite of love is not hate, but indifference? Why or why not?

2. Using that definition, consider for a moment your typical day at home or at work. Think about getting ready, the drive to work or school, the people at the office or the grocery store, and your evening activities. Of all the people you encounter, toward which ones do you feel the most indifferent? How is that the "opposite" of loving them?

3. What makes us prone to view people as "problems," "irritations," or "interruptions," instead of viewing them as people we are called to love?

4. What needs to change in you or in your life to allow you to become a better lover of people?

5. What's keeping you from making those changes this week?

NOTES

INTRODUCTION: CHRISTIANITY ISN'T FOR WIMPS

1. Eugene Robinson, *It Takes Endurance* (Sisters, Ore.: Multnomah, 1998), 25–26.

2. As quoted in *The Communion of the Saints*, edited by Horton Davies (Grand Rapids, Mich.: William B. Eerdmans, 1990), 145.

CHAPTER 1: COURAGE TO PRAY

1. Lloyd Thomas, "There's Much More to Intimacy Than Simple Sex," *Reporter-Herald* (Loveland, Colo.), 18 April 1999.

2. From a conversation with the author.

3. As quoted in *God's Little Devotion Book on Prayer* (Tulsa, Okla.: Honor Books, 1997), 122.

4. Steve Brown, *Approaching God* (Nashville, Tenn.: Moorings, 1996), ix.

CHAPTER 2: COURAGE TO THINK

1. John W. Kennedy, "Hate in the Name of God," *Christian Single*, May 1999, 24–30.

2. Ibid.

3. Just so you know, yes, I am strongly opposed to abortion. I have even participated in peaceful antiabortion demonstrations—but I could never condone the killing of other human beings as an appropriate, or godly, means of stopping this kind of tragedy.

4. Dave and Neta Jackson, *Hero Tales* (Minneapolis, Minn.: Bethany House, 1996), 165–75.

5. Ibid.

6. Sam Om's story and quotes are taken from an advertisement for Gordon-Conwell Theological Seminary, on the inside cover of *Christianity Today*, 15 November 1999.

7. From a June 1999 Nappaland Communications, Inc., interview with Philip Yancey.

8. Ibid.

CHAPTER 3: COURAGE TO WORSHIP

1. Desmond Tutu, *An African Prayer Book* (New York: Doubleday, 1995), 5–6.

2. George Barna, *The Habits of Highly Effective Churches* (Ventura, Calif.: Regal, 2000), 83.

3. Ed Hird, "Rediscovering Handel's Messiah," *Deep Cove Crier*, April 1993. Printed at the Web address: http://www3.bc.sympatico.ca/st-simons/cr9304.htm.

4. Barna, *The Habits of Highly Effective Churches*, 95.

5. As quoted in *Praise Prayers*, compiled by James S. Yagow (St. Louis, Mo.: Concordia), 15.

6. As quoted in *The Book of Virtues*, compiled with commentary by William J. Bennett. (New York: Simon & Schuster, 1993), 798–99.

CHAPTER 4: COURAGE TO GIVE YOUR ALL

1. As quoted in *Jesus Freaks* by DC Talk and The Voice of the Martyrs (Tulsa, Okla.: Albury, 1999), 270.

2. Tony Carnes, "Arrests of Pastor Signal Religious Freedom Setback," *Christianity Today*, 7 February 2000, 28.

3. I know some of you will take offense to the fact that I have referred to Christianity as a "religion." Please understand that I definitely believe our faith is more than just a systematized philosophy— that it is, at its core, a relationship with Jesus Christ himself. But please also realize that Christianity is still often categorized and known by the world as a "religion," so for the sake of familiarity I use it here. Don't let the semantics of the reference interfere with the message of this chapter. Thank you!

4. Lynn Miller, "What Your Retirement Planner Doesn't Tell You," *Christianity Today*, 6 March 2000, 52–55.

5. Associated Press, "Husker's Wills Peels Off Cross," *Reporter-Herald* (Loveland, Colo.), 22 October 1999, B-3.

6. Associated Press, "Patton to Stop Prayers," *Reporter-Herald*, 24 February 2000, D-2.

7. Ibid.

8. Associated Press, "Park Managers Ban Religious Symbols," *Reporter-Herald*, 9 May 1999, A-5.

9. "Bible Study Challenge Dropped" *Reporter-Herald*, 23 December 1999, A-3.

10. Jody Veenker, "Can I Get a Witness," *Christianity Today*, 7 February 2000, 26–27; also, "Southern Baptist Leaders Disagree with Chicago Leaders' 'Hate Crimes' Assertion," Zondervan News Service, 1 December 1999.

11. Charles Colson, "The Ugly Side of Tolerance," *Christianity Today*, 6 March 2000, 136.

12. Ibid.

13. "Late Night Food for Thought" as quoted from CCM in *Christian Reader*, January/February 2000, 92.

CHAPTER 5: COURAGE TO SERVE

1. Paul Enns, *Manners and Customs of Bible Times* (Nashville, Tenn.: Broadman & Holman, 2000), 25.

2. From the song "Be Our Guest" on Disney's *Beauty and the Beast* soundtrack CD (The Walt Disney Company, 1991).

3. As quoted in the article "Servanthood" at the Acts 17:11 Bible Studies home page: http://www.acts17-11.com/servant.html.

4. One other interesting thing to note: Roman law during the time of Christ stipulated that any free person simply *acting* like a slave could *legally be declared* a slave and barred ever after from claiming his freedom. That means when Jesus performed the slave function of washing the disciples' feet, he was not only swallowing his pride but risking his freedom as well! For a more complete explanation, see the *Expository Dictionary of Bible Words* by Lawrence O. Richards (Grand Rapids, Mich.: Regency Reference Library/ Zondervan, 1985), 553.

5. As quoted in the Internet archives of Quote World at: www.quoteworld.org.

6. Linda Carlson Johnson, *Mother Teresa: Protector of the Sick* (Woodbridge, Conn.: Blackbirch, 1991), 5–6.

7. As quoted in *The Tale of the Tardy Oxcart* by Charles R. Swindoll (Nashville, Tenn.: Word, 1998), 513.

CHAPTER 6: COURAGE TO LEAD—AND FOLLOW

1. *Spartacus*, directed by Stanley Kubrick (Universal Pictures Company, Inc., 1960).

2. From a conversation with the author.

3. Bob Briner and Ray Pritchard, *The Leadership Lessons of Jesus* (Nashville, Tenn.: Broadman & Holman, 1997), 107–108.

4. Herbert Lockyear, *All the Men of the Bible.* (Grand Rapids, Mich.: Zondervan, 1958), 231–33.

5. Ibid., 233.

6. Swindoll, *The Tale of the Tardy Oxcart*, 586.

CHAPTER 7: COURAGE TO SAY NO—TO YOURSELF AND OTHERS

1. Zig Ziglar, *Zig Ziglar's Little Instruction Book* (Tulsa, Okla.: Honor Books, 1997), 46.

2. Bob Briner and Ray Pritchard, *The Leadership Lessons of Jesus*, 11.

3. Swindoll, *The Tale of the Tardy Oxcart*, 468–69.

4. W. H. Lewis, ed., *Letters of C. S. Lewis* (New York: Harcourt Brace Jovanovich, 1966), 228.

5. Joni Eareckson Tada, *Holiness in Hidden Places* (Nashville, Tenn.: J. Countryman, 1999), 30–32.

CHAPTER 8: COURAGE TO BE CHRISTIAN AT HOME

1. Retold in *Hot Illustrations for Youth Talks* by Wayne Rice (El Cajon, Calif.: Youth Specialties, 1994), 112–15.

2. "Christians Are More Likely to Experience Divorce Than Are Non-Christians," Barna Research Group, 21 December 1999, press release. Found at www.barna.org/cgi-bin/MainTrends.asp.

3. As quoted in the Internet archives of Quote World at: www.quoteworld.org.

4. Ibid.

5. As quoted in *Legacy of Joy: A Devotional for Fathers* by Mike Nappa and Dr. Norm Wakefield. (Uhrichsville, Ohio: Promise, 1998), 90. Originally in *The Jesus I Never Knew* by Philip Yancey (Grand Rapids, Mich.: Zondervan, 1995).

6. Nappaland Communications, Inc., phone interview with Karyn Henley, March 2000.

7. "Ringling Brothers and Barnum and Bailey Circus Program: The Living Carousel" (Vienna, Va.: Feld Entertainment, 1999), 14.

8. From a conversation with the author.

9. As quoted in *Eerdmans' Book of Famous Prayers*, compiled by Veronica Zundel (Grand Rapids, Mich.: William B. Eerdmans, 1983), 30.

CHAPTER 9: COURAGE TO BE CHRISTIAN AT WORK

1. Michael Hodgin, *1001 More Humorous Illustrations for Public Speaking* (Grand Rapids, Mich.: Zondervan, 1998), 344.

2. Ibid.

3. Frederick Talbott, *Churchill on Courage* (Nashville, Tenn.: Thomas Nelson, 1996), 60–61.

4. Edward K. Rowell, ed., *Fresh Illustrations for Preaching and Teaching* (Grand Rapids, Mich.: Baker Books, 1997), 143.

5. James Patterson and Peter Kim, *The Day America Told the Truth* (New York: Prentiss Hall, 1991), 150–56.

6. Thomas J. Stanley, Ph.D., *The Millionaire Mind* (Kansas City, Mo.: Andrews McMeel, 2000), 33–34.

7. As quoted in *Joke Soup*, edited by Judy Brown (Kansas City, Mo.: Andrews McMeel, 1998), 295.

8. Patterson and Kim, *The Day America Told the Truth*, 142–43.

9. As quoted in *The Moral of the Story*, compiled and edited by Jerry Newcombe (Nashville, Tenn.: Broadman & Holman, 1996), 287–89.

10. From the Internet newsletter *Gators Music Party*, 20 February 2000, at the Web site: GatorsMusicParty@yahoo.com.

11. As quoted in *The Book of Wisdom* (Sisters, Ore.: Multnomah, 1997), 89.

CHAPTER 10: COURAGE TO BE CHRISTIAN IN YOUR COMMUNITY

1. Philip Yancey, *The Jesus I Never Knew* (Grand Rapids, Mich.: Zondervan, 1995), 228.

2. Selwyn Hughes, *Discovering Life's Greatest Purpose* (Nashville, Tenn.: Broadman & Holman, 2000), 34–35, 144.

3. Warner Brothers Studios (1967). As quoted on The Internet Movie Database at: http://uk.imdb.com/a2z.html.

4. As quoted in Hughes, *Discovering Life's Greatest Purpose*, 4.

5. From an e-mail message to the author dated 30 March 1999.

6. Edgar R. Trexler, "Judgment and Grace at Nuremberg." *Christian Reader*, March-April 2000, 11–12.

CHAPTER 11: COURAGE TO BE CHRISTIAN AT LEISURE

1. As quoted in *The Communion of the Saints*, edited by Horton Davies, 32.

2. As quoted in the Internet archives of Quote World at: www.quoteworld.org.

3. Craig S. Keener, *The IVP Bible Background Commentary: New Testament* (Downers Grove, Ill.: InterVarsity, 1993), 268–69.

4. As quoted in the Internet archives of Quote World at: www.quoteworld.org.

5. Swindoll, *The Tale of the Tardy Oxcart*, 342.

6. Ibid., 343.

7. Robert Banks and R. Paul Stevens, eds., *The Complete Book of Everyday Christianity* (Downers Grove, Ill.: InterVarsity, 1997), 853–54.

CHAPTER 12: COURAGE TO BE CHRISTIAN WHEN YOU'RE ALONE

1. Peg Tyre, "Trend Toward Solitary Confinement Worries Experts," *CNN Interactive*, located on the Internet at http://www.cnn.com/US/9801/09/solitary.confinement/index.html.

2. "Ask the Expert—Solitary Confinement" by Ron Pies, M.D. *Mental Health Infosource*, located on the Internet at http://www.mhsource.com/expert/exp1031797g.html.

3. As quoted in the Internet archives of Quote World at: www.quoteworld.org.

4. From personal correspondence with the author.

5. As quoted in *1001 Great Stories and Quotes* by R. Kent Hughes (Wheaton, Ill.: Tyndale House, 1998), 392.

6. All the quotes in this section are from Quote World.

7. Ibid.

8. Ibid.

9. From a conversation with the author.

10. As quoted in *The Book of Wisdom*, 356.

11. Rowell, ed., *Fresh Illustrations for Teaching and Preaching*, 93.

12. Rowell, ed., *Humor for Preaching and Teaching* (Grand Rapids, Mich.: Baker Books, 1996), 130.

13. Patterson and Kim, *The Day America Told the Truth*, 38.

14. Ibid., 37.

15. Not his real name.

16. C. S. Lewis, *Mere Christianity* (New York: Macmillan, 1952), 124–25.

17. Swindoll, *The Tale of the Tardy Oxcart*, 519.

CHAPTER 13: COURAGE TO RELY ON GOD

1. Twentieth Century Fox, 1947. As quoted on The Internet Movie Database at www.uk.imdb.com.

2. Charles Swindoll, *Perfect Trust* (Nashville, Tenn.: J. Countryman, 2000), 53–54.

3. As quoted in the Internet archives of Quote World at: www.quoteworld.org.

4. Please understand that I'm not advocating that we abandon common sense or medicine when faced with an illness! I'm only using this as an example of how we can lull ourselves into thinking we have no need to trust God in situations where we believe we can take care of ourselves.

5. Bruce Bickel and Stan Jantz, *God Is in the Small Stuff—And It All Matters* (Uhrichsville, Ohio: Promise, 1998) on the book cover.

6. As quoted in *More Holy Humor* by Cal and Rose Samra (Colorado Springs, Colo.: WaterBrook, 1997), 108.

7. As quoted in *3000 Quotations from the Writings of George MacDonald,* compiled by Harry Verploegh (Grand Rapids, Mich.: Fleming H. Revell, 1996), 117.

8. C. S. Lewis, *Miracles* (New York: Macmillan, 1960), 124.

CHAPTER 14: COURAGE TO MULTIPLY YOUR GIFTS AND TALENTS

1. As quoted in *Multiple Streams of Income* by Robert G. Allen (New York: John Wiley and Sons, 2000), 1.

2. Adapted from the biographical booklet *Nat King Cole,* from the album *Nat King Cole: The Man and His Music* (Capitol Records).

3. As quoted in Allen, *Multiple Streams of Income,* 39.

4. Donna I. Douglas, "Saved by a Wrinkled Dress," *Christian Reader*, January/February 2000, 79.

5. Russ Busby, "The Secret to Billy's Success," *Christian Reader*, January/February 2000, 79.

6. "Spiritual-Gifts Indicator" by Mike Nappa. Reprinted by permission from Apply-It-To-Life Bible Curriculum *The Church: What Am I Doing Here?*, copyright © 1995 by Group Publishing Inc., PO Box 481, Loveland, CO 80539. www.grouppublishing.com.

CHAPTER 15: COURAGE TO GO IN OVER YOUR HEAD
—AND RISK IT ALL

1. "Dive" by Steven Curtis Chapman, from his CD *Speechless* (Sparrow Records, 1999).

2. From the *Speechless* CD's press kit, "Speechless Song by Song."

3. Charles R. Swindoll, *Improving Your Serve* (Nashville, Tenn.: Word, 1981), 50.

4. Ibid., 49–50.

5. L. M. Boyd, "Difference Isn't Night and Day," *Reporter-Herald*, 14 October 1999, D-6.

6. As quoted in *It's Just a Thought...But It Could Change Your Life* by John Maxwell (Tulsa, Okla.: Honor Books, 1996), 42.

7. As quoted in *Churchill on Courage*, compiled by Frederick Talbott (Nashville, Tenn.: Thomas Nelson, 1996), 68.

8. For those of you who are curious, the book *was* eventually published by Promise Press in 1998 under the title *Legacy of Joy: A Devotional for Fathers*, and it sold respectably. But the deal to publish that book didn't come together until more than a year after my little revelation—and after I'd totally given up on having it published at all. It was really a miracle of God—but that's another story.

9. From a conversation with the author.

CHAPTER 16: COURAGE TO RISK IT ALL...AGAIN

1. As quoted in Allen, *Multiple Streams of Income*, 295.

2. Hughes, *1001 Great Stories and Quotes*, 147–48.

3. Randall Bedwell, ed., *Brink of Destruction* (Nashville, Tenn.: Cumberland House, 1999), 86, 95.

4. Newcombe, *The Moral of the Story*, 290, 292.

5. As quoted in Allen, *Multiple Streams of Income*, 291, 315.

6. Swindoll, *The Tale of the Tardy Oxcart*, 192.

7. Rice, *Hot Illustrations for Youth Talks*, 104–105.

8. Quotes drawn from *The Coaches' Little Playbook* by George Hetzel, Jr. (Nashville, Tenn.: Cumberland House, 1996), 143, 147, 152; *Bible Illustrator 3* CD-ROM (Parsons Technology, 1998); and *The Tale of the Tardy Oxcart* by Charles R. Swindoll, 193.

9. Rice, *Hot Illustrations for Youth Talks*, 186–88.

10. Ibid., 199.

11. William J. Petersen and Randy Petersen, *The One Year Book of Psalms* (Wheaton, Ill.: Tyndale House, 1999), March 11 devotional page.

CHAPTER 17: COURAGE TO FORGIVE—YOURSELF AND OTHERS

1. Greg Stebben and Jim Morris, *White House: Confidential* (Nashville, Tenn.: Cumberland House, 1998), 100–102, 250–52.

2. Ibid., 103.

3. As quoted in Rowell, *Fresh Illustrations for Preaching and Teaching*, 80.

4. As quoted in Swindoll, *The Tale of the Tardy Oxcart*, 216.

5. Pope John Paul II, *Forgiveness* (Kansas City, Mo.: Andrews McMeel, 1999), 22.

6. You can check out this free Internet magazine for families at: www.nappaland.com. If you'd like me to add your e-mail address to our subscriber list so you can receive once-a-month updates about the webzine, send me an e-mail at: mike@nappaland.com. Thanks!

7. Dennis Jernigan, *This Is My Destiny* (West Monroe, La.: Howard, 1999), 182.

8. Not his real name.

9. Pope John Paul II, *Forgiveness*, 41.

10. If you or someone you know is contemplating suicide, get help immediately. One call to the national hotline number 1-800-SUICIDE will connect you with a suicide prevention center near you.

11. As quoted in Verploegh, *3000 Quotations from the Writings of George MacDonald*, 91.

CHAPTER 18: COURAGE TO CHOOSE YOUR RESPONSE TO LIFE CIRCUMSTANCES

1. Mary Hollingsworth, *Fireside Stories of Love and Laughter* (Nashville, Tenn.: Word, 2000), 32.

2. Information and quotes from Viktor Frankl are drawn from the Web site: http://www.rjgeib.com/thoughts/frankl/frankl.html, and also from *Bible Illustrator 3* CD-ROM (Parsons Technology). The original source is *Man's Search for Meaning* by Victor Frankl, published by Simon & Schuster, Washington Square Press, and Beacon Press.

3. As quoted in the Internet archives of Quote World at: www.quoteworld.org.

4. Herbert Lockyer, *All the Women of the Bible* (Grand Rapids, Mich.: Zondervan), 99–103.

5. *The Book of Wisdom*, 16–18.

6. As rendered on the soundtrack CD *Fiddler on the Roof—London Cast* (Columbia Records).

7. Ibid.

8. As quoted in *The Book of Wisdom*, 25.

CHAPTER 19: COURAGE TO HOPE

1. As quoted in *The Quotable Christian*, compiled by Helen Hosier (Uhrichsville, Ohio: Barbour, 1998), 129.

2. J. I. Packer and Carolyn Nystrom, *Never Beyond Hope* (Downers Grove, Ill.: InterVarsity, 2000), 9–10.

3. Dennis Jernigan's story and quotes are from a May 1999 interview with the author. If you'd like to learn more about Dennis Jernigan or send him an e-mail, you can do both through his Web site at: www.dennisjernigan.com.

4. Adapted from the DVD *Galaxy Quest* (Dreamworks Home Entertainment, 2000). And no, I'm not going to tell you what happens to our heroes—that would ruin the movie for you!

5. As quoted in Verplough, *3000 Quotations from the Writings of George MacDonald*, 163.

6. Billy Graham, *Hope for the Troubled Heart* (Nashville, Tenn.: Word, 1991), 215.

7. Ibid., 213.

8. Hodgin, *1001 More Humorous Illustrations for Public Speaking*, 95.

CHAPTER 20: COURAGE TO PERSEVERE

1. From the video *First Love: Volume 2* (Monument, Colo.: Reel Productions, 1998)

2. Frederick Talbott, *Churchill on Courage*, 95, 83, 99–101, 107, 109, 110, 124, 133, 152, 159.

3. As quoted in *Success One Day at a Time* by John C. Maxwell (Nashville, Tenn.: J. Countryman, 2000), 47.

4. Ibid., 61.

5. As quoted in Hetzel, *The Coaches' Little Playbook*, 42.

6. Gerald Harris, *Olympic Heroes* (Nashville, Tenn.: Broadman & Holman, 1996), 53–56.

7. Author unknown.

CHAPTER 21: COURAGE TO LOVE—NO MATTER WHAT

1. Johnson, *Mother Teresa: Protector of the Sick*, 6, 27–28.

2. As quoted in Swindoll, *The Tale of the Tardy Oxcart*, 360.

3. As quoted at the Quote World Web site.

4. As quoted in Johnson, *Mother Teresa: Protector of the Sick*, 49.

5. Ibid., 35–36.

6. Author unknown. As quoted in *A Third Serving of Chicken Soup for the Soul* by Jack Canfield and Mark Victor Hansen (Deerfield Beach, Fla.: Health Communications Inc., 1996), 65.

7. Johnson, *Mother Teresa: Protector of the Sick*, 20, 29, 34–35.

8. As quoted in *The Christian Daily Planner 2000* (Nashville, Tenn.: J. Countryman, 1999), 204.

9. From a June 1999 interview with the author.

10. As quoted in the Internet archives of Quote World at: www.quoteworld.org.

11. Ibid.

12. As quoted in *The Book of Wisdom*, 182–83.